T0207103

Learn to Program with Kotlin

From the Basics to Projects with Text and Image Processing

Tim Lavers

Apress®

Learn to Program with Kotlin: From the Basics to Projects with Text and Image Processing

Tim Lavers
Woonona, NSW, Australia

ISBN-13 (pbk): 978-1-4842-6814-8
https://doi.org/10.1007/978-1-4842-6815-5

ISBN-13 (electronic): 978-1-4842-6815-5

Copyright © 2021 by Tim Lavers

This work is subject to copyright. All rights are reserved by the Publisher, whether the whole or part of the material is concerned, specifically the rights of translation, reprinting, reuse of illustrations, recitation, broadcasting, reproduction on microfilms or in any other physical way, and transmission or information storage and retrieval, electronic adaptation, computer software, or by similar or dissimilar methodology now known or hereafter developed.

Trademarked names, logos, and images may appear in this book. Rather than use a trademark symbol with every occurrence of a trademarked name, logo, or image we use the names, logos, and images only in an editorial fashion and to the benefit of the trademark owner, with no intention of infringement of the trademark.

The use in this publication of trade names, trademarks, service marks, and similar terms, even if they are not identified as such, is not to be taken as an expression of opinion as to whether or not they are subject to proprietary rights.

While the advice and information in this book are believed to be true and accurate at the date of publication, neither the authors nor the editors nor the publisher can accept any legal responsibility for any errors or omissions that may be made. The publisher makes no warranty, express or implied, with respect to the material contained herein.

Managing Director, Apress Media LLC: Welmoed Spahr
Acquisitions Editor: Steve Anglin
Development Editor: Matthew Moodie
Coordinating Editor: Mark Powers

Cover designed by eStudioCalamar

Cover image by Christian Lue on Unsplash (www.unsplash.com)

Distributed to the book trade worldwide by Apress Media, LLC, 1 New York Plaza, New York, NY 10004, U.S.A. Phone 1-800-SPRINGER, fax (201) 348-4505, e-mail orders-ny@springer-sbm.com, or visit www.springeronline.com. Apress Media, LLC is a California LLC and the sole member (owner) is Springer Science + Business Media Finance Inc (SSBM Finance Inc). SSBM Finance Inc is a **Delaware** corporation.

For information on translations, please e-mail booktranslations@springernature.com; for reprint, paperback, or audio rights, please e-mail bookpermissions@springernature.com.

Apress titles may be purchased in bulk for academic, corporate, or promotional use. eBook versions and licenses are also available for most titles. For more information, reference our Print and eBook Bulk Sales web page at http://www.apress.com/bulk-sales.

Any source code or other supplementary material referenced by the author in this book is available to readers on GitHub via the book's product page, located at www.apress.com/9781484268148. For more detailed information, please visit http://www.apress.com/source-code.

Printed on acid-free paper

Table of Contents

About the Author

Tim Lavers has 25 years' experience in commercial software engineering. He has worked on a variety of applications using many different programming languages. He loves learning new programming technologies and passing that knowledge on to his colleagues. He also taught mathematics for several years, and from that knows how to help people learn difficult things. Apart from programming, Tim enjoys running, bushwalking, and playing the piano.

About the Technical Reviewer

Ted Hagos is a software developer by trade; at the moment, he's Chief Technology Officer and Data Protection Officer of RenditionDigital International, a software development company based out of Dublin. He wore many hats in his 20+ years in software development, for example, team lead, project manager, architect, and director for development. He also spent time as a trainer for IBM Advanced Career Education, Ateneo ITI, and Asia Pacific College. He has written *Learn Android Studio 4* (2020) and *Beginning Android Games Development* (2020) for Apress.

Preface

This book is for anyone who wants to learn computer programming.

Whether you are an absolute beginner, or you have experience with JavaScript, R, Python, or another programming language, this is your path to developing a clear understanding of important fundamental concepts used by software engineering professionals and gaining the skills to implement those concepts in interesting and realistic projects.

I learned programming in my mid-20s, more than 25 years ago, and have worked as a software engineer since then. My opinion, based on this experience, is that the very best way to learn coding is by doing lots of it.

This book gives you the opportunity to get that essential practice. At the same time, you will be working on fascinating programs such as text analysis, image manipulation, and computer vision. These programs progress in a series of small steps that you, the reader, implement. Each step is a simple change to a working program, so that you are never outside your comfort zone and learning becomes a pleasure. Fully worked solutions are provided for each step.

The book is organized into four parts, as follows: In Part I, you will set up the tools needed, get a first program running, and then learn just enough syntax that you can start working on the projects. Part II concentrates on software for text analysis and word games. This introduces the concepts of Object-Oriented Programming and Unit Testing, which are two cornerstones of modern software engineering. Part III is about image processing and concludes with a CGI (computer-generated imagery) program. By doing this project, you will learn Functional Programming, which is an extremely important feature of modern computer languages. Finally, in Part IV, you will consolidate your skills by developing a computer vision system that reads speed signs.

Throughout the book, you will use the same language and tools that are used by professional software engineers worldwide. The language, Kotlin, is very modern and has a simpler syntax than almost any other language used today. Not only is Kotlin a beautiful and powerful language, but it is employed in a wide variety of situations, from hugely complex business software to web programming, to data science, to Android apps. The skills that you learn here will be applicable in any of these areas.

Kotlin programs are written with an editor that highlights errors and offers genuinely useful corrections in most cases. By using professional-grade tools, you should feel the excitement of knowing that the programs that you are working on are of industry standard. If you get stuck, the large and active community of Kotlin users can help you out.

When you finish the projects in this book and move on to your own programs, you will have all the skills required for success and will have a working knowledge of one of the best programming languages that I have used in my 25 years of professional software engineering. Happy coding!

January 2021   *Tim Lavers*

PART I

Basics

In Part I, we set up Kotlin and learn the most important features of the language.

CHAPTER 1

Getting Started

In this chapter, we set up our programming environment and get our first program running.

1.1 What Is Programming?

A computer program is a set of instructions that tell a computer to perform an action such as showing an image or printing out some text.

These instructions are written using special sets of words and symbols, called programming languages. In this book, we are going to use a language called Kotlin. Kotlin is quite new and is closely related to another language, called Java, which is extremely popular in industry and in universities around the world. While Java is an excellent language, it is over 20 years old, which is ancient in computing terms. Additionally, since Java was first developed, there have been many improvements in programming that Kotlin takes advantage of. These improvements mean that Kotlin programs tend to be simpler than their Java equivalents, and many sources of mistakes are avoided outright.

Unlike human beings, computers do not understand vague instructions and are not able to move beyond the simple typographical errors that we easily make. This can make programming a very frustrating task, as even tiny mistakes, such as a missing comma, can stop an otherwise perfect program from working. To avoid these problems, some introductory programming books use very simple languages or even Lego-style visual programming tools in which syntax errors are not possible.

We've decided to stick with Kotlin in this book because by learning it you will be gaining skills in a language that is the first choice for thousands of other programmers and can be used to program lots of different kinds of devices, such as personal computers (obviously), Android devices, microcomputers, and so on. Also, there are lots of code samples that can be found for solving particular problems.

© Tim Lavers 2021
T. Lavers, *Learn to Program with Kotlin*, https://doi.org/10.1007/978-1-4842-6815-5_1

To handle the problems brought about by the complexity of a full-powered language, we will work by modifying existing programs using a code editor that highlights errors and offers sensible corrections.

1.2 Installing Java

As mentioned before, Kotlin is related to an older language called Java. In fact, in order to write and run Kotlin programs, we will need to install the programming tools for Java. These are bundled as what is called the *Java Development Kit* or *Java Platform*, or *JDK*, which is a free download from Oracle at the site `www.oracle.com/java/technologies/javase-downloads.html`.On this page, shown in Figure 1-1, click the "JDK Download" link. This will take you to a page that provides download links for a variety of operating systems. Choose the one that suits your system and download and install the software.

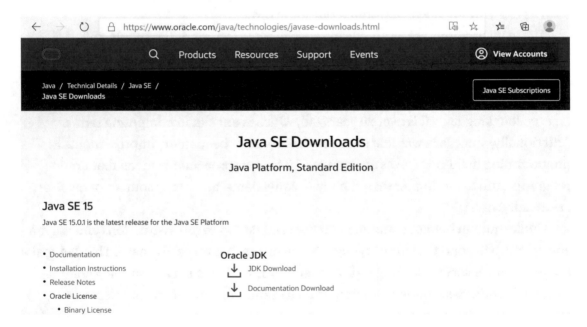

Figure 1-1. *The Java download site. Click the "JDK Download" link*

1.3 Installing Git

Git is a program that is used to share source code between programmers. All of the code in this book can be obtained using Git. This is extremely convenient, but the downside is that we need to install another piece of software. To begin, visit `https://git-scm.com/`.

From this site, download the version for your operating system. Running the installer is a pretty lengthy process, as there are lots of screens that present different setup options. Just accept the default options at each screen.

1.4 Installing IntelliJ

A good code editor is extremely helpful in avoiding and correcting errors in programs. IntelliJ is the best code editor for Kotlin and is very popular with professional programmers. We will be using the "Community Edition" of the tool, which is free for noncommercial use. IntelliJ can be downloaded from the JetBrains website, `www.jetbrains.com/idea/`, and the installation process is simple and well documented.

1.5 Our First Program

Our first program is available from a Git repository that can be opened with IntelliJ. The IntelliJ tool for opening a Git repository is available from the "Welcome to IntelliJ IDEA" screen shown in Figure 1-2.

Figure 1-2. *The IntelliJ welcome screen*

To get the first program:

1. Click the **Get from VCS** button.

2. Wait for the "Get from Version Control" dialog, shown in Figure 1-3, to show.

3. Copy this address: `https://github.com/Apress/learn-to-program-w-kotlin-basics.git` into the **URL** field.

4. Create a new directory, also known as a "folder" in Windows, and copy the location into the **Directory** field.

5. Press the **Clone** button.

Figure 1-3. *The IntelliJ dialog for getting a Git repository*

After some time, which depends on your Internet connection and computer speed, IntelliJ will present the downloaded project, as in Figure 1-4. In the bottom right-hand corner, there might be a pop-up (not shown here) asking about adding files to Git. Just click the **Don't ask again option**.

The upper left-hand side of this screen has what is called the project tree. We will use this later to locate our first program and run it. The project tree can be shown or hidden by pressing the `Alt` and `1` keys at the same time. If, for whatever reason, the project tree is not showing, use this key combination to reveal it. If that does not work, use the menu `Windows` ➤ `Restore Default Layout` to put things right.

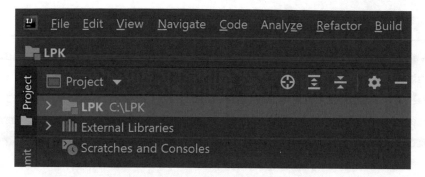

Figure 1-4. *The project in IntelliJ. This part of the IntelliJ user interface is called the project tree. It contains the source files for our programs*

1.6 Changing the Appearance of IntelliJ

As with many programs, the appearance of IntelliJ is configurable. This is done by selecting a visual "theme." The default theme uses the dark colors that can be seen in the preceding screenshots—in fact, the theme is called "Darcula." To change the theme, use the menu File ➤ Settings to display the Settings dialog. Then select **Appearance** in the tree on the left of the settings screen. The **Theme** drop-down has a number of built-in themes from which you can select one you like, as shown in Figure 1-5. In the interests of producing clearer screenshots, I will be using the "IntelliJ Light" theme from now on, as shown.

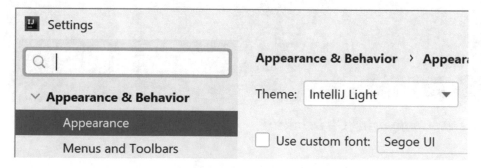

Figure 1-5. *Setting the visual theme*

1.7 Troubleshooting

If IntelliJ was installed before Git, you may get an error message about the path to the Git executable not being found. This can generally be fixed by setting the path within IntelliJ. To do this, choose File ➤ Settings and then select Git under the Version Control heading, as in Figure 1-6. The **Test** button in the top right-hand corner can be used to check that IntelliJ knows where Git is installed. If this test fails, you may need to adjust the setup in IntelliJ by changing the **Path to Git executable** value.

1.8 Running Our First Program

By clicking the folder icons (they look like > signs) in the project tree, you should be able to navigate to the file FirstProgram.kt. Double-click this to open it in the main editor pane. To run the program, click the little green triangle at line 7 of the program text. A pop-up will show, with the option **Run 'FirstProgramKt'**. Select this option.

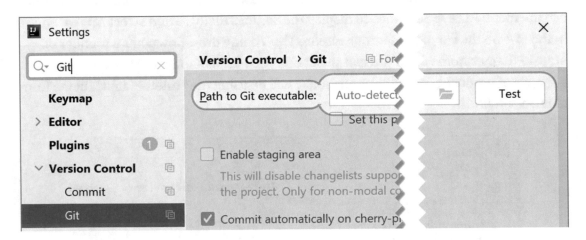

Figure 1-6. *Configuring Git in IntelliJ*

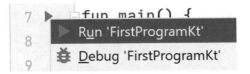

Figure 1-7. *The program is run by clicking the green triangle*

After a half-minute or so of background activity, you should see an application frame with a pattern of black and white squares. Congratulations! You've got the first program running! If you click the small cross at the upper right-hand corner, the display will close and the program will terminate.

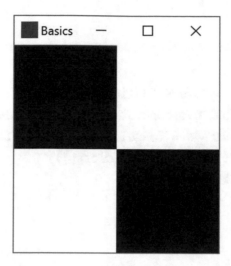

Figure 1-8. *Our first program shows a simple pattern of black and white tiles*

1.9 Source Code for Our Program

As a wrap-up for this chapter, let's have a quick look at the code for our program, just to get a bit more familiar with what Kotlin code looks like. The aim here is just to understand a little of the broad outline of a program. The details will come later.

```
1    package lpk.basics
2
3    import javax.swing.ImageIcon
4    import javax.swing.JFrame
5    import javax.swing.SwingUtilities
6
7    fun main() {
8        SwingUtilities.invokeLater { FirstProgram().doLaunch() }
9    }
10   class FirstProgram {
11
```

```
12        fun tileColors() : Array<Array<Int>> {
13            return arrayOf(
14                    arrayOf(0, 255),
15                    arrayOf(255, 0)
16            )
17        }
18
19        fun doLaunch() {
20            val frame = JFrame("Basics")
21            frame.defaultCloseOperation = JFrame.EXIT_ON_CLOSE
22            frame.iconImage = ImageIcon("./src/lpk/basics/icon.png").image
23            frame.add(TilePanel(tileColors()))
24            frame.pack()
25            frame.isVisible = true
26        }
27    }
```

Note that some of the import statements (lines 3 to 5) might not be showing. Instead, they might appear as a collapsed code block that can be expanded by clicking the + sign.

```
3        ⊞import ...
```

Figure 1-9. *The import statements might be hidden as a collapsed code block*

Even this short program contains a lot of detail that will be totally incomprehensible to a first-time programmer. Don't worry! You don't need to understand everything at once. The main parts of the program can be understood in the following terms:

1. The first line tells the system what package our program belongs in. The complete name of a program includes its package, just as the combination of street name plus other details makes a postal address unique.

2. The import statements let the system know what other programs are needed in our code. All software that does anything remotely complex, such as showing a user interface, makes use of prebuilt components. The import statements are used to make them available to our code.

3. The block containing `tileColors()` sets up a grid of color values. We'll look at this in detail in the next few chapters.

4. Lines 19 to 26 tell the system how to turn the block of colors into a user interface element that can be drawn on the screen.

5. The function called `main` on line 7 is the starting point for the system to launch the program.

In the next chapter, we will begin modifying this code to produce new patterns.

CHAPTER 2

Simple Patterns

In this chapter, we will see how black, white, and other shades of gray can be represented in Kotlin. This will allow us to modify our program from the previous chapter to show different tile patterns. In making these changes, we will be getting familiar with basic Kotlin syntax and with the programming environment.

2.1 Shades of Gray

Software engineering is about modeling aspects of the real world, such as colors, shapes, sounds, and so on, using simple mathematical constructs such as numbers. For now, we are working with shades of gray, and there are many ways that these can be represented in a computer program, for example:

1. Giving specific shades names such as `black`, `white`, `light gray`, `dark gray`, and so on

2. Representing black by 0, white by 1, and intermediate shades by numbers between these values

3. Representing black as 0 and white as 255, with each intermediate shade given by a whole number between these values

The first method is fine if there are just a few shades used in a program. In fact, a similar approach is used in writing web pages. The second method is used in a lot of applications but can be confusing as there are infinitely many numbers between 0 and 1, but only a finite set of shades can be displayed on computer screens, so different decimals might end up producing the same shade. The third approach allows for 256 different shades of gray, which is probably as many as can be discerned by most people, with each number representing a different shade, and a fairly simple way of estimating the shade for a value. This is the model that we have used in our program.

© Tim Lavers 2021
T. Lavers, *Learn to Program with Kotlin*, https://doi.org/10.1007/978-1-4842-6815-5_2

The part of our program that sets up the colors of the squares that are to be displayed is

```
1    fun tileColors() : Array<Array<Int>> {
2        return arrayOf(
3                arrayOf(0, 255),
4                arrayOf(255, 0)
5        )
6    }
```

This code is an example of what is called a *function*, which is a block of code that does one job, and is called from one or more places in a program. Let's look at this function in detail.

1. The keyword fun identifies this as a function.

2. tileColors is the name of the function. When we want to use it, we call it by this name.

3. The empty brackets () signal the end of the function name and mean that the function has no inputs. Inputs to functions are usually called *parameters* (when talking of a function definition) or *arguments* (when talking of an actual call to a function).

4. The complicated bit Array<Array<Int>> describes what the function produces. This particular function produces what is called an Array. An array is just a list of things. Our function produces an array in which the objects are themselves arrays, and these inner arrays hold whole numbers, representing colors. So the function returns an Array of Arrays of Ints. The angle brackets are part of the precise specification of what can go into these arrays. We will discuss these in detail in later chapters.

5. The left brace, {, is the start of the function body, which is the set of instructions in which the logic of the function is implemented.

6. The word return defines what the output, or result, of the function will be.

7.   The word `arrayOf` on line 2 is a call to another function, called `arrayOf`, which produces an array from whatever is passed into it.

8.   The left bracket (at the end of line 2 is the start of the list of arguments that we are passing into the `arrayOf` function. This left bracket is matched by the right bracket on line 5.

9.   On lines 3 and 4, we are setting up the arguments to the `arrayOf` function call made on line 2. We are passing in two arguments, one from line 3 and one from line 4. The comma at the end of line 3 separates these.

10. Line 3 creates an `Array` of two `Ints`. This is done with a call to the `arrayOf` function. The arguments in this call are 0 and 255.

11. Line 4 creates an array that has 255 in the first position and 0 in the second.

12. The closing right brace on line 6 completes the function.

There are lots of details here. Don't let them overwhelm you! By writing code (and making mistakes), you will become familiar with this syntax. Let's make some changes to this program now.

2.2 Changing the Pattern

Now it's your turn for some coding! By modifying the numbers on lines 3 and 4 of the preceding code block, you can change the program from Chapter 1 to produce different tile patterns.

If you make an error, you can just use the menu sequence Edit ➤ Undo Typing to get back to a version of the program that worked. You can also undo changes using the key combination Ctrl + z.

Tip   The solutions to these challenges are at the end of this chapter.

PROGRAMMING CHALLENGE 2.1

Change the program so that it produces this pattern:

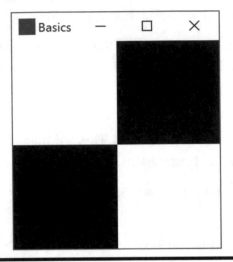

PROGRAMMING CHALLENGE 2.2

Change the program to give

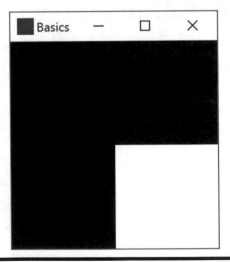

PROGRAMMING CHALLENGE 2.3

Change the program so that it produces this 3-by-3 pattern:

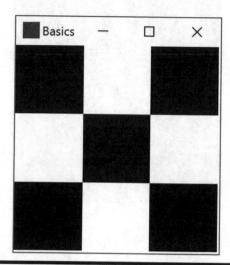

PROGRAMMING CHALLENGE 2.4

If we change the getTileColors function to

```
fun tileColors() : Array<Array<Int>> {
    return arrayOf(
            arrayOf(0, 64),
            arrayOf(128, 192)
    )
}
```

we get this pattern:

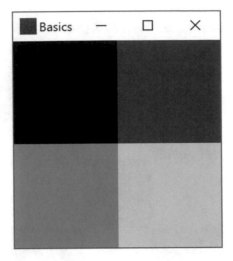

Modify the code again to give

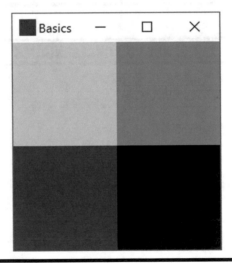

2.3 Solutions to Challenges

For each challenge, we need only change the implementation of the getTileColors function. The changes are as follows.

SOLUTION 2.1

The top-left and bottom-right tiles need to have shade 255, whereas the other tiles are black and so have value 0:

```
fun tileColors() : Array<Array<Int>> {
    return arrayOf(
            arrayOf(255, 0),
            arrayOf(0, 255)
    )
}
```

SOLUTION 2.2

In this pattern, the only white tile is in the bottom-right corner. This corresponds to the second item in the second array:

```
fun tileColors() : Array<Array<Int>> {
    return arrayOf(
            arrayOf(0, 0),
            arrayOf(0, 255)
    )
}
```

SOLUTION 2.3

This pattern has three rows and columns, so we need three arrays of three elements each:

```
fun tileColors() : Array<Array<Int>> {
    return arrayOf(
            arrayOf(0, 255, 0),
            arrayOf(255, 0, 255),
            arrayOf(0, 255, 0)
    )
}
```

SOLUTION 2.4

In the following code, we've used 192 for the brightest tile and then 128 and 64 for the dark gray tiles. Slightly different values will give similar patterns to that shown.

```kotlin
fun tileColors() : Array<Array<Int>> {
    return arrayOf(
            arrayOf(0, 64),
            arrayOf(128, 192)
    )
}
```

CHAPTER 3

Arrays and Loops

In the previous chapter, we worked on a program that built patterns of black and white tiles that corresponded to the elements of a square array. In this chapter, we will introduce a powerful syntax that allows us to build larger patterns from shorter programs.

3.1 Array Indexes

Recall from Chapter 2 that an array is a list of values. An array of arrays is effectively a grid, and our programs so far have used these to represent rectangular patterns of black and white tiles. In these programs, we have used the library function arrayOf to create arrays. However, we can also create arrays from scratch, for example:

```
1    fun tileColors(): Array<Array<Int>> {
2        val shades = Array(2) {
3            Array(2) { 0 }
4        }
5        shades[0][0] = 192
6        shades[0][1] = 128
7        shades[1][0] = 64
8        shades[1][1] = 0
9        return shades
10   }
```

This version of tileColors works as follows. On lines 2 to 4, we are setting up an array of arrays with two rows and two columns in each row and with each value 0. Don't worry too much about the details of this yet; we will return to it later on. It is the next four

© Tim Lavers 2021
T. Lavers, *Learn to Program with Kotlin*, https://doi.org/10.1007/978-1-4842-6815-5_3

lines that are of interest for now. In these lines, we refer to the values in the array using their row and column indexes, just like looking at the grid of a map. The values are then set using the equals sign, which has the meaning "is set to," for example:

```
shades[1][0] = 64
```

means "the array value that is in row 1 and column 0 is set to 64."

In this grid system, we work from the top down, and the first row has index 0. Within each row, we work from left to right, and the first column has index 0. Figure 3-1 shows the correspondence between array indexes and the squares in the tile array.

[0][0]	[0][1]
[1][0]	[1][1]

Figure 3-1. *The row and column indexes of an array*

Referring to the preceding code listing, the top-left square, which has grid references [0][0], is given the value 192. The top-right square, which has grid references [0][1], is assigned value 128. The bottom-left corner has references [1][0] and is assigned value 64. Finally, the bottom-right corner has references [1][1] and is assigned value 0. Remember that a high value is a light shade of gray, so the top-left corner is light gray, whereas the bottom-right corner is black. In fact, if we run the code, we get the pattern shown in Figure 3-2.

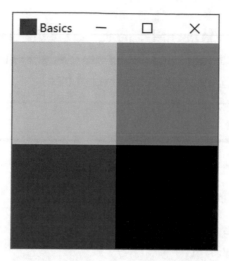

Figure 3-2. *The pattern produced by our first code listing*

This method of building arrays is more fiddly than what we are used to from Chapter 2, but will allow us to use loops and other constructions to build much more interesting patterns. Before we go on with this, let's get some practice using array notation.

PROGRAMMING CHALLENGE 3.1

Consider the following version of `tileColors`:

```
fun tileColors(): Array<Array<Int>> {
    val shades = Array(2) {
        Array(2) { 0 }
    }
    shades[0][0] = 0
    shades[0][1] = 255
    shades[1][0] = 255
    shades[1][1] = 0
    return shades
}
```

By hand, draw a grid of squares with two rows and two columns. Into each of the cells, write the assigned value. Use this to shade in the cells. Finally, run the program and check your hand-drawn picture against what gets shown.

Tip   To save readers of the paper-bound version of the book from too much typing, the code snippets from this chapter are available in a file called `chapter3_code_to_copy.txt` in the project tree.

```
┌──────────────────────────────────────────────────────────────┐
│                    PROGRAMMING CHALLENGE 3.2                    │
└──────────────────────────────────────────────────────────────┘
```

Now consider another different version of `tileColors`:

```
fun tileColors(): Array<Array<Int>> {
    val shades = Array(3) {
        Array(3) { 0 }
    }
    shades[0][0] = 255
    shades[0][1] = 255
    shades[0][2] = 0
    shades[1][0] = 255
    shades[1][1] = 0
    shades[1][2] = 0
    shades[2][0] = 0
    shades[2][1] = 0
    shades[2][2] = 0

    return shades
}
```

How many rows and columns of tiles will there be? Draw a grid and write in the grid references. Which squares are black, and which are white? Run the program to check your answers.

3.2 Loops

Suppose that we wanted to produce a tile pattern like the one shown in Figure 3-3. With so many cells, it would be tedious to set each of the colors in the `getTileColors` function individually. However, we can take advantage of the fact that within each row all of the cells are the same color, to automate the process of setting the colors within a row. To do this, we need to use a programming structure called a for-loop.

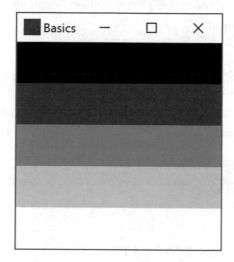

Figure 3-3. *We will use for-loops to produce this pattern*

The first step in producing the pattern is to initialize an array, which we call shades, with five rows and columns:

```
val shades = Array(5) {
    Array(5) { 0 }
}
```

With the array created, we can set the colors of the first row using a for-loop:

```
//Set each cell in row 0 to be black
for (col in 0..4) {
    shades[0][col] = 0
}
```

The structure of the for-loop that we are using is

```
for (COUNTER in RANGE) {
  LOOP BODY: CODE THAT MAY USE THE COUNTER
}
```

In our preceding for-loop, the counter is called col. It represents the column index and therefore has values from 0 to 4. A list of consecutive numbers is represented in

Kotlin by what is called a *range*. There are various ways of defining a range in Kotlin. Here, we are using the expression 0..4. (In fact, ranges in Kotlin can be nonconsecutive numbers too, but we won't need those.) The loop body simply sets the color of the cell corresponding to the column:

```
shades[0][col] = 0
```

Note that each cell in the row gets the same value, 0.

To produce the full pattern, we use similar loops for each of the rows, but with progressively lighter shades of gray:

```
fun tileColors(): Array<Array<Int>> {
    val shades = Array(5) {
        Array(5) { 0 }
    }
    //Set each cell in row 0 to be black
    for (col in 0..4) {
        shades[0][col] = 0
    }
    //Row 1 is dark gray.
    for (col in 0..4) {
        shades[1][col] = 65
    }
    //Row 2 is gray.
    for (col in 0..4) {
        shades[2][col] = 130
    }
    //Row 3 is light gray.
    for (col in 0..4) {
        shades[3][col] = 195
    }
    //Row 4 is white.
    for (col in 0..4) {
        shades[4][col] = 255
    }
    return shades
}
```

Copy the preceding code into your program and run it to verify that it produces the pattern shown earlier.

PROGRAMMING CHALLENGE 3.3

Modify the preceding code so that it produces this pattern of black and white stripes:

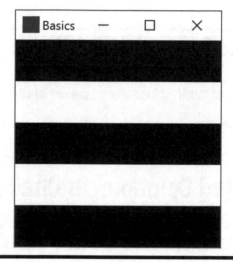

3.3 Nested Loops

We have seen that a for-loop makes it easy to set all cells in a row to have the same color. Suppose that we wanted to give *all* of the tiles in a pattern the same color. To do this, we could have a series of nearly identical loops, one for each row. A better approach is to loop over the rows, and for the body of the loop, have another loop, which sets the values within a row. This pattern, of having a loop inside another loop, is very common in programming and is called a *nested loop*. Here is a nested loop that sets each cell to be white:

```
fun tileColors(): Array<Array<Int>> {
    val shades = Array(5) {
        Array(5) { 0 }
    }
}
```

```
    for (row in 0..4) {
        for (col in 0..4) {
            shades[row][col] = 255
        }
    }
    return shades
}
```

PROGRAMMING CHALLENGE 3.4

Run the preceding code. Then modify it to produce a pattern in which each tile is gray (value 128).

3.4 Summary and Solutions to Challenges

In this chapter, we have seen how array indexes are like map references that allow us to set and read particular values. We have also seen for-loops, which provide a convenient syntax for setting array values in bulk. In the next chapter, we will see how it is possible to build nested loops that set array values in a way that depends on the row and column values, resulting in yet more interesting patterns.

SOLUTION 3.1

The grid of values is

0	255
255	0

This produces a pattern with black tiles in the top-left and bottom-right corners, corresponding to values 0:

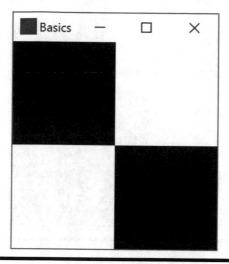

SOLUTION 3.2

There are three rows and three columns. The grid references are

[0][0]	[0][1]	[0][2]
[1][0]	[1][1]	[1][2]
[2][0]	[2][1]	[2][2]

The values for the grid cells are

255	255	0
255	0	0
0	0	0

The corresponding image is

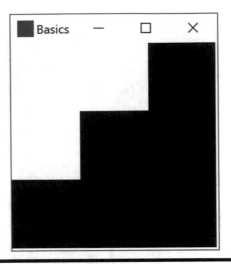

SOLUTION 3.3

The form of the code is the same as the example from the text, with the difference being that we give all cells within a row either the value 0 or 255:

```
fun tileColors(): Array<Array<Int>> {
    val shades = Array(5) {
        Array<Int>{ 0 }
    }
    //Set each cell in row 0 to be black
    for (col in 0..4) {
        shades[0][col] = 0
    }
    //Row 1 is white.
    for (col in 0..4) {
        shades[1][col] = 255
    }
    //Row 2 is black
    for (col in 0..4) {
        shades[2][col] = 0
    }
```

```
//Row 3 is white.
for (col in 0..4) {
    shades[3][col] = 255
}
//Row 4 is black.
for (col in 0..4) {
    shades[4][col] = 0
}
return shades
}
```

SOLUTION 3.4

The code is

```
fun tileColors(): Array<Array<Int>> {
    val shades = Array(5) {
        Array(5) { 0 }
    }
    for (row in 0..4) {
        for (col in 0..4) {
            shades[row][col] = 128
        }
    }
    return shades
}
```

CHAPTER 4

Binary Choices

In the previous chapter, we learned how to iterate over the elements of an array, using a for-loop. This allowed us to automate the coloring of our tiles rather than setting the color of each individually. Now we will learn to make choices in our code based on expressions that evaluate as either true or false. Combined with looping, this will allow us to generate complex tile patterns with very few lines of code.

4.1 If-Else Statements

Consider the pattern in Figure 4-1. There are eight rows and columns, and the tiles are either black or white. All of the white tiles are below the diagonal that goes from the top-left to the bottom-right corner.

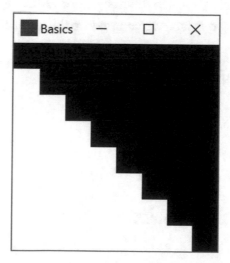

Figure 4-1. *A pattern produced using if-else logic*

© Tim Lavers 2021
T. Lavers, *Learn to Program with Kotlin*, https://doi.org/10.1007/978-1-4842-6815-5_4

What might the corresponding `getTileColors` code be? Something like this, perhaps:

```
fun getTileColors() : Array<Array<Int>> {
  CODE TO INITIALIZE AN 8-BY-8 ARRAY

  FOR EACH ROW
    FOR EACH COLUMN
      IF BELOW DIAGONAL
        shades[row][column] = WHITE
      ELSE
        shades[row][column] = BLACK

  RETURN ARRAY
}
```

To implement this algorithm, we need to be able to decide whether an arbitrary cell is below the top-to-bottom diagonal. Consider a cell with coordinates `[row][column]`. If `row` and `column` are the same, then the cell is on the diagonal. If `column` is greater than `row`, then the cell is to the right and above the diagonal. If, however, `row` is greater than `column`, the cell is to the bottom and to the left of the diagonal. You can check these statements by looking at actual cells in the image. For example, where is cell `[5][3]`? Where is cell `[3][5]`? Using this fact, we can rewrite the algorithm as

```
fun getTileColors() : Array<Array<Int>> {
  CODE TO INITIALIZE AN 8-BY-8 ARRAY

  FOR EACH ROW
    FOR EACH COLUMN
      if (row > column) {
        shades[row][column] = WHITE
      } else {
        shades[row][column] = BLACK
      }

  RETURN ARRAY
}
```

To turn this into Kotlin code, we need to

1.   Implement the code for initializing the array

2.   Replace the FOR EACH pseudo-code with for-loops

3.   Use the correct values for white and black

4.   Write a proper return statement

The result is

```kotlin
fun tileColors(): Array<Array<Int>> {
    val shades = Array(8) {
        Array(8) { 0 }
    }
    for (row in 0..7) {
        for (column in 0..7) {
            if (row > column) {
                shades[row][column] = 255
            } else {
                shades[row][column] = 0
            }
        }
    }
    return shades
}
```

Tip   As with the previous chapter, there's a file in the project tree: chapter4_code_to_copy.txt from which this and other code can be copied.

PROGRAMMING CHALLENGE 4.1

Change the program so that it produces the inverse to the preceding pattern:

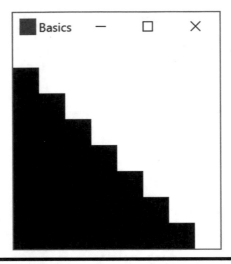

PROGRAMMING CHALLENGE 4.2

To check if two values are the same, we use the == (two equals signs) operator. For example, to check if the row and column have the same value in an `if` statement, we would use `if (row == column)`. Using this operation, can you change the preceding code to produce a pattern with black tiles on the main top-left to bottom-right diagonal?

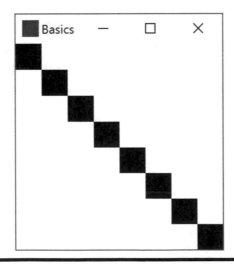

PROGRAMMING CHALLENGE 4.3

By choosing a color based just on the column index, we can produce a vertical stripe. See if you can produce this pattern:

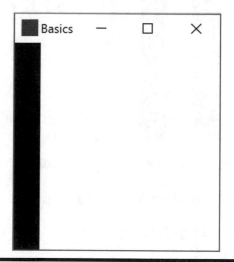

4.2 The Or Operator

Suppose that we'd like to produce a tile pattern with both column 0 and column 2 being entirely filled with black tiles, as in Figure 4-2. We could produce this if the body of our if statement was something like

```
if (column == 0 OR column == 2) ....
```

In fact, this is possible, but Kotlin uses two pipe characters instead of the word OR:

```
if (column == 0 || column == 2) ....
```

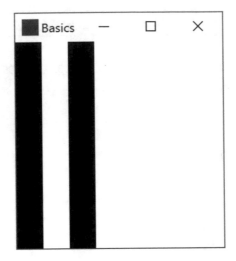

Figure 4-2. *A pattern produced using the* or *operation*

Here is a version of getTileColors that gives the pattern:

```
fun tileColors(): Array<Array<Int>> {
    val shades = Array(8) {
        Array(8) { 0 }
    }
    for (row in 0..7) {
        for (column in 0..7) {
            if (column == 0 || column == 2) {
                shades[row][column] = 0
            } else {
                shades[row][column] = 255
            }
        }
    }
    return shades
}
```

PROGRAMMING CHALLENGE 4.4

It is possible to use multiple || operators in a single statement: a || b || c || d means "a OR b OR c OR d." Use this to change the code so that it produces this pattern:

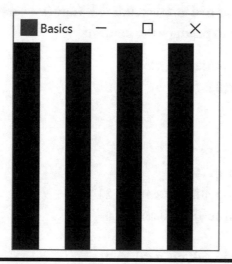

PROGRAMMING CHALLENGE 4.5

Change the code so that it produces this pattern:

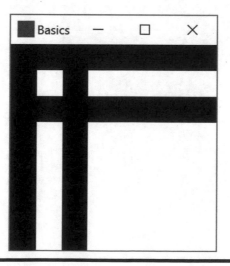

4.3 The And Operator

Suppose that we want to produce a pattern that has a single black tile, which occurs at position [1][1], as in Figure 4-3. This is the single array location for which both row == 1 *and* column == 1. To express a requirement that two conditions are true, we use the *and* operator, which is written as two ampersands: &&. Here is a version of tileColors that uses && in an if statement to produce the pattern:

```
fun tileColors(): Array<Array<Int>> {
    val shades = Array(8) {
        Array(8) { 0 }
    }
    for (row in 0..7) {
        for (column in 0..7) {
            if (row == 1 && column == 1) {
                shades[row][column] = 0
            } else {
                shades[row][column] = 255
            }
        }
    }
    return shades
}
```

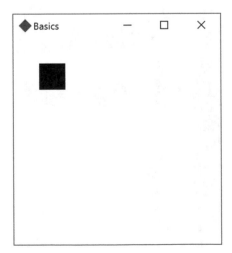

Figure 4-3. *A pattern produced using the and operator*

PROGRAMMING CHALLENGE 4.6

To test if one number is greater than another, we can use the > operator. For example, row > 2 will return the value true if row is 3, 4, 5, … and will return false if row is 0, 1, or 2. Using the > operator for both rows and columns produces this pattern:

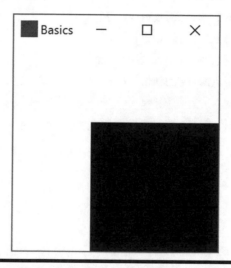

PROGRAMMING CHALLENGE 4.7

The preceding pattern can also be produced using an || operator. For which values of row are the cells white? For which values of column?

Note   You might want to use the "less than" operator, <, to express the conditions on rows and columns.

4.4 If-Else-If Statements

It is possible to make more complex choices by an extension of the if-else syntax in which the else part is itself an if-else statement. For example, suppose that we want to produce the "two dots" pattern in Figure 4-4. We can do this using an if-else-if combination:

```kotlin
fun tileColors(): Array<Array<Int>> {
    val shades = Array(8) {
        Array(8) { 0 }
    }
    for (row in 0..7) {
        for (column in 0..7) {
            if (row == 1 && column == 1) {
                shades[row][column] = 0
            } else if (row == 1 && column == 6) {
                shades[row][column] = 0
            } else {
                shades[row][column] = 255
            }
        }
    }
    return shades
}
```

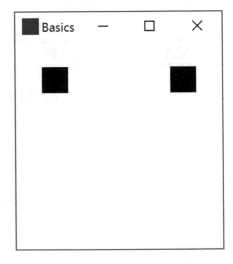

Figure 4-4. *A pattern produced using* `if-else-if` *logic*

PROGRAMMING CHALLENGE 4.8

See if you can produce this pattern:

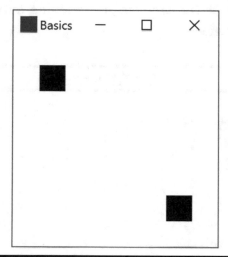

PROGRAMMING CHALLENGE 4.9

It is possible to have repeated else-if blocks. See if you can produce this pattern:

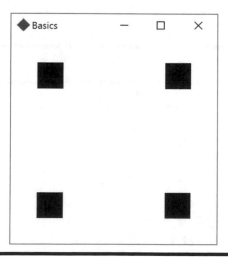

4.5 Summary and Solutions to Challenges

In this chapter, we have learned how to express logical choices as code. We have also learned how to write complex logical conditions using the && and || operators. These concepts are some of the most important in programming, and we will be using them in almost every program we write.

SOLUTION 4.1

```kotlin
fun tileColors(): Array<Array<Int>> {
    val shades = Array(8) {
        Array(8) { 0 }
    }
    for (row in 0..7) {
        for (column in 0..7) {
            if (row > column) {
                shades[row][column] = 0
            } else {
                shades[row][column] = 255
            }
        }
    }
    return shades
}
```

SOLUTION 4.2

```kotlin
fun tileColors(): Array<Array<Int>> {
    val shades = Array(8) {
        Array(8) { 0 }
    }
    for (row in 0..7) {
        for (column in 0..7) {
            if (row == column) {
                shades[row][column] = 0
```

```
        } else {
            shades[row][column] = 255
        }
    }
}
return shades
}
```

SOLUTION 4.3

```
fun tileColors(): Array<Array<Int>> {
    val shades = Array(8) {
        Array(8) { 0 }
    }
    for (row in 0..7) {
        for (column in 0..7) {
            if (column == 0) {
                shades[row][column] = 0
            } else {
                shades[row][column] = 255
            }
        }
    }
    return shades
}
```

SOLUTION 4.4

```
fun tileColors(): Array<Array<Int>> {
    val shades = Array(8) {
        Array(8) { 0 }
    }
    for (row in 0..7) {
        for (column in 0..7) {
            if (column == 0 || column == 2 || column == 4 || column == 6) {
                shades[row][column] = 0
```

```
        } else {
            shades[row][column] = 255
        }
    }
}
return shades
}
```

SOLUTION 4.5

```kotlin
fun tileColors() : Array<Array<Int>> {
    val shades = Array(8) {
        Array(8) { 0 }
    }
    for (row in 0..7) {
        for (column in 0..7) {
            if (column == 0 || column == 2 || row == 0 || row == 2) {
                shades[row][column] = 0
            } else {
                shades[row][column] = 255
            }
        }
    }
    return shades
}
```

SOLUTION 4.6

```kotlin
fun tileColors(): Array<Array<Int>> {
    val shades = Array(8) {
        Array(8) { 0 }
    }
    for (row in 0..7) {
        for (column in 0..7) {
            if (row > 2 && column > 2) {
                shades[row][column] = 0
```

```
        } else {
            shades[row][column] = 255
        }
    }
}
return shades
}
```

```
fun tileColors(): Array<Array<Int>> {
    val shades = Array(8) {
        Array(8) { 0 }
    }
    for (row in 0..7) {
        for (column in 0..7) {
            if (row < 3 || column < 3) {
                shades[row][column] = 255
            } else {
                shades[row][column] = 0
            }
        }
    }
    return shades
}
```

```
fun tileColors(): Array<Array<Int>> {
    val shades = Array(8) {
        Array(8) { 0 }
    }
    for (row in 0..7) {
        for (column in 0..7) {
            if (row == 1 && column == 1) {
                shades[row][column] = 0
```

```
            } else if (row == 6 && column == 6) {
                shades[row][column] = 0
            } else {
                shades[row][column] = 255
            }
        }
    }
    return shades
}
```

SOLUTION 4.9

```
fun tileColors(): Array<Array<Int>> {
    val shades = Array(8) {
        Array(8) { 0 }
    }
    for (row in 0..7) {
        for (column in 0..7) {
            if (row == 1 && column == 1) {
                shades[row][column] = 0
            } else if (row == 6 && column == 1) {
                shades[row][column] = 0
            } else if (row == 1 && column == 6) {
                shades[row][column] = 0
            } else if (row == 6 && column == 6) {
                shades[row][column] = 0
            } else {
                shades[row][column] = 255
            }
        }
    }
    return shades
}
```

CHAPTER 5

Integers

Whole numbers, such as 1, 2, 0, –1, –194, and so on, are known as *integers*. We have already used these as the row and column indexes for our tile patterns and also to define shades of gray. In this chapter, we will be seeing how to combine integers using the familiar arithmetical operators, plus some that you might not have seen before.

5.1 Addition, Subtraction, and Multiplication

To add two integer values together in Kotlin, we use the + operator, and subtraction uses -. The asterisk, *, is used for multiplication.

To see Kotlin's arithmetical operators in action, let's write a new program that does some calculations and prints out the results. In the project tree, right-click the item lpk.basics. A menu will pop up. From it, choose New ➤ Kotlin File/Class. A dialog will show that asks for the name and type of the file. Type "Arithmetic" as the name, and select **File** for the type, as in Figure 5-2. When you press enter, a file will be created. You may also get a dialog that asks you if you'd like to add the new file to a Git repository. If so, click the **Cancel** button.

Figure 5-1. *The right-click menu*

The new file will contain a package declaration and a comment about when the file was created. Delete all of this text and replace it by this code:

© Tim Lavers 2021
T. Lavers, *Learn to Program with Kotlin*, https://doi.org/10.1007/978-1-4842-6815-5_5

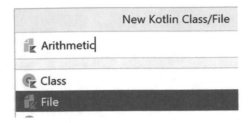

Figure 5-2. *Creating a new Kotlin file*

```
package lpk.basics

fun main() {
    val x = 7 + 5
    println(x)
}
```

When you have done this, you should get a green triangle just to the left of the main function. Right-click this and then choose the Run... option, just like running programs in previous chapters. A panel should show at the bottom of the IntelliJ screen, with some printout, including the number 12.

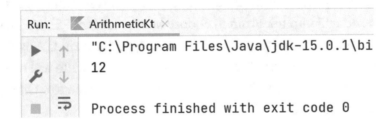

Figure 5-3. *The printout after running the program*

The program works as follows. On line 1, we declare it to be in the lpk.basics package, as we did with earlier programs. The main function, which is the starting point, is declared on line 3. Line 4 is where the arithmetic happens. We define a value called x using the keyword val. The equals sign sets x to be equal to 5 + 7, which of course is 12. On line 5, we call the library function println to print out x.

PROGRAMMING CHALLENGE 5.1

Modify the program so that it prints out 7 minus 5.

PROGRAMMING CHALLENGE 5.2

There is no × symbol on the keyboard, so for multiplication, programmers use an asterisk. Modify the program so that it prints out 7 * 5.

PROGRAMMING CHALLENGE 5.3

Let's rewrite the program so that it prints out the seven times table. To do this, we will need a loop that has values from 1 through to 10. The body of this loop will print out 7 times the loop value. Here is the program with the loop outlined:

```
package lpk.basics

fun main() {
    for (i in 1..10) {
        //Loop body goes here
    }
}
```

Replace the //Loop body goes here comment with code that

1. Declares a variable x with value 7 times i

2. Prints x

The last challenge prints out a list of multiples of seven. We can do something a bit fancier. Change the program to the following:

```
package lpk.basics

fun main() {
    for (i in 1..10) {
        val x = 7 * i
        println("7 times $i is $x")
    }
}
```

When you run the program, you should see the output shown in Figure 5-4.

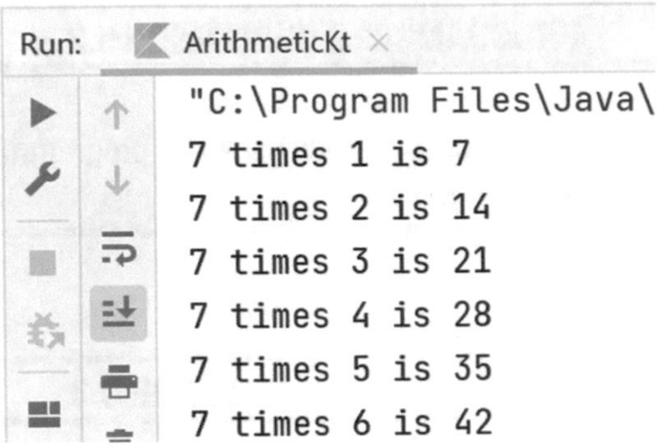

Figure 5-4. *Printing out a times table*

On line 6, we are printing out what is called a String rather than just a number. We will work more with Strings in later chapters. For now, it is enough to think of a String just as a mixture of letters, digits, and other characters. Kotlin has a great feature that allows us to insert variable values into a String. This is done using the dollar signs on line 6: $i means "the current value of i" and similarly for $x. This is called *string interpolation.*

This output can be made a bit more compact by replacing words with symbols. We will also put a tab character instead of a newline between each group. To do this, we replace the line that does the printing with

```
print("7*$i=$x\t")
```

In this code, we have called print rather than println. The latter function prints out its argument and then prints a newline character (which is like pressing the enter key). Also, we have used the "backslash t" combination, which means "print a tab." (Tabs are special invisible characters that are used to regulate spacing when printing a series of items of slightly different lengths.) With these changes, the printout is as shown in Figure 5-5.

```
"C:\Program Files\Java\jdk-15.0.1\bin\java.exe" "-javaa
7*1=7    7*2=14   7*3=21   7*4=28   7*5=35   7*6=42   7*7=49
Process finished with exit code 0
```

Figure 5-5. *The times table on a single line*

Let's modify the program to print out all times tables from 1 to 10. We need to do, for each number from 1 to 10, what we are currently doing for the number 7. In very rough terms, our program has the form

```
1    package lpk.basics
2
3    fun main() {
4        for (s in 1..10) {
5            //Print out the s times table
6            println()
7        }
8    }
```

Notice that on line 6 we are printing an empty line so that each inner loop prints on its own line. The code to print out the s times table is a loop almost identical to what we have previously used in the seven times table program. So a more complete outline of the required program is

```
package lpk.basics

fun main() {
    for (s in 1..10) {
        for (i in 1..10) {
            //Define x to be s times i
            //Print out s, i and the result
        }
        println()
    }
}
```

PROGRAMMING CHALLENGE 5.4

Can you make the final changes to finish this program?

When you run it, the output should begin:

```
"C:\Program Files\Java\jdk-15.0.1\bin\java.exe" "-java
1*1=1    1*2=2    1*3=3    1*4=4    1*5=5    1*6=6    1*7=7
2*1=2    2*2=4    2*3=6    2*4=8    2*5=10   2*6=12   2*7=14
3*1=3    3*2=6    3*3=9    3*4=12   3*5=15   3*6=18   3*7=21
4*1=4    4*2=8    4*3=12   4*4=16   4*5=20   4*6=24   4*7=28
5*1=5    5*2=10   5*3=15   5*4=20   5*5=25   5*6=30   5*7=35
6*1=6    6*2=12   6*3=18   6*4=24   6*5=30   6*6=36   6*7=42
```

5.2 Division

With addition, subtraction, and multiplication, we combine two integers in a simple way to produce another integer. Division is more complicated because it is not always possible to divide one number into another. Division by 0 is not defined. And how do we divide 13 by 4 to obtain another integer? In programming, division of whole numbers is handled by two operations: / and %.

By x / y, we mean the number of times that y goes completely into x. For example, 8/3 is 2 and 8/4 is also 2.

By x % y, we mean the remainder after dividing x by y. For example, 8 % 3 is 2 and 8 % 4 is 0. To see these operations in action, run the following program:

```
1   package lpk.basics
2
3   fun main() {
4       for (i in 1..20) {
5           val div = i / 5
6           val rem = i % 5
7           println("i: $i, div: $div, rem: $rem")
8       }
9   }
```

Line 4 sets up a for-loop with variable i that goes from 1 to 20. On line 5, we define a val called div, which is set to be the integer part of i divided by 5. The next line defines a val, called rem, which is the remainder after dividing i by 5. On line 7, we print out i and the two vals. The result of our program begins:

```
i: 1, div: 0, rem: 1
i: 2, div: 0, rem: 2
i: 3, div: 0, rem: 3
i: 4, div: 0, rem: 4
i: 5, div: 1, rem: 0
i: 6, div: 1, rem: 1
i: 7, div: 1, rem: 2
i: 8, div: 1, rem: 3
i: 9, div: 1, rem: 4
i: 10, div: 2, rem: 0
```

5.3 Making Patterns Using Arithmetic

We can modify our tiles program to produce patterns using the arithmetical operations. For example, let's change the getTileColors function in FirstProgram to

```
1    fun tileColors(): Array<Array<Int>> {
2        val shades = Array(16) {
3            Array(16) { 0 }
4        }
5        for (row in 0..15) {
6            for (col in 0..15) {
7                shades[row][col] = row * col
8            }
9        }
10       return shades
11   }
```

We get the pattern shown in Figure 5-6. Notice that this contains 16 rows and columns.

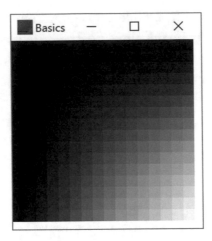

Figure 5-6. *A pattern in which the tile shade is obtained by multiplying its row index by its column index*

These dimensions are set up on lines 2 and 3. The pattern is symmetrical about the diagonal between the top-left and bottom-right corners. This is because the reflection of cells in this diagonal has the effect of swapping row and column coordinates. For example, consider the cell with row 5 and column 3. The reflection of this cell in the diagonal has row 3 and column 5. Since 5 times 3 is 3 times 5, these cells will have the same shade of gray. The cells along the first row and the first column are all black because 0 times any other number is 0.

Now let's use the remainder operation, %, to build the pattern of alternating black and white rows shown in Figure 5-7.

Figure 5-7. *A pattern in which the tile shade is either black or white depending on the remainder of the row index divided by 2*

The code that produces this is

```
1    fun tileColors(): Array<Array<Int>> {
2        val shades = Array(16) {
3            Array(16) { 0 }
4        }
5        for (row in 0..15) {
6            for (col in 0..15) {
7                val remainder = row % 2
8                if (remainder == 0) {
9                    shades[row][col] = 0
10               } else {
11                   shades[row][col] = 255
12               }
13           }
14       }
15       return shades
16   }
```

PROGRAMMING CHALLENGE 5.5

Change the tileColors function so that it produces a pattern of alternating black and white columns:

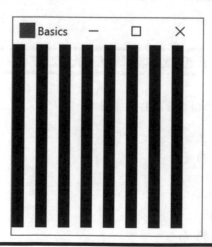

PROGRAMMING CHALLENGE 5.6

Can you change the `tileColors` function so that it produces a pattern of alternating black and white squares?

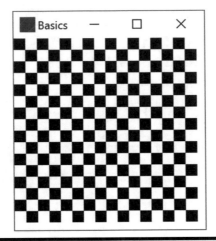

PROGRAMMING CHALLENGE 5.7

Can you produce a chessboard pattern, which is the same as in the previous challenge, but with only eight rows and columns, and with white squares on the top-left to bottom-right diagonal?

PROGRAMMING CHALLENGE 5.8

Consider this implementation of getTileColors:

```
fun tileColors(): Array<Array<Int>> {
    val shades = Array(7) {
        Array(7) { 0 }
    }
    for (row in 0..6) {
        for (col in 0..6) {
            val remainder = (row * col) % 2
```

```
            if (remainder == 0) {
                shades[row][col] = 255
            } else {
                shades[row][col] = 0
            }
        }
    }
    return shades
}
```

How many rows and columns will the pattern have?

What color will cells (0, 0), (1, 4), (3, 2), and (5, 5) be?

In general, what can we say about a cell if it lies in an even-numbered column?

What can we say about cells that lie in even-numbered rows?

What cells will be white?

What do you think the pattern looks like? Run the code and see for yourself.

5.4 Summary and Solutions to Challenges

We now know how to do integer arithmetic in Kotlin, including division into whole numbers and remainders.

SOLUTION 5.1

```
package lpk.basics

fun main() {
    val x = 7 - 5
    println(x)
}
```

SOLUTION 5.2

```
package lpk.basics

fun main() {
    val x = 7 * 5
    println(x)
}
```

SOLUTION 5.3

```
package lpk.basics

fun main() {
    for (i in 1..10) {
        val x = 7 * i
        println(x)
    }
}
```

SOLUTION 5.4

```
package lpk.basics

fun main() {
    for (s in 1..10) {
        for (i in 1..10) {
            val x = s * i
            print("$s*$i=$x\t")
        }
        println()
    }
}
```

SOLUTION 5.5

```kotlin
fun tileColors(): Array<Array<Int>> {
    val shades = Array(16) {
        Array(16) { 0 }
    }
    for (row in 0..15) {
        for (col in 0..15) {
            val remainder = col % 2
            if (remainder == 0) {
                shades[row][col] = 0
            } else {
                shades[row][col] = 255
            }
        }
    }
    return shades
}
```

SOLUTION 5.6

```kotlin
fun tileColors(): Array<Array<Int>> {
    val shades = Array(16) {
        Array(16) { 0 }
    }
    for (row in 0..15) {
        for (col in 0..15) {
            val remainder = (row + col) % 2
            if (remainder == 0) {
                shades[row][col] = 0
```

```
        } else {
            shades[row][col] = 255
        }
    }
}
return shades
}
```

SOLUTION 5.7

```kotlin
fun tileColors(): Array<Array<Int>> {
    val shades = Array(8) {
        Array(8) { 0 }
    }
    for (row in 0..7) {
        for (col in 0..7) {
            val remainder = (row + col) % 2
            if (remainder == 0) {
                shades[row][col] = 255
            } else {
                shades[row][col] = 0
            }
        }
    }
    return shades
}
```

SOLUTION 5.8

There are seven rows and seven columns.

If the product of the row index of a cell by its column index is even, then the cell is white. This means that any cell for which the row index or column index is even is white.

Only cells for which both the row and column are odd are black.

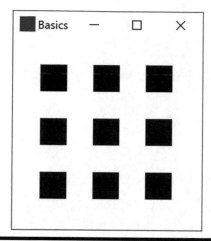

CHAPTER 6

Values and Variables

When we are writing a program, we may have a piece of information that will need to be referred to from other places in our program. *Values* and *variables* are used for this. They are defined using the keywords val and var, respectively. We can think of vals and vars as boxes containing items of data. A var is a box from which the data may be removed and replaced with some other data item. With a val, however, the data item is set once and can never be replaced.

6.1 Using **vars**

One common use of vars is to store the partial results of a calculation. For example, if we want to write a program to add up the numbers from 1 to 10, we can

- Create a var called sum, with an initial value of 0.

- Define a loop with counter i that starts at 1 and goes to 10.

- Add i to sum at each step in the loop.

Here's how this algorithm looks as code:

```
1   package lpk.basics
2
3   fun main() {
4       var sum = 0
5       for (i in 1..10) {
6           sum = sum + i
7       }
8       print(sum)
9   }
```

Copy this into the Arithmetic.kt file that we used in the previous chapter. Check that when you run it, the number 55 is printed out.

© Tim Lavers 2021
T. Lavers, *Learn to Program with Kotlin*, https://doi.org/10.1007/978-1-4842-6815-5_6

The code works as follows. On line 4, we define the var called sum. The equals sign in this line of code actually means "set the data in the sum box to be 0." Line 6 at first seems confusing because sum is used on both sides of the equals sign. But as in line 4, the equals sign actually means "set the value to." So line 6 is actually interpreted as "replace the contents of the sum box with the current contents plus i."

One of the trickiest things about working with variables is the use of = for setting their values. Some programming languages use := for this job, which is less confusing. Remember that to test to see if two objects are equal, we use ==.

PROGRAMMING CHALLENGE 6.1

Modify the preceding program to add up the numbers between 1 and 100.

Then modify it to add up the numbers between 11 and 20.

PROGRAMMING CHALLENGE 6.2

Now change the program to add up the squares of the numbers between 1 and 10. (The square of a number is that number times itself. Remember to use * for multiplication.)

PROGRAMMING CHALLENGE 6.3

By using an if statement, we can add just the even numbers to the sum variable. See if you can work out the sum of the even numbers between 0 and 10.

PROGRAMMING CHALLENGE 6.4

The *factorial* of a number is defined as follows:

- 1 factorial is 1
- 2 factorial is 2×1
- 3 factorial is $3 \times 2 \times 1$

and so on. Modify the program for sums to find the factorial of 5.

6.2 Using `vals`

As mentioned earlier, we can think of a val as a box containing an item of data that cannot be replaced with another item. You might well ask: "Why bother? Why not just use vars everywhere? They can do more so aren't they better?" In fact, a lot of languages do not have vals and only have vars. The problem with vars is that because the contents can be replaced, it can become very hard to keep track of what is in them. This difficulty really becomes important in two situations.

Firstly, with very complex programs, it's hard for us humans to keep track of what is inside each var. This makes it hard to write and maintain large programs that use a lot of vars.

The second problem with vars is that modern software has lots of things happening simultaneously. If one computer activity is trying to retrieve the contents of a var but other activities are changing these contents, unpredictable behavior can ensue. It's very hard to write software in which multiple independent activities are changing shared data. In "the old days," prior to 2005, it was quite unusual to find computers that were capable of doing several tasks at the same time, whereas now it is almost impossible to find ones that do not have at least two so-called processing cores. For this reason, modern languages such as Kotlin distinguish between vals and vars.

We will use vals a lot in later chapters. Right now, let's just write a program that uses a val in a temporary variable. The *Fibonacci* numbers are 1, 1, 2, 3, 5, 8, and so on. Each number in the sequence is obtained by adding up the previous two numbers. Here is the outline of a program that prints the first ten or so Fibonacci numbers:

```
1   package lpk.basics
2
3   fun main() {
4       var current = 1
5       var previous = 1
```

```
6        for (i in 1..10) {
7               //Print previous
8               //Calculate the next one
9               //Re-assign previous to current
10              //Re-assign current to next
11           }
12    }
```

On lines 4 and 5, we define vars to hold the current and previous Fibonacci numbers. These vars are initialized with the first two elements of the sequence and will be changed in the loop to hold further elements of the sequence as these are calculated.

Within the loop, the first thing that we want to do is print previous. So line 7 can be changed to

```
println(previous)
```

On line 8, we need to calculate the next number. The Fibonacci recipe says that this is the sum of previous and next. We can store this sum in a val, which we might as well call next. So line 8 becomes

```
val next = current + previous
```

Now that we've calculated the next number, what was the current becomes the previous. So line 9 can be changed to

```
previous = current
```

Remember, this is to be understood as "take the contents of current and put them in previous."

Finally, we need to switch the contents of current to contain the contents of next:

```
current = next
```

PROGRAMMING CHALLENGE 6.5

Implement these changes and run the program.

This program would work with next defined as a var rather than as a val, but whenever we can use a val, we should. Notice that in IntelliJ the vars are written with a slightly annoying underline. That is a subtle hint to use vals when possible. If you change next from being a val to being a var, then IntelliJ will write var with an off-putting yellow background, as in Figure 6-1. This is a less subtle hint that we can do better.

```
println(previous)
var next = current + previous
```

Figure 6-1. *An IntelliJ hint to use a val*

6.3 Scope

Consider this program:

```
1    package lpk.basics
2
3    fun main() {
4        for (i in 1..10) {
5            val square = i * i
6            val cube = i * square
7            println("$i, $square, $cube")
8        }
9    }
```

There are three vals: the loop counter, i; square, defined on line 5; and cube, defined on line 6. These vals have meaning within the body of the for-loop, that is, between the left brace at the end of line 4 and the matching right brace on line 8. If we copy line 7 and put it after the brace on line 8, the i, square, and cube references have no meaning, so we get errors, as in Figure 6-2. In languages such as Kotlin, symbols have meaning within the pair of braces in which they are defined, and outside they have either no meaning or another meaning. Within a pair of braces, symbols cannot be referred to by a line above the line in which they are defined. For example, we can't use square before it has been defined, as has been attempted in Figure 6-3. The section of code in which a val or var has meaning is called its *scope*.

```
for (i in 1..10) {
    val square = i * i
    val cube = i * square
}
println("$i, $square, $cube")
```

Figure 6-2. *IntelliJ shows out-of-scope symbols as errors*

```
for (i in 1..10) {
    val cube = i * square
    val square = i * i
    println("$i, $square, $cube")
}
```

Figure 6-3. *We can't use a symbol before it has been defined*

The rules for scoping are very much common sense, and IntelliJ will make it obvious when there's a problem, so don't worry too much about this issue.

One thing that might be confusing is that loop counters, which are described as vals earlier, seem to be reassigned with each iteration of the loop. In fact, this is not the case. A loop such as

```
for (i in 1..3) {
    val square = i * i
    println("$i, $square")
}
```

gets converted by Kotlin into code along the lines of

```
val i1 = 1
val square1 = i1 * i1
println("$i1, $square1")

val i2 = 2
val square2 = i2 * i2
println("$i2, $square2")

val i3 = 3
val square3 = i3 * i3
println("$i3, $square3")
```

6.4 Summary and Solutions to Challenges

To write complex programs, we need to store information, and we do this in vals and vars.

SOLUTION 6.1

This is done by changing the limits of the loop. The sum to 100 is calculated using

```
package lpk.basics

fun main() {
    var sum = 0
    for (i in 1..100) {
        sum = sum + i
    }
    print(sum)
}
```

This should give result 5050.

The sum from 11 to 20 is given by

```
package lpk.basics

fun main() {
    var sum = 0
    for (i in 11..20) {
        sum = sum + i
    }
    print(sum)
}
```

This should give result 155.

SOLUTION 6.2

```
package lpk.basics

fun main() {
    var sum = 0
    for (i in 1..10) {
        sum = sum + i * i
    }
    print(sum)
}
```

In the expression sum + i * i, the multiplication is done before the addition. In Kotlin, as in standard mathematical notation, multiplication takes precedence over addition.

SOLUTION 6.3

```
package lpk.basics

fun main() {
    var sum = 0
    for (i in 1..10) {
        if (i % 2 == 0) {
            sum = sum + i
        }
    }
    print(sum)
}
```

SOLUTION 6.4

This is similar to calculating the sum, but we begin with 1 and multiply the partial result within the loop body:

```
package lpk.basics
```

```
fun main() {
    var factorial = 1
    for (i in 1..5) {
        factorial = factorial * i
    }
    print(factorial)
}
```

The sequence of factorials grows very fast. In fact, if you try to calculate the factorial of a number like 30 using something like the preceding code, you will get a crazy answer. This is because of a limit to the memory allocated to store Ints in Kotlin. It is possible to work with larger numbers, though we won't be doing so in this book.

SOLUTION 6.5

```
package lpk.basics

fun main() {
    var current = 1
    var previous = 1
    for (i in 1..10) {
        println(previous)
        val next = current + previous
        previous = current
        current = next
    }
}
```

CHAPTER 7

Strings

A lot of software deals with text in some form or another, and there are a couple of data types in Kotlin for this.

Char is used to represent symbols such as letters, digits, and punctuation marks. We can define a Char by writing it between single quotes, for example, 'a'. The uppercase and lowercase versions of a character are represented by distinct Chars. Apart from the so-called Latin characters that are on most computer keyboards, Chars can represent accented letters, symbols from languages all around the world, and mathematical notation.

Strings are used to represent words, sentences, or even whole books. We define Strings by writing them between double quotes, as we did in some of our previous programs. If we want an empty String, we simply write two double quotes: "". We'll see this a lot in the code in this chapter.

7.1 Strings as Objects

As has been mentioned before, programming is a process of modeling the real world using lists of instructions that can be performed by a computer. The String data type is used to model text. If we have some text, we might be interested in questions such as how many characters it has, for example, to find out how many lines it will take to print it. In Kotlin, and in many other languages, information is obtained by "asking" data items about themselves. We "ask" questions of data items with a special "dot" notation. Here's an example:

```
1   fun main() {
2       val str = "Hello World!"
3       val l = str.length
4       println("Length: $l" )
5   }
```

© Tim Lavers 2021
T. Lavers, *Learn to Program with Kotlin*, https://doi.org/10.1007/978-1-4842-6815-5_7

On line 2, we define a val called `str`, which is a `String` having the value "Hello World!". On the next line, we define a val called `l` to be equal to the `length` of `str`. This value is obtained using the notation:

```
str.length
```

Note that on line 4 we are printing out the `String`:

```
"Length: $l"
```

Kotlin interprets this by replacing the text:

```
$l
```

with the value of `l`, so that what gets printed is

```
Length: 12
```

This is `String` interpolation again. It is used a lot in Kotlin programming, and you will quickly get used to it.

Tip   As usual, there's a file in the project tree from which all of the code examples in this chapter can be copied:

```
chapter7_code_to_copy.txt
```

This is especially useful in this chapter because some of the code samples will not copy correctly from the electronic version of the book.

Let's get a bit more practice using this dot notation. Create a file called `Strings.kt`, following the instructions from Chapter 5. Then copy this code into the new file:

```
1    package lpk.basics
2
3    fun main() {
4        val str = "Hello World!"
5        val l = str.length
6        println("Length: $l")
7        val upperCase = str.toUpperCase()
8        println(upperCase)
```

```
9        val lowerCase = str.toLowerCase()
10       println(lowerCase)
11   }
```

When you run this program, you should see output like this:

```
Length: 12
HELLO WORLD!
hello world!
```

On line 7 of this program, we create a val by asking str "What is an uppercase version of you?" using the toUpperCase function. Similarly, on line 9, we ask str for a lowercase version of itself.

How do we know which questions we can ask a String? In the old days, programmers spent a lot of time learning all of the functions that were available for different data types, and this knowledge was a large part of their skill set. These days, tools such as IntelliJ put this information at our fingertips. If we type in the code

```
str.
```

and then press the Ctrl and space keys simultaneously, a pop-up will show that contains a list of the available functions, as shown in Figure 7-1. We will get a lot of practice in using these "dot" functions and will define our own data types, which will demystify things considerably! For now, take heart from the fact that IntelliJ will do a lot of the hard work for us when we write code.

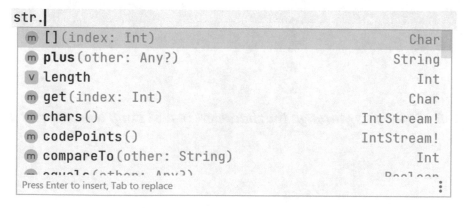

Figure 7-1. *IntelliJ lists the functions that may be called on a data type*

7.2 **String** Iteration

One of the most common operations on Strings is to *iterate*, or loop, through the Chars in them, one by one, from the first to the last, just as we can with the elements of an Array. To see how this works, copy the following code into your Strings.kt file:

```
1    package lpk.basics
2
3    fun main() {
4        val str = "Kotlin!"
5        for (c in str) {
6            println(c)
7        }
8    }
```

Line 4 defines a val called str, just like we saw in earlier programs. The next line introduces a for-loop in which there is a loop val called c. The body of the loop, which here is just a println call, is executed once for each of the Chars in str. If we run this program, we get the characters of "Kotlin!" printed out, one per line, as shown in Figure 7-2.

```
"C:\Program File
K
o
t
l
i
n
!
```

Figure 7-2. *By iterating through the characters in a* String, *we can print it vertically*

```
PROGRAMMING CHALLENGE 7.1
```

Suppose that we change the body of the loop in the preceding code listing to be a print rather than a println statement. What do you think the result of running the program will be?

```
PROGRAMMING CHALLENGE 7.2
```

Consider this variation on the program:

```
fun main() {
    val str = "Kotlin!"
    var numberOfSpaces = 0
    for (c in str) {
        for (n in 0..numberOfSpaces) {
            print(" ")
        }
        println(c)
        numberOfSpaces = numberOfSpaces + 1
    }
}
```

Notice the var called numberOfSpaces defined on line 3. It gets incremented each time the loop body is executed, as the last statement of the loop body, on line 9.

What is the value of numberOfSpaces when the loop val c is 'K'?

What is the value when c is 'o'?

What is the effect of the inner loop on lines 5 to 7?

What do you think the result of the program will be?

A common reason for iterating (looping) through a String is to find certain Chars within it. For example, here's a program that uses a loop to count the spaces in a String:

```
1    package lpk.basics
2
3    fun main() {
4        val str = "How long is a piece of string?"
```

```
5          var spaceCount = 0
6          for (c in str) {
7              if (c == ' ') {
8                  spaceCount = spaceCount + 1
9              }
10         }
11         println("Number of spaces: $spaceCount")
12     }
```

On line 5, we define a var to hold the number of spaces seen so far. Line 6 sets up a for-loop that will go through the Chars in the String, with a loop val called c. On line 7, the val c is compared with the Char that represents a space. If the comparison is true, spaceCount is incremented, on line 8. Finally, the count is printed out after the loop, on line 11.

PROGRAMMING CHALLENGE 7.3

Copy the preceding code from the file:

chapter7_code_to_copy.txt

Can you modify the code to count the number of times that the letter 'a' appears?

Can you count the number of times that either 'a' or 'e' appears?

Now change the program to count the number of times that vowels appear.

7.3 Building New **Strings**

Often, in programming, we need to produce text automatically—a message to users, for example—and in Kotlin this is very easy because we can join Strings together using the same + operator that is used for adding numbers:

```
1    fun main() {
2        val msg = "Hello" + " " + "World!"
3        println(msg)
4    }
```

The val msg on line 2 is defined by joining three Strings, the middle of which is just a space, to produce the single String "Hello World!".

We can remove certain Chars from text by looping through it and, as we do so, adding the letters that we want to keep to a result var. For example, suppose that we want to remove the spaces from a String. We can look at each Char in the String, and if it is not a space, we add it to a result var. The way we check that a Char c is *not* the space Char is by using the not equals operator, written !=:

```
1    if (c != ' ') {
2        //add it
3    }
```

Here's the complete program:

```
fun main() {
    val str = "There is a bunker!"
    var noSpaces = ""
    for (c in str) {
        if (c != ' ') {
            noSpaces = noSpaces + c
        }
    }
    println(noSpaces)
}
```

PROGRAMMING CHALLENGE 7.4

Copy the preceding code from the file:

chapter7_code_to_copy.txt

Change the program to remove all vowels from the String "Can you understand this?".

PROGRAMMING CHALLENGE 7.5

(Super difficult.) In some typesetting programs, when we have more than one space between words, our formatted text will look "gappy." Write a program to compact all multiple spaces between words into a single space character. For example, given the input

`"Mind the    gap!"`

the output will be

`"Mind the gap!"`

Note   If you copy the text from this document, the triple space may get converted to a single space.

Hint   This is similar to the space removal program, but we need a `var` that remembers whether or not the previous `Char` was a space. This `var` can be called `previousCharWasSpace`. Its values are either `true` or `false`. The initial value of it is `false`. A type that is either `true` or `false` is called a Boolean.

7.4 More on **String** Iteration

Consider this simple program:

```
package lpk.basics

fun main() {
    val str = "abc"
    for (c in str) {
        println(c)
    }
}
```

The Kotlin system treats this as if it were written:

```
package lpk.basics

fun main() {
    val str = "abc"
    val c_0 = 'a'
    println(c_0)
    val c_1 = 'b'
    println(c_1)
    val c_2 = 'c'
    println(c_2)
}
```

This is why we can talk about c as a val in a loop such as

```
for (c in str) {
    //Loop body. c is a val here.
}
```

PROGRAMMING CHALLENGE 7.6

Consider this program:

```
package lpk.basics

fun main() {
    val str = "back"
    var result = ""
    for (c in str) {
        result = result + c
    }
    println(result)
}
```

Write an equivalent "long form" version of this program that does not use a loop.

PROGRAMMING CHALLENGE 7.7

The solution to the previous challenge is a program in which a var called result is initialized (created) as an empty String and then reset four times. For each reset, write on a piece of paper the value before and after the reset.

Each of the resets is of the form

result = result + c_0

What happens if we switch the order of the Strings in the + operations? That is, if we change them to put the next Char before result:

result = c_0 + result

Write out "before" and "after" values for result with these switched resets.

Using these insights, convert the program of the previous challenge to one that uses a loop to reverse a String.

7.5 Summary and Solutions to Challenges

This chapter introduced the hugely important String data type. One of the most common operations on Strings is to loop through the characters of it, just as can be done with arrays. The expansion of such loops as equivalent code blocks, one for each element of the String, gives some insight into the nature of loop variables.

SOLUTION 7.1

The output will be just "Kotlin!" on a single line.

SOLUTION 7.2

When c is 'K', numberOfSpaces is 0.

When c is 'o', numberOfSpaces is 1.

The inner loop prints out numberOfSpaces spaces, one after the other, on a single line.

Running the program gives a printout of "Kotlin!" on the diagonal:

```
"C:\Program Files\Java\jdk-15.0.1\
 K
   o
     t
       l
         i
           n
             !


Process finished with exit code 0
```

SOLUTION 7.3

Counting the 'a's:

```kotlin
package lpk.basics

fun main() {
    val str = "How long is a piece of string?"
    var count = 0
    for (c in str) {
        if (c == 'a') {
            count = count + 1
        }
    }
    println("Count: $count")
}
```

To count the 'a's and the 'e's, we can use an or in our comparison:

```kotlin
package lpk.basics

fun main() {
    val str = "How long is a piece of string?"
    var count = 0
```

```
    for (c in str) {
        if (c == 'a' || c == 'e') {
            count = count + 1
        }
    }
    println("Count: $count")
}
```

An alternative is to have two if statements:

```
package lpk.basics

fun main() {
    val str = "How long is a piece of string?"
    var count = 0
    for (c in str) {
        if (c == 'a') {
            count = count + 1
        }
        if (c == 'e') {
            count = count + 1
        }
    }
    println("Count: $count")
}
```

To count the vowels, we can list them all in the if statement:

```
package lpk.basics

fun main() {
    val str = "How long is a piece of string?"
    var count = 0
    for (c in str) {
        if (c == 'a' || c == 'e' || c == 'i'|| c == 'o'|| c == 'u') {
            count = count + 1
        }
    }
    println("Count: $count")
}
```

Actually, this is incorrect because it is not taking into account uppercase vowels. To fix this problem, we can insert a `val` that is the lowercase version of `c` and make the comparison against this. To get the lowercase version of a `Char`, we call the `toLowerCase` "dot" function on it. (This function is defined on `Char`s as well as `String`s.) Here is the corrected code:

```
package lpk.basics

fun main() {
    val str = "Are we there yet?"
    var count = 0
    for (c in str) {
        val l = c.toLowerCase()
        if (l == 'a' || l == 'e' || l == 'i'|| l == 'o'|| l == 'u') {
            count = count + 1
        }
    }
    println("Count: $count")
}
```

(And in fact this is still not counting "y" as a vowel when it acts as such, in a word like "rhythm.")

SOLUTION 7.4

```
package lpk.basics

fun main() {
    val str = "Can you understand this?"
    var result = ""
    for (c in str) {
        val l = c.toLowerCase()
        if (l != 'a' && l != 'e' && l != 'i' && l != 'o' && l != 'u') {
            result = result + 1
        }
    }
    println(result)
}
```

```
┌─────────────────────────────────────────────────────────────┐
│                        SOLUTION 7.5                           │
└─────────────────────────────────────────────────────────────┘
```

```kotlin
package lpk.basics

fun main() {
    val str = "Mind the gap!"
    var compacted = ""
    var previousCharWasASpace = false
    for (c in str) {
        if (c == ' ') {
            if (!previousCharWasASpace) {
                compacted = compacted + c
            }
            previousCharWasASpace = true
        } else {
            compacted = compacted + c
            previousCharWasASpace = false
        }
    }
    println(compacted)
}
```

```
┌─────────────────────────────────────────────────────────────┐
│                        SOLUTION 7.6                           │
└─────────────────────────────────────────────────────────────┘
```

Here is a version with no loop:

```kotlin
package lpk.basics

fun main() {
    val str = "back"
    var result = ""

    val c_0 = 'b'
    result = result + c_0

    val c_1 = 'a'
    result = result + c_1
```

```
    val c_2 = 'c'
    result = result + c_2

    val c_3 = 'k'
    result = result + c_3

    println(result)
}
```

SOLUTION 7.7

The values that result takes on are b, ba, bac, and back.

With the symbols around the plus signs switched, the values that result takes on are b, ab, cab, and kcab. Here is a String reversal program:

```
package lpk.basics

fun main() {
    val str = "That's weird!"
    var reversed = ""
    for (c in str) {
        reversed = c + reversed
    }
    println(reversed)
}
```

CHAPTER 8

Data Structures

Suppose that we go on a bird-watching expedition and want to keep a record of the birds that we see. We might wish to answer the following questions:

- What types of birds did we see?
- In what order did we see them?
- How many times were the different species seen?

In this chapter, we will look at the tools that Kotlin provides for answering these kinds of questions.

8.1 Lists

A `List` is a collection of objects that keeps track of the order in which they were added. Here is how we create a `List` of `Strings`:

```
val stringList = mutableListOf<String>()
```

This line of code declares a `val` called `stringList` that contains the value returned by a call to the `mutableList` function. The funny-looking `<String>` term is called a *type parameter*. It tells the Kotlin system what kind of objects the `List` will hold. For a `List` of `Ints`, the call would be

```
val intList = mutableListOf<Int>()
```

Suppose that on our bird-watching trip we see

- An emu
- A magpie
- A galah
- Another emu

© Tim Lavers 2021
T. Lavers, *Learn to Program with Kotlin*, https://doi.org/10.1007/978-1-4842-6815-5_8

The following code records these sightings and then answers some questions about what was seen:

```
1    package lpk.basics
2
3    fun main() {
4        val sightings = mutableListOf<String>()
5        sightings.add("emu")
6        sightings.add("magpie")
7        sightings.add("galah")
8        sightings.add("emu")
9
10       println("Number of bird sightings: " + sightings.size)
11       if (sightings.contains("emu")) {
12           println("Saw an emu!")
13       }
14       if (sightings.contains("brolga")) {
15           println("Saw a brolga!")
16       }
17       println("Third sighting: " + sightings[2])
18   }
```

Note that we use the code birds[2] to find the third bird seen. Like Arrays, Lists use zero-based indexing.

PROGRAMMING CHALLENGE 8.1

Create a new Kotlin file called DataStructures.kt and copy the preceding code into it. Run the program. What output do you get?

Suppose that on a second trip you saw a pee-wee, a cockatoo, a thick-knee, and then a brolga. Change lines 5 to 8 of the preceding code to record these sightings.

8.2 Sets

A Set is a collection of objects, of which no two are the same. A Set does not record the order in which the objects were added to it. To create a Set, we can use the mutableSetOf function. As with the mutableListOf function, we need to pass in a type parameter. So to create a Set of Strings, we use

```
val stringList = mutableSetOf<String>()
```

PROGRAMMING CHALLENGE 8.2

Change the code from the List challenge to the following:

```
package lpk.basics

fun main() {
    val birds = mutableSetOf<String>()
    birds.add("emu")
    birds.add("magpie")
    birds.add("galah")
    birds.add("emu")

    println("Number of bird species: " + birds.size)
    if (birds.contains("emu")) {
        println("Saw an emu!")
    }
    if (birds.contains("brolga")) {
        println("Saw a brolga!")
    }
}
```

Run the program. What output do you get?

Note that there is no call to find out what the "third" species seen was. This is because the elements of a Set are not in any order, so we cannot access the element at a particular position, as we can with Lists and Arrays.

8.3 Maps

We use Maps to record information about objects, for example, the ages of the members of a club. The objects about which we are storing information are called the *keys*. For each key in a map, there is exactly one *value*. As with Lists and Sets, we specify the types of objects to be stored in a Map. However, we need to specify a type for the keys and also a type for the values.

If we would like a Map to store people's ages, we might use their names, which are Strings, for the keys, and we might use Ints for their ages. To create a Map with these type parameters, we use this code:

```
val nameToAge = mutableMapOf<String, Int>()
```

To store a key and its value in a Map, we use the put function, which has two parameters: one for the key and one for the value. To get the value for a particular key, we use square bracket notation, similar to that for getting Array and List items for a particular index. Let's see these in action.

PROGRAMMING CHALLENGE 8.3

Run the following code:

```
package lpk.basics

fun main() {
    val nameToAge = mutableMapOf<String, Int>()
    nameToAge.put("Harry", 15)
    nameToAge.put("Luna", 16)
    nameToAge.put("Snape", 36)

    println("Harry's age: " + nameToAge["Harry"])
    println("Luna's age: " + nameToAge["Luna"])
    println("Snape's age: " + nameToAge["Snape"])
}
```

What output do you get?

If the value for a key in the map needs to be updated, we call put again, with the key and the new value. This simply overwrites the previous value for that key. If we are no longer interested in the value for a key, we remove the key from the map using the remove function. Another operation of interest is to iterate over the keys in a map.

PROGRAMMING CHALLENGE 8.4

Consider the following code:

```
package lpk.basics

fun main() {
    val nameToAge = mutableMapOf<String, Int>()
    nameToAge.put("Harry", 15)
    nameToAge.put("Luna", 16)
    nameToAge.put("Snape", 36)

    nameToAge.put("Luna", 17)//Happy birthday!

    nameToAge.remove("Snape")//So long Snape!

    for (name in nameToAge.keys) {
        val age = nameToAge[name]
        println("$name is $age years old")
    }
}
```

What output do you expect?

8.4 **null Objects**

Consider the following code:

```
1   package lpk.basics
2
3   fun main() {
4       //Record the sightings.
5       val sightings = mutableListOf<String>()
6       sightings.add("emu")
```

```
7        sightings.add("magpie")
8        sightings.add("galah")
9        sightings.add("emu")
10
11       //Count the species.
12       val speciesToCount = mutableMapOf<String, Int>()
13       for (sighting in sightings) {
14           val countSoFar = speciesToCount[sighting]
15           val updatedCount = countSoFar + 1
16           speciesToCount.put(sighting, updatedCount)
17       }
18
19       //Print the species counts.
20       for (species in speciesToCount.keys) {
21           val count = speciesToCount[species]
22           println("Number of $species sightings: $count")
23       }
24   }
```

On lines 5 to 9, we are recording bird sightings in a List, which is straightforward. The next block of code, lines 12 to 17, is an attempt to count the species by using a map where the keys are the species and the values are the number of times sighted. The final block of code is printing out the species counts, just as we printed out ages in the last challenge.

If we look at this code in IntelliJ, we see a red line under the plus sign on line 15, indicating an error, as shown in Figure 8-1. To understand what the problem is, it helps to remember that the for-loop of lines 13 to 17 is equivalent to a series of blocks, as follows:

```
//Count the species.
val speciesToCount = mutableMapOf<String, Int>()
for (sighting in sightings) {
    val countSoFar = speciesToCount[sighting]
    val updatedCount = countSoFar + 1
    speciesToCount.put(sighting, updatedCount)
}
```

Figure 8-1. *There is something wrong with using + here*

```
1    val sighting_0 = "emu"
2    val countSoFar_0 = speciesToCount[sighting_0]
3    val updatedCount_0 = countSoFar_0 + 1
4    speciesToCount.put(sighting_0, updatedCount_0)
5
6    val sighting_1 = "magpie"
7    val countSoFar_1 = speciesToCount[sighting_1]
8    val updatedCount_1 = countSoFar_1 + 1
9    speciesToCount.put(sighting_1, updatedCount_1)
10
11   val sighting_2 = "galah"
12   val countSoFar_2 = speciesToCount[sighting_2]
13   val updatedCount_2 = countSoFar_2 + 1
14   speciesToCount.put(sighting_2, updatedCount_2)
15
16   val sighting_3 = "emu"
17   val countSoFar_3 = speciesToCount[sighting_3]
18   val updatedCount_3 = countSoFar_3 + 1
19   speciesToCount.put(sighting_3, updatedCount_3)
```

Now consider the declaration of countSoFar_0 on line 2 of this expanded code. We are trying to set this val to hold the value that the map speciesToCount associates with the key sighting_0. At this point in the program, speciesToCount does not hold any values at all, so

speciesToCount[sighting_0]

will return a special value called null. This null value is not an Int, so the + operator cannot apply to it.

At line 7, the program is trying to get the value that speciesToCount associates with magpie. At this point, there is a value in the map for the key emu, but not for our black and white friend, so countSoFar_1 is also set to null.

Line 17 is a little different, because there *is* a value (1) for the key (emu) at this point, so line 18 will actually be adding two Ints. However, the compiler is not smart enough to know this, so this line will also get an error.

To fix this problem, we use some special syntax which means "use 0 instead of null." This is written using the so-called *Elvis operator*: "?:".

Here is a corrected version of the program:

```
1    package lpk.basics
2
3    fun main() {
4        //Record the sightings.
5        val sightings = mutableListOf<String>()
6        sightings.add("emu")
7        sightings.add("magpie")
8        sightings.add("galah")
9        sightings.add("emu")
10
11       //Count the species.
12       val speciesToCount = mutableMapOf<String, Int>()
13       for (sighting in sightings) {
14           val countSoFar = speciesToCount[sighting] ?: 0
15           val updatedCount = countSoFar + 1
16           speciesToCount.put(sighting, updatedCount)
17       }
18
19       //Print the species counts.
20       for (species in speciesToCount.keys) {
21           val count = speciesToCount[species]
22           println("Number of $species sightings: $count")
23       }
24   }
```

PROGRAMMING CHALLENGE 8.5

What output do you expect from the program? Run it and see.

You might wonder why Kotlin returns null when getting a value from a map for an unknown key. Why not return 0? Well, there are lots of situations where 0 would *not* be correct, and the code would then need to check for 0, which would be annoying and error-prone. By possibly returning null, Kotlin is forcing us to think about what might go wrong. The strict rules that Kotlin enforces actually allow the system to detect errors that programmers need to test for manually in other languages. In fact, some languages are very lax, and for them 0, `false`, and `null` are all the same thing. This makes them easy to learn, but in the long run, it's very hard to know what is going on, which leads to faulty software.

8.5 Summary and Solutions to Challenges

This chapter has been a very brief introduction to a broad area of programming. However, we now have enough knowledge of data structures to write some complex programs, which we will start doing in the next part of the book.

SOLUTION 8.1

The output is

```
Number of bird sightings: 4
Saw an emu!
Third sighting: galah
```

The code for the second trip is

```
package lpk.basics

fun main() {
    val sightings = mutableListOf<String>()
    sightings.add("pee-wee")
    sightings.add("cockatoo")
    sightings.add("thick-knee")
    sightings.add("brolga")

    println("Number of bird sightings: " + sightings.size)
    if (sightings.contains("brolga")) {
        println("Saw a brolga!")
    }
    println("Third sighting: " + sightings[2])
}
```

SOLUTION 8.2

```
Number of bird species: 3
Saw an emu!
```

SOLUTION 8.3

```
Harry's age: 15
Luna's age: 16
Snape's age: 36
```

SOLUTION 8.4

```
Harry is 15 years old
Luna is 17 years old
```

The order in which these lines are printed may vary, because the keys of the map are not in any particular order.

SOLUTION 8.5

```
Number of emu sightings: 2
Number of magpie sightings: 1
Number of galah sightings: 1
```

The order in which these lines are printed may vary.

CHAPTER 9

The File System

Computers can store information on a wide variety of hardware, such as magnetic disks, thumb drives, optical drives, and so on. To save programmers from having to write code that is specific to each storage device, operating systems present an abstraction called the *file system*. In turn, Kotlin provides us with the tools we need in order to be able to explore the files on a computer and read and write information. In this chapter, we will make use of some of these tools to read and write text files.

In this chapter, we are using a new project in IntelliJ. To download this, use the menu sequence File ➤ New ➤ Project from Version Control ➤ Git. As in Chapter 1, a **Clone Repository** dialog should be shown. Copy the address https://github.com/Apress/learn-to-program-w-kotlin-files.git into the **Git Repository URL** field, choose a destination directory, and click the **Clone** button.

Again, as in Chapter 1, you may be presented with an almost entirely empty screen. If so, follow the same tricks as on page 6 to show the project file tree. As well as a Kotlin program called HelloWorldFile.kt, there should be several text files, as shown in Figure 9-1.

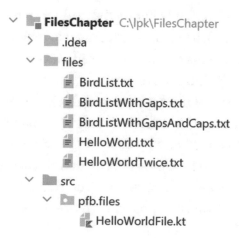

Figure 9-1. *The project for this chapter includes text files in addition to a Kotlin file*

© Tim Lavers 2021
T. Lavers, *Learn to Program with Kotlin*, https://doi.org/10.1007/978-1-4842-6815-5_9

9.1 Reading

The file HelloWorldFile.kt contains the following code:

```
1    package lpk.files
2
3    import java.nio.file.Files
4    import java.nio.file.Paths
5
6    fun main() {
7        val helloWorld = Paths.get("files/HelloWorld.txt")
8        val strings = Files.readAllLines(helloWorld)
9        println("strings = $strings")
10   }
```

As usual, the first line names the package in which this program is located. In this chapter, we are working in a package called lpk.files. Following the package definition, we have a list of import statements. As mentioned in Chapter 1, these are special instructions that tell Kotlin what preexisting programs our code will rely on. In our programs dealing with Strings, Lists, and so on, we have been using classes that are almost always needed, so are made available by default. As we write more complex programs, we will rely heavily on other code libraries and will therefore use import statements almost all the time.

Line 7 defines a val, called helloWorld, as the return value of the function Paths. get. This function is defined in a code library that was written in Java (remember that Java is the precursor to Kotlin), which is why we need to include a file name (Paths) in the function name. The functions that we have used previously, such as mutableListOf, are "Kotlin native," so are a little bit easier to use.

You may be wondering what the data type of helloWorld is. Is it an Int? A String? Something else? Good question! In fact, it is a Path. We can tell this by putting the cursor in or near the word "helloWorld" and pressing Ctrl and q simultaneously. When we do this, a little pop-up is shown that gives information about the val, including its data type, as shown in Figure 9-2. Path is a class that is used to model the file system on a computer. Essentially, a Path object represents a file or directory (folder).

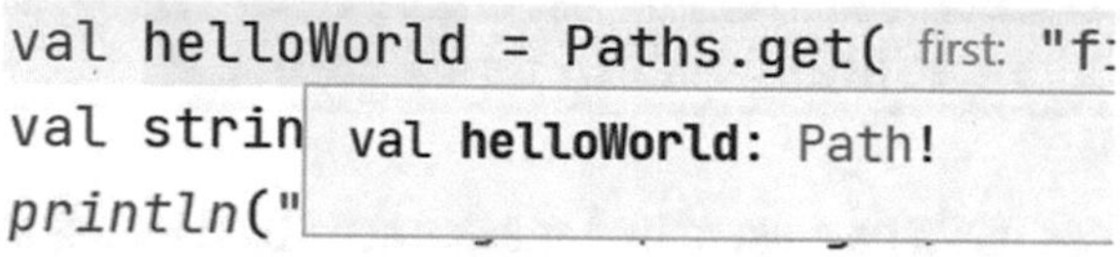

```
val helloWorld = Paths.get( first: "f:
val strin  val helloWorld: Path!
println("
```

Figure 9-2. *The type information pop-up*

When defining a location, we can use either "absolute" or "relative" terms. An absolute path is one such as

C:\lpk\FilesChapter\files\HelloWorld.txt

which defines exactly one location in the machine's file system. A relative path needs to be interpreted with respect to the current location. This is just like defining geographical locations. For example, if someone asks us "Where is Bondi Beach?" and they are actually in Bondi, we can reply "On Campbell Parade." However, if they are in Jakarta, we might reply "On Campbell Parade in Bondi, Sydney, Australia." On line 7, we are defining a Path relative to the FilesChapter directory, which is the "current location" when running the program in IntelliJ.

On line 8, the val helloWorld is passed as argument to the function called Files. readAllLines. This is another function from a Java library, which is why the full name, including "File", is used when calling it. The function reads the file at the location described by its parameter and returns a List of Strings, with one list entry for each line of the file.

As usual, we can run the program from the menu that shows when we right-click the green triangle beside the main function. When we do this, we get the list of lines printed as a String. There is in fact only one line, and the printout is

strings = [Hello world!]

PROGRAMMING CHALLENGE 9.1

You can open text files in IntelliJ by double-clicking them. Open the file HelloWorldTwice. txt. How many lines of text are there? Modify the program to read in and print the contents of this file. What do you expect to be printed?

PROGRAMMING CHALLENGE 9.2

The file `BirdList.txt` contains a list of bird species seen by a tourist in inland Australia.

Modify the program to read this file.

Then add code to create a `Set` of `<String>`s. Finally, add a `for`-loop that iterates through the list and adds each list entry to the `Set`.

How many types of bird were seen?

PROGRAMMING CHALLENGE 9.3

The file `BirdListWithGaps.txt` was compiled by a careless typist and contains empty lines.

Can you modify your program to ignore these? You can test to see if a `String`, `str`, is not empty using this code:

```
if (bird != "") {
    //add it to set
}
```

What happens if these lines are not ignored?

9.2 Writing

To store information, we can use the function `Files.write`. This requires a parameter for the storage location and a parameter for the data that is to be written. The following program reads a list of bird sightings, converts it to a list with no blanks, and then writes the filtered list to a file, called `Reformatted.txt`, in the `files` directory:

```
package lpk.files

import java.nio.file.Files
import java.nio.file.Paths
```

```kotlin
fun main() {
    val helloWorld = Paths.get("files/BirdListWithGaps.txt")
    val sightings = Files.readAllLines(helloWorld)

    val noGaps = mutableListOf<String>()
    for (sighting in sightings) {
        if (sighting != "") {
            noGaps.add(sighting)
        }
    }
    val reformatted = Paths.get("files/Reformatted.txt")
    Files.write(reformatted, noGaps)
}
```

If we run the modified program, a new file will be created in the files directory. To see this, right-click the directory and then select **Reload from Disk**, as in Figure 9-3. The file will then appear as shown in Figure 9-4. If you double-click this file, IntelliJ will open it, and you can check that it contains no empty lines.

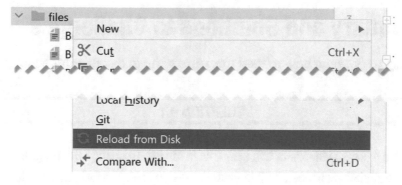

Figure 9-3. *Reloading the files directory*

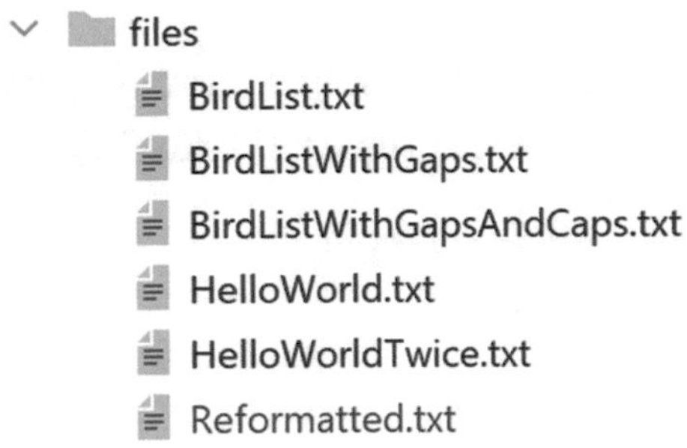

Figure 9-4. *The newly written file appears in red in IntelliJ*

PROGRAMMING CHALLENGE 9.4

In the file `BirdListWithGapsAndCaps.txt`, we have the observations of someone who not only left some empty lines but also got overexcited by a couple of sightings and recorded these in uppercase. Modify the program so that empty lines are removed and all text is in lowercase.

9.3 Summary and Solutions to Challenges

In this chapter, we've seen how to read from and write to a computer's file system.

SOLUTION 9.1

There are two lines, so we expect two elements in the list. To change the program to read in this file, we can simply change line 7 to point to the `HelloWorldTwice.txt` file:

```
package lpk.files

import java.nio.file.Files
import java.nio.file.Paths

fun main() {
    val helloWorld = Paths.get("files/HelloWorldTwice.txt")
    val strings = Files.readAllLines(helloWorld)
    println("strings = $strings")
}
```

The result should be

strings = [Hello world!, And hello again!]

SOLUTION 9.2

```kotlin
package lpk.files

import java.nio.file.Files
import java.nio.file.Paths

fun main() {
    val file = Paths.get("files/BirdList.txt")
    val sightings = Files.readAllLines(file)

    val birdTypes = mutableSetOf<String>()
    for (bird in sightings) {
        birdTypes.add(bird)
    }

    val numberOfTypes = birdTypes.size
    println("Number of species = $numberOfTypes")
}
```

There are six species.

SOLUTION 9.3

```kotlin
package lpk.files

import java.nio.file.Files
import java.nio.file.Paths

fun main() {
    val file = Paths.get("files/BirdListWithGaps.txt")
    val sightings = Files.readAllLines(file)
```

```kotlin
    val birdTypes = mutableSetOf<String>()
    for (bird in sightings) {
        if (bird != "") {
            birdTypes.add(bird)
        }
    }

    val numberOfTypes = birdTypes.size
    println("Number of species = $numberOfTypes")
}
```

If we don't do this filtering, then the count incorrectly includes a species for the blank lines. The total number of species is six.

SOLUTION 9.4

```kotlin
package lpk.files

import java.nio.file.Files
import java.nio.file.Paths

fun main() {
    val original = Paths.get("files/BirdListWithGapsAndCaps.txt")
    val sightings = Files.readAllLines(original)

    val noGaps = mutableListOf<String>()
    for (sighting in sightings) {
        if (sighting != "") {
            noGaps.add(sighting.toLowerCase())
        }
    }
    val reformatted = Paths.get("files/Reformatted.txt");
    Files.write(reformatted, noGaps)
}
```

PART II

Text

In Part II, we learn the fundamentals of Object-Oriented Programming and Unit Testing by completing some fascinating programs on text analysis and word games.

CHAPTER 10

Project Austen

The previous chapters have given us enough basic skills to start on the first of our programming projects. The goal of this project will be to make a statistical analysis of the novels of Jane Austen. For each of Austen's major works, we will calculate

- The number of words in the book

- The set of distinct words

- Frequency histograms of word usage

This project introduces two of the cornerstones of modern software engineering: *Object-Oriented Programming* and *Unit Testing*.

10.1 Object-Oriented Programming

Object-Oriented Programming, or OOP, has been the dominant software development methodology of the last three decades. When we develop software using OOP, we write a collection of programs called *classes*. These are the data types used to model different aspects of the real-world problem that our software solves. We've actually been using some aspects of OOP already: String is a prebuilt class to represent real-world text and List, Set, and Map model collections of data.

As stated earlier, we are going to analyze the books of Jane Austen. How might we think about book as a collection of objects? The answer depends on what problem our software is trying to solve. If we are writing an inventory system for a book distributor, we will need classes to represent authors, publishers, subjects, and so on. If we are writing a program to control the printing process, we will need classes to describe the layout and text of a book, plus details of the paper and binding.

In Project Austen, we will start with text files for books, and our purpose is to extract word count information from these. We know from Chapter 9 how to read a text file into a List of Strings, one for each line of the book. We can encapsulate this task into a data type.

© Tim Lavers 2021
T. Lavers, *Learn to Program with Kotlin*, https://doi.org/10.1007/978-1-4842-6815-5_10

The lines of the book will need to be split apart into individual words, which might not be an easy job. This anticipated difficulty is a clue that it is probably worthwhile having a class for splitting lines.

Finally, we will probably want a class for collecting the statistics themselves. Putting this all together, here is a first guess at the classes that we will need for Project Austen:

Histogram: Records the statistics for the usage of the words in a book

Line: Splits a String into individual words to be recorded in a Histogram

Book: Reads Lines from a File and populates a Histogram

The great thing about software is that it is easy to change, so we don't need to agonize about getting the design of our classes right straight away. As we develop our software, we will get new ideas about how to implement the system, and we can rework it without much loss. In fact, the continual rewriting of software is such a big part of modern programming that it has a special name: *refactoring*.

10.2 Unit Tests

The downside of software being easy to change is that we can easily introduce errors. Our defense against such is *Unit Testing*. A unit test of a class is a program that creates instances of the class, makes function calls on them, and checks the outputs of these calls. This is actually very simple, and the unit tests that we write later will make these concepts very clear.

There are various programs that can help us write and run our tests, and we are going to use one called JUnit, which is an industry standard and which integrates very well with IntelliJ.

10.3 Project Structure and Setup

To get started, create a new project in IntelliJ by cloning this repository: https://github.com/Apress/learn-to-program-w-kotlin-projectausten.git. (If you've forgotten how to do this, have a look at Chapter 1 or 9.) The project structure, shown in Figure 10-1, is a little bit more complicated than we have previously seen. The src directory has two subdirectories: main and test. Our programs will be put into the main directory, and the unit tests for them will be put into test.

If we expand the `main` directory, we see two directories, one called `kotlin` and one called `resources`, as shown in Figure 10-2a. The `kotlin` directory contains the code that we will be working on. There are files for the three classes that we identified, and they have been put in a package called `lpk.austen`. At this stage, these Kotlin files are just stubs: there is no real code written yet. The `resources` directory contains text files for each of four books by Austen. These were downloaded from Project Gutenberg.

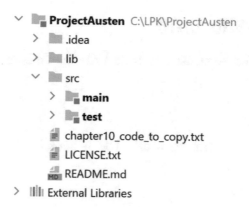

Figure 10-1. *The structure of Project Austen*

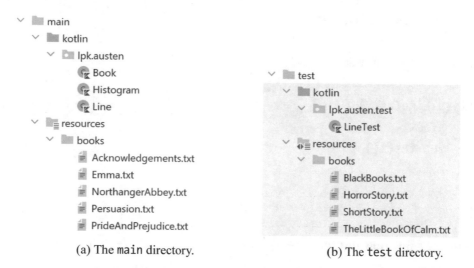

(a) The `main` directory.   (b) The `test` directory.

Figure 10-2. *Expansion of the project tree*

The test directory has a structure that is parallel to that of main, as shown in Figure 10-2b. In the kotlin subdirectory, there is a single file, called LineTest, in a package called lpk.austen.test. This is a stub for the unit test of Line. In the resources directory, there are some very short books (not by Austen!) that will be used in our unit tests of the Book class, when we come to write it.

10.4 LineTest and Line

At present, the Line stub class consists of little more than a comment:

```
package lpk.austen

/**
 * Represents a line of text read in from a book.
 */
class Line
```

LineTest, however, is a bit more interesting:

```
1    package lpk.austen.test
2
3    import org.junit.Test
4
5    class LineTest {
6        @Test
7        fun test1() {
8
9        }
10   }
```

There are a few new things here:

1. On line 3, we are importing org.junit.Test, which is a special kind of class called an annotation. These are used as labels within code.

2. On lines 6 and 7, we have declared a function called test1, which is labeled using the @Test annotation that we imported on line 3. This label allows the JUnit framework to identify test1 as a test and for Kotlin to run it.

3. The body of `test1` is currently empty, because we have no code in
    Line to test.

We can use IntelliJ to run `test1` by clicking the little green triangle that appears to the left of the code, as shown in Figure 10-3a. Figure 10-3b shows the **Run** tab of IntelliJ after the test has been run. The test passed because it made no assertions at all.

Now that we have the basic framework in place, we can start implementing and testing Line. We know that we will want to create Lines from Strings (the lines of text in the book). To express this in code, we change the contents of Line.kt to this code:

```
1   package lpk.austen
2
3   /**
4    * Represents a line of text read in from a book.
5    */
6   class Line(line : String) {
7
8   }
```

The major change here is the replacement of the bare declaration Line with

`Line(line : String)`

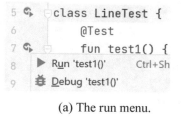

(a) The run menu.

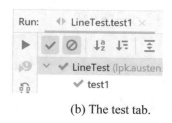

(b) The test tab.

Figure 10-3. *Running JUnit tests from IntelliJ*

This is what is called a *constructor*. For now, the constructor does nothing; we are only sketching out our code.

We will also need a function to retrieve the words that were contained in the line of text. This will need to return a List of Strings and might as well be called words. This is expressed in Kotlin as

`fun words() : List<String>`

You can think of this as saying "there is a function called words that returns a List of Strings." Finally, for our code to compile, we need to add a function body. The simplest way of doing this is to return an empty List:

```
1   fun words() : List<String> {
2       return mutableListOf()
3   }
```

Something of interest here is that we didn't need to include the type parameter <String> on line 2 of this code snippet. The reason for this is that the Kotlin compiler is so clever that it can work out—from the return type on line 1—exactly what kind of List is needed on line 2. This is called type inferencing and is one of the things that makes Kotlin such a productive and enjoyable language to work in.

So far, our Line class does almost nothing, but it is just enough that we can now write some meaningful tests. It's best to write tests early as these clarify our thinking about the classes we are working on.

PROJECT STEP 10.1

Implement the preceding code changes. When you have finished, Line.kt should be as follows:

```
package lpk.austen

/**
 * Represents a line of text read in from a book.
 */
class Line(line : String) {

    fun words(): List<String> {
        return mutableListOf()
    }
}
```

Now check that the unit test still passes.

Let's now think about some very simple tests for Line. First, if we create a Line with an empty String, we should expect the Line to have an empty word list. We can replace the do-nothing test1 with this code:

```
1    @Test
2    fun testEmpty() {
3        val line = Line("")
4        Assert.assertEquals(0, line.words().size)
5    }
```

Line 3 here creates a Line from an empty String. The next line calls a function called Assert.assertEquals, which is provided by JUnit. This function takes two parameters and compares them for equality. If they are not equal, the test will fail. So line 4 is checking that 0 is equal to the size of the words returned by line, which was created from an empty String.

If you go ahead and change test1 to the preceding testEmpty code, IntelliJ will display some errors because we need to add a couple of import statements. For line 4, we need to import the class org.junit.Assert. Less obviously, we also need to import the class lpk.austen.Line. The reason that we need to import this is that we are working in the package lpk.austen.test, and this does not "know" about classes in lpk.austen or any other package.

PROJECT STEP 10.2

With the correct import statements and the implementation of testEmpty, LineTest.kt should be as follows:

```
package lpk.austen.test

import org.junit.Test
import org.junit.Assert
import lpk.austen.Line

class LineTest {
    @Test
    fun testEmpty() {
        val line = Line("")
```

```
        Assert.assertEquals(0, line.words().size)
    }
}
```

Copy the code into ListTest.kt. Run the test and check that it passes.

The second simplest test is to check that if a Line is created from a String that contains just one word, then precisely that word is returned by the words function:

```
1   @Test fun oneWord() {
2       val line = Line("hello")
3       val words = line.words()
4       Assert.assertEquals(1, words.size)
5       Assert.assertEquals("hello", words[0])
6   }
```

This test creates a Line from the String "hello". The words List for this object is then extracted as a val. On line 4, we begin making assertions about the extracted List. Our first assertion is that this contains exactly one item. Next, we assert that this single item is equal to hello.

PROJECT STEP 10.3

Copy this new test into ListTest, then run it and check that the test fails.

Before we return to work on Line, let's write one more test, as this will really help us think about how to proceed. This test is to check that a Line constructed from a String with two words will have those words, in the correct order, and no others. Here's an implementation of such a test:

```
@Test fun twoWords() {
    val line = Line("hello there")
    val words = line.words()
    Assert.assertEquals(2, words.size)
    Assert.assertEquals("hello", words[0])
    Assert.assertEquals("there", words[1])
}
```

We can run all three of our tests at once by clicking the little green triangle to the left of the word LineTest and choosing the Run 'LineTest' option. When we do this, the test report should show that one test passes and two fail.

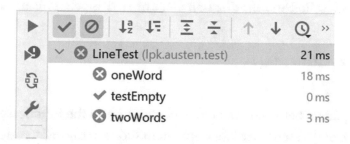

Figure 10-4. *Two of the unit tests fail*

PROJECT STEP 10.4

Copy the test twoWords into LineTest and check that you get the same test report as shown earlier.

Let's now turn to the implementation of List. To do this, we need to introduce the concept of a *field* or *instance variable*. This is just a fancy name for a val or var that is available to all functions in a class. (Even if the field is a val, so in fact does not vary, it is still called an instance variable. The terminology predates Kotlin.) Fields are usually declared just after the constructor. Our Line class will have as a field a List of Strings, which will be returned by the words function. Here is Line with these changes:

```
1    package lpk.austen
2
3    /**
4     * Represents a line of text read in from a book.
5     */
6    class Line(line : String) {
7        val words = mutableListOf<String>()
8
9        fun words(): List<String> {
10           return words
11       }
12   }
```

There is still one key section of code missing, which is the connection between the parameter line passed into the constructor on line 6 and the field words declared on line 7. Somehow we need to extract information from line and put it into words. To do this, we use what is called an *initialization block* or init block. This uses the syntax

```
init {
    //initialization code...
}
```

and is generally placed between the field declarations and the functions.

There are lots of different possible implementations of the init code. Here is a fairly simple approach:

1. Declare a var called currentWord to store the Chars of each word as it is being built.

2. Iterate through the Chars in line. For each:

   a. If it is a letter, we add it to currentWord.

   b. If it is a space, then the word is complete. We add it to the word list and reset currentWord.

3. When have been through all of the Chars in line, we need to take care to add the currentWord to the word list.

In code, this becomes

```
1    package lpk.austen
2
3    /**
4     * Represents a line of text read in from a book.
5     */
6    class Line(line : String) {
7        val words = mutableListOf<String>()
8
9        init {
10           var currentWord = ""
11           for (c in line) {
```

```
12                  if (c == ' ') {
13                      words.add(currentWord)
14                      currentWord = ""
15                  } else {
16                      currentWord = currentWord + c
17                  }
18              }
19              words.add(currentWord)
20          }
21
22          fun words(): List<String> {
23              return words
24          }
25      }
```

If we now run our unit tests, we discover that oneWord and twoWords both pass, but that testEmpty now fails. This is an example of a unit test protecting us from coding errors.

PROJECT STEP 10.5

Copy the code into List and verify that two tests pass, but that testEmpty fails.

A problem with our code is the way that, on line 19, we add currentWord to words. It's possible that at this point currentWord is empty, in which case we shouldn't add it. We can prevent this by wrapping line 19 in an if block:

```
if (currentWord != "") {
    words.add(currentWord)
}
```

PROJECT STEP 10.6

Make this code change and then check that all of the unit tests now pass.

10.5 Further Tests of Line

Our last change to Line got all three tests passing, but actually there's still a problem. The old version of the code was adding an empty String to the words field. We prevented this by adding an if statement that ignored empty Strings. But there's another place where we are adding a String to words: inside the loop. If the input String contains multiple spaces, then two Chars in a row will satisfy the condition of the if statement on line 12. This will result in an empty word being added. Let's prove this with a test.

PROJECT STEP 10.7

Add this new test to LineTest:

```
@Test fun doubleSpace() {
    val line = Line("a  b")
    val words = line.words()
    Assert.assertEquals(2, words.size)
    Assert.assertEquals("a", words[0])
    Assert.assertEquals("b", words[1])
}
```

Then confirm that the test fails. *If the test does not fail, it is probably because the double spaces in "a b" did not copy properly. As with all chapters, there's a file in the project tree from which all required code can be copied—use this.*

One way of fixing the problem would be to wrap line 8 in an if statement, just as line 14 was. If we were to do this, we would have exactly the same logic repeated in two places, which is almost always a bad thing. Instead, we will create a new function to add Strings to the word list and use this function in both places.

PROJECT STEP 10.8

Create the following new function in Line:

```
fun addWord(str: String) {
    if (str != "") {
        words.add(str)
```

```
    }
}
```

Then change the `init` block to make use of the new function:

```
package lpk.austen

/**
 * Represents a line of text read in from a book.
 */
class Line(line: String) {
    val words = mutableListOf<String>()

    init {
        var currentWord = ""
        for (c in line) {
            if (c == ' ') {
                addWord(currentWord)
                currentWord = ""
            } else {
                currentWord = currentWord + c
            }
        }
        addWord(currentWord)
    }

    fun words(): List<String> {
        return words
    }

    fun addWord(str: String) {
        if (str != "") {
            words.add(str)
        }
    }
}
```

Confirm that all four unit tests now pass.

Our tests so far have only used lowercase text. Do we want to count capitalized words differently from lowercase versions of the same word? No. Let's make sure that the words in a List are always converted to lowercase. Again, we start with a unit test.

PROJECT STEP 10.9

Add this to `ListTest`:

```
@Test fun wordsAreLowerCase() {
    val line = Line("Hello THERE")
    val words = line.words()
    Assert.assertEquals(2, words.size)
    Assert.assertEquals("hello", words[0])
    Assert.assertEquals("there", words[1])
}
```

Check that the test fails. Think about how we might change `Line` so that the test passes: where are `Strings` added to `words`, and how can we convert them to lowercase?

One way of fixing `List` is to modify `addWord` to convert the input `String` to lowercase before adding it:

```
fun addWord(str: String) {
    if (str != "") {
        words.add(str.toLowerCase())
    }
}
```

Here, the strategy of "not repeating ourselves" has paid off. If we had calls to `words.add` in two places, then we would have to add the `toLowerCase` call in both instances. It would have been very easy to forget one of these.

PROJECT STEP 10.10

Fix the `addWord` function in your code and check that all of the tests pass.

10.6 HistogramTest and Histogram

At this point, we have a basic implementation of Line together with a basic unit test class. Rather than continue work on these, let's turn our attention to Histogram. From our discussions earlier, we have a pretty good idea of what functions this will require. We will need to be able

- To record that a word has occurred

- To retrieve the Set of words that have been recorded

- To get the number of times that any word has been given

We can provide stubs for the corresponding functions and then begin testing.

PROJECT STEP 10.11

Change Histogram as follows:

```kotlin
package lpk.austen

/**
 * Collects word usage data.
 */
class Histogram {

    fun record(word: String) {}

    fun allWords(): Set<String> {
        return mutableSetOf()
    }

    fun numberOfTimesGiven(word: String): Int {
        return 0
    }
}
```

To create a unit test, right-click lpk.austen.test in the project tree and select the option for a new Kotlin file, as shown in Figure 10-5. When the **New Kotlin File/Class** dialog shows, enter "HistogramTest" as the name. With a file created ready to contain our tests, let's think about some test cases. When faced with the problem of designing unit tests, a good starting point is to consider what happens to "small" test objects. What "small" means will depend on the problem at hand. With HistogramTest, we can start with an empty Histogram and then record zero, one, or two words. This approach gives us a few scenarios straight away:

Scenario	Description
Empty	There are no words in a Histogram when it is first created.
Unknown word	If we ask for the count of an unrecorded word, we get 0.
One word	If we record just one word, then the Set of allWords will contain just that word, and it will have count 1.
Same word twice	If we record a word twice, then it will have count 2.
Two words	If we record two different words, then they will both occur in allWords, and they will each have count 1.

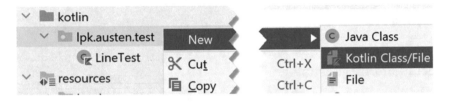

Figure 10-5. *Creating HistogramTest*

PROJECT STEP 10.12

Let's implement the first of these test scenarios. Replace whatever text is in HistogramTest.kt with this code:

```
package lpk.austen.test

import org.junit.Assert
import org.junit.Test
import lpk.austen.Histogram

public class HistogramTest {
    @Test
    fun emptyToStartWith() {
        val histogram = Histogram()
```

```
        Assert.assertEquals(0, histogram.allWords().size)
    }
}
```

Why is there an import statement for `Histogram`?

Do you think this test will pass or fail?

Run it and find out.

The test for an unknown word is also easy to write. When a `Histogram` is first created, any word is unknown to it. So a test could work by creating a `Histogram` object and then calling `numberOfTimesGiven` with any `String` as parameter. We would expect 0 as the result of this call.

PROJECT STEP 10.13

Here Is the shell of the test described earlier:

```
@Test
fun unknownWord() {
}
```

Add a line to create a `Histogram` called `histogram`.

Now add a line that creates a `val` called `given` that contains the result of calling

```
histogram.numberOfTimesGiven("xylophone")
```

Finally, add a line that asserts that `given` is equal to 0. Your completed test should be something like this:

```
@Test
fun unknownWord() {
    val histogram = Histogram()
    val given = histogram.numberOfTimesGiven("xylophone")
    Assert.assertEquals(0, given)
}
```

Do you expect this to pass or fail?

Run it and see.

PROJECT STEP 10.14

Now let's write a test that checks the state of a Histogram after one word has been recorded. Here's some code that creates a Histogram, records the single word "piano", and then extracts the result of allWords as a val called words:

```
@Test
fun recordOneWord() {
    val histogram = Histogram()
    histogram.record("piano")
    val words = histogram.allWords()
}
```

Copy this code into HistogramTest.

How many elements do you expect the words to contain?

Add a line that checks (asserts) this.

The Assert.assertTrue function can be used to check that a statement is true. Add the following line, which checks that words contains "piano":

```
Assert.assertTrue(words.contains("piano"))
```

Together, these two lines check precisely what is in words: we have checked that there is a single element, and we have checked what that element is.

Finally, add a line that checks that the result of numberOfTimesGiven applied to "piano" is 1.

The completed test should look like this:

```
@Test
fun recordOneWord() {
    val histogram = Histogram()
    histogram.record("piano")
    val words = histogram.allWords()
    Assert.assertEquals(1, words.size)
    Assert.assertTrue(words.contains("piano"))
    Assert.assertEquals(1, histogram.numberOfTimesGiven("piano"))
}
```

PROJECT STEP 10.15

The next test scenario we want to look at is when the same word is recorded twice. Here is the setup code for this:

```
@Test
fun recordOneWordTwice() {
    val histogram = Histogram()
    histogram.record("piano")
    histogram.record("piano")
    val words = histogram.allWords()
}
```

What do you expect words to contain? Remember that this is a Set. Add assertions that check this.

What should the value of

```
histogram.numberOfTimesGiven("piano")
```

be? Add an assertion for this.

The completed test should be something like this:

```
@Test
fun recordOneWordTwice() {
    val histogram = Histogram()
    histogram.record("piano")
    histogram.record("piano")
    val words = histogram.allWords()
    Assert.assertEquals(1, words.size)
    Assert.assertTrue(words.contains("piano"))
    Assert.assertEquals(2, histogram.numberOfTimesGiven("piano"))
}
```

PROJECT STEP 10.16

Let's test what happens when we record two different words. Create a test function called `recordTwoWords`.

In the test function, create a `Histogram` called `histogram`. Add lines in which the words "piano" and "violin" are recorded. Create a `val` called `words` which is the value returned by calling `allWords` on `histogram`.

How many elements should `words` contain? Add an assertion for this.

Add a line checking that `words` contains "piano".

Add a line checking that `words` contains "violin".

Add lines checking that each of these words is given once.

The completed test should look like this:

```
@Test
fun recordTwoWords() {
    val histogram = Histogram()
    histogram.record("piano")
    histogram.record("violin")
    val words = histogram.allWords()
    Assert.assertEquals(2, words.size)
    Assert.assertTrue(words.contains("piano"))
    Assert.assertTrue(words.contains("violin"))
    Assert.assertEquals(1, histogram.numberOfTimesGiven("piano"))
    Assert.assertEquals(1, histogram.numberOfTimesGiven("violin"))
}
```

With these tests in place, we can implement `Histogram`. There are many ways to do this, and we are free to choose any implementation that makes our tests pass. One approach is to use a `Map<String,Int>` to record the word counts, just as we used a `Map` to record bird counts in Chapter 8. The `Map` will need to be available to all of the functions in `Histogram`, so we will declare it as a field, which we will call `counter`.

PROJECT STEP 10.17

Change Histogram to

```
1    package lpk.austen
2
3    /**
4     * Collects word usage data.
5     */
6    class Histogram {
7
8        val counter = mutableMapOf<String, Int>()
9
10       fun record(word: String) {
11       }
12
13       fun allWords(): Set<String> {
14           return counter.keys
15       }
16
17       fun numberOfTimesGiven(word: String): Int {
18           return counter[word] ?: 0
19       }
20   }
```

Line 8 declares our counter field. This is used on line 14 in the implementation of allWords. The keys for a Map<String, Int> are all of the Strings for which the Map contains an Int.

On line 18, we get the count for a String directly from the Map. Do you remember why we use the Elvis operator? If not, check the explanation on page 97.

Something you might wonder, with regard to the code listed earlier, is why there is no constructor and no init block. Unlike Line, there is no information needed to create Histogram, so there is no need to add a constructor. As to the absence of init, the only field initialization that is needed is done as part of the field declaration.

The only remaining part of Histogram to implement is the record function. As mentioned before, we've already seen something like this.

PROJECT STEP 10.18

Let's implement `record`. There are three lines of code. In the first, we retrieve the current count for the word passed in as a parameter:

```
val currentCount = counter[word] ?: 0
```

Next, we define a new `val` which is the old count plus 1:

```
val newCount = currentCount + 1
```

Finally, we put the newCount into counter with key word:

```
counter.put(word, newCount)
```

Make these changes then rerun the unit tests. They should all now pass.

If you ran into problems, you can use this code for `Histogram.kt`:

```
package lpk.austen

/**
 * Collects word usage data.
 */
class Histogram {

    val counter = mutableMapOf<String, Int>()

    fun record(word: String) {
        val currentCount = counter[word] ?: 0
        val newCount = currentCount + 1
        counter.put(word, newCount)
    }

    fun allWords(): Set<String> {
        return counter.keys
    }

    fun numberOfTimesGiven(word: String): Int {
        return counter[word] ?: 0
    }

}
```

10.7 BookTest and Book

From our brief design discussion earlier, we know that a Book is created from a text file and will have a Histogram object in which the words in the book are to be recorded. The text file can be passed in as a constructor parameter, and the extraction of information from it can be done in an init block. Here's a partial implementation of Book:

```
package lpk.austen

import java.nio.file.Files
import java.nio.file.Path
import java.nio.file.Paths

/**
 * Reads a book from a text file and produces word usage information.
 */
class Book(bookFile : Path) {
    val histogram = Histogram()

    init {
        //Code to read the book here.
    }
}
```

PROJECT STEP 10.19

Paste this code into Book.kt, replacing whatever is currently in that file.

Our unit tests for Book will work by creating Books from the short text files in the test/resources/books directory. These files are all so small that we can easily count the words in them, and our unit tests will compare our counts with values returned by the code. Let's get started!

PROJECT STEP 10.20

Create an empty file BookTest.kt alongside the other unit test files. Replace whatever is in this file with this code:

```
package lpk.austen.test

import org.junit.Assert
import org.junit.Test
import lpk.austen.Book
import java.nio.file.Paths

class BookTest {
    @Test fun shortStory() {
        val book = Book(Paths.get(
        "src/test/resources/books/ShortStory.txt"))
        val allWords = book.histogram.allWords()
    }
}
```

The messy part of this code is the path to the file ShortStory.txt, but this is just another of the kind of Path construction that we had in Chapter 9. Now double-click the file ShortStory.txt and inspect the text. How many different words are there? What are they?

PROJECT STEP 10.21

Add an assertion to the test function, shortStory, that checks that there are four words.

For each of the words in ShortStory.txt, add a line to the test that checks that the word is in the Set.

For each of the words in ShortStory.txt, add a line to the test that checks that book. histogram has the correct count for that word.

After completing this step, your test code should look something like this:

```
@Test fun shortStory() {
    val book = Book(Paths.get(
     "src/test/resources/books/ShortStory.txt"))
    val allWords = book.histogram.allWords()

    Assert.assertEquals(4, allWords.size)

    Assert.assertTrue(allWords.contains("the"))
    Assert.assertTrue(allWords.contains("beginning"))
    Assert.assertTrue(allWords.contains("middle"))
    Assert.assertTrue(allWords.contains("end"))

    Assert.assertEquals(3, book.histogram.numberOfTimesGiven("the"))
    Assert.assertEquals(1, book.histogram.numberOfTimesGiven("beginning"))
    Assert.assertEquals(1, book.histogram.numberOfTimesGiven("middle"))
    Assert.assertEquals(1, book.histogram.numberOfTimesGiven("end"));
}
```

Of course, this test will fail, because we have not yet implemented the init block of Book.

We can implement the init block by having the Line and Histogram classes work together to record all of the words in the Book. The lines of the book file will be turned into Line objects, and then these Lines will provide the words to be recorded by the Histogram:

```
1    init {
2        val lines = Files.readAllLines(bookFile)
3        for (str in lines) {
4            val line = Line(str)
5            for (word in line.words()) {
6                histogram.record(word)
7            }
8        }
9    }
```

Let's go through this code in detail, as it is a bit complicated. On line 2, we read the bookFile from the constructor into a val called lines. As with the bird sightings example from page 92, lines is a List of Strings, with an entry for each line of the text file. On line 3, we iterate through the elements of lines. Line 4 creates a Line instance, called line, from the line of text currently represented by the loop val. Since line is of type Line, it offers the "dot" function words. On line 5, we iterate over the elements of line.words, and on line 6 we add the current word to our histogram field.

PROJECT STEP 10.22

Copy this code into Book and check that the unit test now passes.

PROJECT STEP 10.23

Add a test to BookTest that uses HorrorStory.txt. This test should be something like this:

```
@Test fun horrorStory() {
    val book = Book(Paths.get(
      "src/test/resources/books/HorrorStory.txt"))
    val allWords = book.histogram.allWords()

    Assert.assertEquals(7, allWords.size)

    Assert.assertTrue(allWords.contains("it"))
    Assert.assertTrue(allWords.contains("was"))
    Assert.assertTrue(allWords.contains("a"))
    Assert.assertTrue(allWords.contains("and"))
    Assert.assertTrue(allWords.contains("stormy"))
    Assert.assertTrue(allWords.contains("night"))
    Assert.assertTrue(allWords.contains("dark"))

    Assert.assertEquals(1, book.histogram.numberOfTimesGiven("it"))
    Assert.assertEquals(1, book.histogram.numberOfTimesGiven("was"))
    Assert.assertEquals(1, book.histogram.numberOfTimesGiven("a"))
    Assert.assertEquals(1, book.histogram.numberOfTimesGiven("dark"));
    Assert.assertEquals(1, book.histogram.numberOfTimesGiven("and"));
```

```
Assert.assertEquals(1, book.histogram.numberOfTimesGiven("stormy"));
Assert.assertEquals(1, book.histogram.numberOfTimesGiven("night"));
}
```

Run the test. It should pass.

PROJECT STEP 10.24

Open the file TheLittleBookOfCalm.txt in IntelliJ. This text is a little more complex
than either ShortStory or HorrorStory because it contains a blank line and because the
sentences end with full stops. Add a test to BookTest that is based on this text file. It should
look something like this:

```
1    @Test
2    fun littleBookOfCalmTest() {
3        val book = Book(Paths.get(
4          "src/test/resources/books/TheLittleBookOfCalm.txt"))
5        //This book has two lines with several repeated words.
6        //There is also a blank line.
7        //The two non-blank lines end in full stops.
8        val histogram = book.histogram
9        Assert.assertEquals(2, histogram.numberOfTimesGiven("this"))
10       Assert.assertEquals(1, histogram.numberOfTimesGiven("is"))
11       Assert.assertEquals(1, histogram.numberOfTimesGiven("a"))
12       Assert.assertEquals(3, histogram.numberOfTimesGiven("very"))
13       Assert.assertEquals(2, histogram.numberOfTimesGiven("short"))
14       Assert.assertEquals(2, histogram.numberOfTimesGiven("book"))
15       Assert.assertEquals(1, histogram.numberOfTimesGiven("we"))
16       Assert.assertEquals(1, histogram.numberOfTimesGiven("hope"))
17       Assert.assertEquals(1, histogram.numberOfTimesGiven("that"))
18       Assert.assertEquals(1, histogram.numberOfTimesGiven("you"))
19       Assert.assertEquals(1, histogram.numberOfTimesGiven("find"))
20       Assert.assertEquals(1, histogram.numberOfTimesGiven("calming"))
21   }
```

Run this test. It should fail.

Why is TheLittleBookOfCalm.txt not processed properly? To investigate, we can add a line to our test that prints out the words in histogram before making any assertions. Add this statement:

```
print(histogram.allWords())
```

after line 8 of littleBookOfCalmTest, and run this test again. It will still fail, but will also print out something like this:

```
[a, very, calming., book, this, is, hope, we, that, find, short, book., you]
```

This reveals the problem: we are not trimming the full stops, so are getting entries for both "book" and "book.". Also, there is an entry for "calming." instead of "calming". This is a bug (error) in Line.

10.8 Back to LineTest and Line

Our implementation of Line is deficient because it does not handle full stops. In fact, it does not handle commas, semicolons, colons, quotation marks, or any other punctuation Chars. If we look at the first 30 or so lines of PrideAndPrejudice.txt, we see that the underscore character has also been used. So let's add checks for these in LineTest.

PROJECT STEP 10.25

Copy the following test functions into LineTest:

```
@Test
fun ignorePunctuation() {
    val line = Line("Hello. Goodbye! Yes? No, no.")
    val words = line.words()
    Assert.assertEquals(5, words.size)
    Assert.assertEquals("hello", words[0])
    Assert.assertEquals("goodbye", words[1])
    Assert.assertEquals("yes", words[2])
    Assert.assertEquals("no", words[3])
    Assert.assertEquals("no", words[4])
}
```

```
@Test fun morePunctuation() {
    val line = Line("Hello; _Goodbye_! X: 5")
    val words = line.words()
    Assert.assertEquals(4, words.size)
    Assert.assertEquals("hello", words[0])
    Assert.assertEquals("goodbye", words[1])
    Assert.assertEquals("x", words[2])
    Assert.assertEquals("5", words[3])
}
```

Run them and confirm that they fail.

Something that we haven't yet written a test for is the double quote character. We use double quotes to *delimit* (define the start and end of) Strings, so we can't just put one in a String and expect it will work. What we need to do is precede a double quote that we want literally in a String with a backslash Char. This is called an *escape* character.

PROJECT STEP 10.26

Add this test for double quotes to LineTest:

```
@Test
fun doubleQuotes() {
    val line = Line("\"It's not.\"")
    val words = line.words()
    Assert.assertEquals(2, words.size)
    Assert.assertEquals("it's", words[0])
    Assert.assertEquals("not", words[1])
}
```

It will fail.

Here is the init block from Line:

```
1   init {
2       var currentWord = ""
3       for (c in line) {
```

```
4              if (c == ' ') {
5                  addWord(currentWord)
6                  currentWord = ""
7              } else {
8                  currentWord = currentWord + c
9              }
10          }
11          addWord(currentWord)
12      }
```

Line 4 is an `if` statement that, when `true`, branches into the code that breaks the word currently being built. This `if` statement is only taking the space `Char` into account. We could fix this by using the `||` operator:

```
if (c == ' ' || c == ',' || c == '.' || ...) {
```

However, this will become a very complex line of code because there are so many possible punctuation characters that can terminate a word. Instead, we will create a function that takes a `Char` as input and returns either `true` or `false`, depending on whether or not the `Char` should break a word. The data type that has values `true` and `false` is called `Boolean`, and this will be the return type for our new function. Instead of comparing c to the space `Char` on line 4, we will make a call to the new function, which is called `isWordTerminator`.

PROJECT STEP 10.27

Replace the existing code for `Line` with this new version:

```
package lpk.austen

/**
 * Represents a line of text read in from a book.
 */
class Line(line: String) {
    val words = mutableListOf<String>()

    init {
        var currentWord = ""
        for (c in line) {
```

```
            if (isWordTerminator(c)) {
                addWord(currentWord)
                currentWord = ""
            } else {
                currentWord = currentWord + c
            }
        }
        addWord(currentWord)
    }

    fun words(): List<String> {
        return words
    }

    fun addWord(str: String) {
        if (str != "") {
            words.add(str.toLowerCase())
        }
    }

    fun isWordTerminator(c: Char): Boolean {
        if (c == ' ') return true
        if (c == '.') return true
        if (c == ',') return true
        if (c == '!') return true
        if (c == '?') return true
        if (c == '\"') return true
        if (c == '_') return true
        if (c == ';') return true
        if (c == ':') return true
        return false
    }
}
```

Check that all of the unit tests for Line now pass.

10.9 Testing with Real Data

With these corrections to Line, all of the unit tests for Book should now pass. To be sure
that our code is correct, we ought to write a test that uses actual text from a book by
Austen.

In IntelliJ, find the file PrideAndPrejudice.txt and open it. Copy the first 32 lines
of text. Right-click the books directory in resources of the test directory (make sure it's
the test directory) as shown in Figure 10-6, and choose the **New ➤ File** option. A dialog
will show, asking for the file name. Enter Page1.txt into this and press the Enter key.
Open the new file (it may even open automatically) and paste in the text copied from
PrideAndPrejudice.txt.

Figure 10-6. *Adding a new test data file*

PROJECT STEP 10.28

Add the following to BookTest:

```
@Test
fun prideAndPrejudice() {
    val book = Book(Paths.get(
      "src/test/resources/books/Page1.txt"))
    //32 lines from the start of Pride and Prejudice
    val histogram = book.histogram

    //Check some words that we have
    //counted using a text editor.
    Assert.assertEquals(1, histogram.numberOfTimesGiven("pride"))
    Assert.assertEquals(5, histogram.numberOfTimesGiven("it"))
    Assert.assertEquals(3, histogram.numberOfTimesGiven("and"))
    Assert.assertEquals(3, histogram.numberOfTimesGiven("bennet"))
```

```
//Check that some words followed by
//punctuation are counted correctly.
Assert.assertEquals(3, histogram.numberOfTimesGiven("you"))
Assert.assertEquals(2, histogram.numberOfTimesGiven("she"))
}
```

Check that the test passes.

The test that we've just added, based on real data, should give us a lot of confidence in our code.

10.10 Almost Finished

In order to analyze the files in main/resources/books, we need to add a main function to Book. Remember, from Chapter 1, that a main function is the starting point for Kotlin programs.

PROJECT STEP 10.29

Copy this code into Book.kt, immediately following the import statement:

```
fun main() {
    val book = Book(Paths.get(
     "src/main/resources/books/PrideAndPrejudice.txt"))
    val histogram = book.histogram
    val allWords = histogram.allWords()
    for (word in allWords) {
        val count = histogram.numberOfTimesGiven(word)
        println("$word $count")
    }
}
```

Figure 10-7 shows the position of the main function in the file.

A green triangle is shown to the left of the main function. Run the program by right-clicking the green triangle.

There should be several thousand lines of output. If we scroll to the top, we see something like:

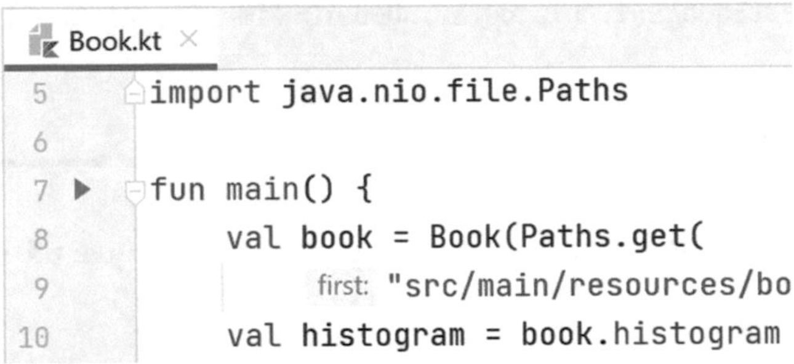

Figure 10-7. *Adding the main function*

```
pride 45
and 3527
prejudice 6
by 634
jane 260
austen 1
chapter 61
1 1
it 1520
is 859
a 1939
truth 27
universally 3
acknowledged 20
```

The actual order of words might be different from what is shown here, because we are not specifying the order in our data structures. If we scroll further through the list, we see a couple of minor problems.

First, there are a few further Chars that should qualify as word delimiters but are being attached to words. For example, the right bracket is not being detached, and so "early)" is counted as a word.

Second, we see that the single quote is apparently used as a word 17 times. If we search the text for single quotes, we see why: when a character is speaking and quotes another person, the single quote is used to delimit the nested speech and can then get mixed up with other punctuation. Here's an example of such nested quoting:

```
"... if ... a friend were to say, 'Bingley, you had better
stay till next week,' you would probably do it ..."
```

Our code is counting the single quote mark that follows "week," as a word.

These issues are examples of how programming with real-world data gets very messy. It can take a lot of work to handle outlier cases such as these.

PROJECT STEP 10.30

Add this test to `LineTest`:

```
@Test
fun brackets() {
    val line = Line("(left, right)")
    val words = line.words()
    Assert.assertEquals(2, words.size)
    Assert.assertEquals("left", words[0])
    Assert.assertEquals("right", words[1])
}
```

Run it and check that it fails.

PROJECT STEP 10.31

Can you fix the `isWordTerminator` function in `Line`? Have a go, and see if the newly added test passes.

Here's one version of the fixed function:

```
fun isWordTerminator(c: Char): Boolean {
    if (c == ' ') return true
    if (c == '.') return true
    if (c == ',') return true
    if (c == '!') return true
    if (c == '?') return true
```

```
    if (c == '\"') return true
    if (c == '_') return true
    if (c == ';') return true
    if (c == ':') return true
    if (c == '(') return true
    if (c == ')') return true
    return false
}
```

PROJECT STEP 10.32

Add this test to LineTest:

```
@Test
fun singleQuoteAfterComma() {
    val line = Line("week,' you")
    val words = line.words()
    Assert.assertEquals(2, words.size)
    Assert.assertEquals("week", words[0])
    Assert.assertEquals("you", words[1])
}
```

This checks that the String "week,' you" gets split into two words (not three). Of course, the test fails.

Our current implementation of List contains this code for adding words:

```
1   fun addWord(str: String) {
2       if (str != "") {
3           words.add(str.toLowerCase())
4       }
5   }
```

On line 2 of this function, we are using an if statement to filter out the empty word. Let's refactor this so that we can filter out all rubbish words easily.

PROJECT STEP 10.33

Add this function:

```
fun isWord(str: String) : Boolean {
    if (str == "") return false
    return true
}
```

to Line. Then change addWord to call the new function in its if statement.

If we run the unit tests for Line at this point, singleQuoteAfterComma will fail. However, the other tests should still pass. The unit tests are checking that we have at least not made things worse with our refactoring.

PROJECT STEP 10.34

Can you modify isWord to filter out the single quote mark?

Here's one way of doing it:

```
fun isWord(str: String) : Boolean {
    if (str == "") return false
    if (str == "'") return false
    return true
}
```

With this most recent change to Line, all of our unit tests should pass. A good thing about our having extracted the isWord function is that we can easily modify it to check for other non-words. For example, in the printout to main on page 144, we saw that the digit 1 is included in the list of words. Now some might argue that this is a word in the book, and some would argue otherwise. The addWord function can be changed to include or exclude numbers, depending on one's own opinion in the matter. For now, we'll leave the numbers in.

10.11 Counting the Words

We have not yet fulfilled our promise of determining the final word count for the book. To get the number of words, we will add a new function called `totalWords` to `Histogram`. This function will take no parameters and will return an `Int`, so a possible stub is

```
fun totalWords() : Int {
    return 0
}
```

PROJECT STEP 10.35

Add the `totalWords` function to `Histogram`.

For the unit test, we can start with an empty `Histogram`, add words to it, and check the totals as we go:

```
@Test
fun totalNumberOfWords() {
    val histogram = Histogram()
    Assert.assertEquals(0, histogram.totalWords())

    histogram.record("piano")
    Assert.assertEquals(1, histogram.totalWords())

    histogram.record("piano")
    Assert.assertEquals(2, histogram.totalWords())

    histogram.record("cello")
    Assert.assertEquals(3, histogram.totalWords())

    histogram.record("guitar")
    Assert.assertEquals(4, histogram.totalWords())

    histogram.record("guitar")
    Assert.assertEquals(5, histogram.totalWords())
}
```

PROJECT STEP 10.36

Copy the new test function into `HistogramTest`. Which line of the unit test do you expect to fail? Run the test to find out.

There are at least two ways that we could implement `totalWords`:

- Add up the counts for each of the words stored in the `Histogram`.

- Have an `Int` field that is incremented each time that `record` is called.

The first method has the advantage that we don't have an extra "moving part" that needs to be kept synchronized with respect to the other field. The second method has the advantage that it is more efficient, because it doesn't involve any calculations. We will choose the first approach because it is simpler and because we're not concerned about efficiency for this function, as it will only be called a few times.

PROJECT STEP 10.37

Replace the stub for `totalWords` with this implementation:

```
fun totalWords() : Int {
    var result = 0
    for (key in counter.keys) {
        val count = counter[key] ?: 0
        result = result + count
    }
    return result
}
```

Check that the unit tests all pass.

PROJECT STEP 10.38

Change the `main` function of Book to

```
fun main() {
    val book = Book(Paths.get(
      "src/main/resources/books/PrideAndPrejudice.txt"))
    val totalWords = book.histogram.totalWords()
    println("Total word count: $totalWords")
}
```

Run the modified function. How many distinct words are in *Pride and Prejudice*?

10.12 Putting Things in Order

The histograms that we can create contain a lot of information about the books that they summarize, but not in a form that is immediately useful. We can scroll through the list of words and their frequencies, but we cannot easily find the most commonly used words, nor can we see the words in alphabetical order.

We could write code to implement these requirements directly, but a better solution is to write the data to a file that can be opened in a spreadsheet application such as Microsoft Excel or Google Sheets.

Both of these programs, and many others, can import data that is in what is called Comma-Separated Variable (CSV) format. In CSV, each row of spreadsheet data is written on a single line. Within lines, commas separate the values for each column, for example:

```
wickham's,32
permit,1
suitable,3
```

PROJECT STEP 10.39

The following import statement should be in `Histogram`, directly after the first line:

```
import java.nio.file.Path
```

If this is missing (IntelliJ sometimes reformats code and, in the process, deletes unused import statements), then add it. Then add this function stub within the body of the class, among the other functions:

```
fun toCSV(file : Path) {
}
```

To test this function, we will need to create a Histogram, populate it with some data, call the function with some known file as the parameter, and then check the contents of the file. Here is a partial implementation of the test, which does just the setup:

```
@Test
fun toCSVTest() {
    val histogram = Histogram()
    histogram.record("piano")
    histogram.record("piano")
    histogram.record("violin")
    val csvFile = Paths.get("HistogramTest.csv")
    histogram.toCSV(csvFile)
}
```

Now let's think about the assertions we can make about the exported file. First of all, it should have two lines, because there are two items in the Histogram. We don't know or care about the order of the lines in the file, but one of them should contain the information piano,2 and the other should show violin as given once. This code does those checks:

```
val lines = Files.readAllLines(csvFile)
Assert.assertEquals(2, lines.size)
Assert.assertTrue(lines.contains("piano,2"))
Assert.assertTrue(lines.contains("violin,1"))
```

PROJECT STEP 10.40

The preceding test needs a couple of `import` statements. Add these lines to the other imports in `HistogramTest`:

```
import java.nio.file.Paths
import java.nio.file.Files
```

Now add this complete test implementation:

```
@Test
fun toCSVTest() {
    val histogram = Histogram()
    histogram.record("piano")
    histogram.record("piano")
    histogram.record("violin")
    val csvFile = Paths.get("HistogramTest.csv")
    histogram.toCSV(csvFile)

    val lines = Files.readAllLines(csvFile)
    Assert.assertEquals(2, lines.size)
    Assert.assertTrue(lines.contains("piano,2"))
    Assert.assertTrue(lines.contains("violin,1"))
}
```

Run the test. You should get some horrible looking error that indicates that the file `HistogramTest.csv` does not exist.

With the test in place, let's consider how we might implement toCSV. There is a useful library function, `Files.write`, for writing a list of `String`s to a file. So if we can get the information we need as a `List` of `String`s, then we are almost finished. We can produce such a `List` by iterating through the words in the `Histogram`, getting the count for the word, and then building a `String` from the word and its count. The following code implements this algorithm:

```
fun toCSV(file : Path) {
    val csvLines = mutableListOf<String>()
    for (word in allWords()) {
        val timesGiven = numberOfTimesGiven(word)
```

```
    val line = "$word,$timesGiven"
    csvLines.add(line)
  }
  Files.write(file, csvLines)
}
```

PROJECT STEP 10.41

Add this import statement to Histogram, if it is not already there:

```
import java.nio.file.Files
```

Then implement toCSV using the preceding code. Run toCSVTest and check that it now passes.

After running the test, you should see a file called HistogramTest.csv in the IntelliJ project tree, as shown in Figure 10-8. If you double-click this, the file will be opened in IntelliJ, and you can check that the contents really are as expected.

With a Histogram now "able to export itself" (this is the kind of language that programmers use when talking about the classes in an object-oriented system), we can enhance main to produce a CSV file.

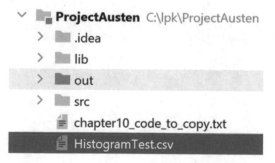

Figure 10-8. *The CSV file in the project tree*

PROJECT STEP 10.42

Change the `main` function of Book to

```
fun main() {
    val book = Book(Paths.get(
      "src/main/resources/books/PrideAndPrejudice.txt"))
    val totalWords = book.histogram.totalWords()
    println("Total word count: $totalWords")
    val file = Paths.get("PandPWords.csv")
    book.histogram.toCSV(file)
}
```

After running this new version of `main`, we get a file called `PandPWords.csv` which can be seen in the project tree, alongside `HistogramTest.csv` shown in Figure 10-8. When imported to Google Sheets, this will look something like what is shown in Figure 10-9. If we click column **A**, then the `Data` menu shows an option to sort the data alphabetically; see Figure 10-10. When we do this, we discover that in fact the first 64 or so rows of the sorted data consist of numbers and a couple of symbols. These are from chapter and section headings in the text and could of course be eliminated by fairly simple enhancements to the software.

	A	B
1	pride	45
2	and	3529
3	prejudice	6
4	by	635
5	jane	260
6	austen	1
7	chapter	61

Figure 10-9. *Histogram exported to CSV as seen in Google Sheets*

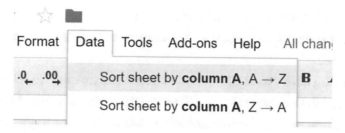

Figure 10-10. *The data can be sorted alphabetically*

We can also sort by column **B**, which reveals the dominance of one-syllable words in English (and also shows the Germanic origins of the language).

	A	B
1	the	4321
2	to	4127
3	of	3598
4	and	3529
5	her	2215
6	i	2050
7	a	1939
8	in	1862
9	was	1842
10	she	1703

Figure 10-11. *The ten most frequently used words in Pride and Prejudice*

10.13 Taking Things Further

If you got stuck on any of the steps in this project, or your code is a mess, you can download a completed version from https://github.com/Apress/learn-to-program-w-kotlin-projectausten-complete.git. Using this, or your own code, there are a few ways that you might want to take the project a bit further. For a start, you can use the supplied text files to analyze some of Austen's other novels. You can also download lots of other books from Project Gutenberg and compare word usage by different authors.

If you want to eliminate the problem of chapter numbers polluting the data, then you may want to tighten up the definition of what a word is and make the corresponding changes to Line. For example, you could test the first Char in a word and, if it is not alphabetical, reject the word. To test if a Char is alphabetical, you can use the function Character.isLetter.

One shortcoming of our analysis is that it counts words that are related as separate entities. See Figure 10-12 for an example. The classification of words by root word is called *stemming*. There are freely downloadable *word banks* for English and other languages that can be used for this kind of analysis. By the time that you have finished this book, you should be able to use a word bank to aggregate the word usage statistics by root word.

1274	condescend	1
1275	condescended	5
1276	condescendingly	1
1277	condescends	1
1278	condescension	7

Figure 10-12. *Words with the same root*

10.14 Summary

This has been a huge chapter. We've covered some really important and difficult topics, such as object-oriented design, and we have written a small but sophisticated text analysis system. The programs that we wrote are of high quality because we wrote unit tests for all of our code.

The enormous amount covered in this chapter puts us in a great position to forge on with more text-related programming in the coming chapters.

CHAPTER 11

Anagrams

This chapter builds on the techniques of object-oriented programming and unit testing that were used in Chapter 10 and introduces a new programming technique, *recursion*. The problem that we will solve is the following: given any English word, what are all the anagrams of it?

11.1 Main Classes

Suppose that we want to find all the anagrams of some given word. One approach is as follows: first, we work out all of the different ways of rearranging the letters in the word, and then we check each arrangement against a list of known English words. The combinations that do not occur in the list are discarded, and the remaining arrangements are the anagrams. For example, suppose that we start with the word rat. The different arrangements of the letters in this word are

```
art
atr
rat
rta
tar
tra
```

The three of these that are actually found in the dictionary are art, rat, and tar.

Given this approach to the problem, two main classes come to mind. The first, which we call Term, encapsulates the algorithm for finding all of the letter arrangements (permutations). The second, called Dictionary, does the checking.

To get started, clone this repository in IntelliJ:

```
https://github.com/Apress/learn-to-program-w-kotlin-anagrams.git
```

© Tim Lavers 2021
T. Lavers, *Learn to Program with Kotlin*, https://doi.org/10.1007/978-1-4842-6815-5_11

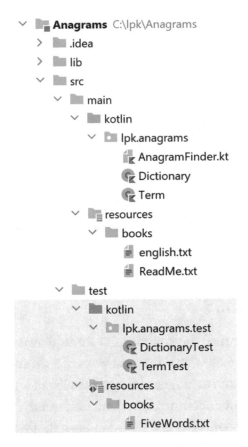

Figure 11-1. *The structure of the Anagrams project*

The expanded project structure should appear as in Figure 11-1. The main parts are

- The lib directory, which contains the files needed by JUnit.

- Three Kotlin files in src/main/kotlin/lpk/anagrams: These are stubs for the two classes described earlier, plus a third, AnagramFinder, that will contain the main function.

- Stubs for the tests of Term and Dictionary, in the directory src/test/ kotlin/lpk/anagrams/test.

- The file english.txt in the resources directory of the main branch: This contains all of the words from Webster's 1913 dictionary, as found at Project Gutenberg.

- The file FiveWords.txt, which is a very small dictionary file, for testing.

- A directory called .idea, which is used by IntelliJ.

AnagramFinder already contains a sketch of the main algorithm:

```
/**
 * Finds and prints the anagrams of a word.
 */
fun main() {
    //Create a dictionary from "english.txt" in resources/books

    //Create a Term from our initial English word.

    //Get all rearrangements of the letters in this word.

    //For each of these,

    //...if it is in the dictionary

    //...print it.
}
```

Our implementation plan is to write the Dictionary and Term classes so they can supply the functions required in the preceding code sketch. In developing Dictionary and Term, we will follow the "test-first" methodology that we used in Project Austen.

11.2 The **Dictionary** Class

When the project is first retrieved, Dictionary should appear as follows:

```
1    package lpk.anagrams
2
3    import java.nio.file.Files
4    import java.nio.file.Path
5
6    /**
7     * Checks words against a list of words read
8     * from a file in which there is one word per line.
9     */
10   class Dictionary(pathToFile: Path) {
11
```

```
12        fun contains(string: String): Boolean {
13            return false
14        }
15    }
```

As usual, the first line names the package to which this class belongs. Lines 3 and 4 import code that will be required for reading the dictionary file. On line 10, the instruction

```
(pathToFile: Path)
```

means that a Dictionary can be constructed from a Path object and that this object will be available in the init block under the name pathToFile.

The contains function is what we will use for checking word validity. Let's get started by testing it. When the project is first retrieved, there is a ready-made test class that has some necessary imports and a test stub:

```
package lpk.anagrams.test

import org.junit.Assert
import org.junit.Test
import java.nio.file.Paths
import lpk.anagrams.Dictionary

class DictionaryTest {
    @Test
    fun containsTest() {

    }
}
```

PROJECT STEP 11.1

We can begin our test by constructing a Dictionary from the file called FiveWords.txt, in the test resources directory.

Copy this code into containsTest:

```
val path = Paths.get("src/test/resources/books/FiveWords.txt")
val dictionary = Dictionary(path)
```

There are as yet no assertions in this test, so it should pass.

The file FiveWords.txt is literally named. It contains precisely these lines:

```
aardvark
bat
cat
dog
eel
```

We can add some meaning to our test by checking that if we call contains for each of these words, the returned value is true.

PROJECT STEP 11.2

Add this line of code into containsTest:

```
Assert.assertTrue(dictionary.contains("aardvark"));
```

Check that the test now fails.

Add equivalent lines for each of the other four words in the dictionary file.

As well as checking what is in the dictionary, we should check what is not. Otherwise, we might have an implementation of contains that always returns true. The test as it is now written would pass, even with such a bad implementation of contains.

PROJECT STEP 11.3

Add these two lines to the test:

```
Assert.assertFalse(dictionary.contains("aardwolf"));
Assert.assertFalse(dictionary.contains("zebra"));
```

Our test should at this point contain five positive assertions and two negative assertions:

```
@Test
fun containsTest() {
    val path = Paths.get("src/test/resources/books/FiveWords.txt")
    val dictionary = Dictionary(path)
```

```
Assert.assertTrue(dictionary.contains("aardvark"))
Assert.assertTrue(dictionary.contains("bat"))
Assert.assertTrue(dictionary.contains("cat"))
Assert.assertTrue(dictionary.contains("dog"))
Assert.assertTrue(dictionary.contains("eel"))

Assert.assertFalse(dictionary.contains("aardwolf"))
Assert.assertFalse(dictionary.contains("zebra"))
}
```

With a complete test in place, we can now think about implementing Dictionary. As usual, there are many ways of doing this. One simple approach is as follows:

- Have a Set<String> field that contains exactly the words in the dictionary file.

- Implement contains by returning the Set's value for contains.

- In the init block, read the lines of the dictionary file one by one, and add each to the Set.

PROJECT STEP 11.4

Add a field called words that is a mutableSetOf<String>().

PROJECT STEP 11.5

Replace the stubbed implementation of contains with

```
fun contains(string: String): Boolean {
    return words.contains(string)
}
```

The only work remaining with Dictionary is to write the init block.

PROJECT STEP 11.6

Can you remember the code to get the contents of a file as a List<String>?

(We used this in the constructor of Book in Project Austen.)

Write an init block for Dictionary. The code should read pathToFile as a List<String>, then iterate over this List and add each item to words.

If each of the last three steps has been implemented correctly, the unit test should pass. You can compare your code with this:

```
package lpk.anagrams

import java.nio.file.Files
import java.nio.file.Path

/**
 * Checks words against a list of words read
 * from a file in which there is one word per line.
 */
class Dictionary(pathToFile: Path) {

    val words = mutableSetOf<String>()

    init {
        val lines = Files.readAllLines(pathToFile)
        for (line in lines) {
            words.add(line)
        }
    }

    fun contains(string: String): Boolean {
        return words.contains(string)
    }
}
```

11.3 The Term Class

A Term object represents any arrangement of Chars. The arrangement may or may not be a real "term" that can be found in a dictionary. Here's the code for Term when the project is first opened:

```
1    package lpk.anagrams
2
3    /**
4     * An arrangement of characters which may
5     * or may not be an English word.
6     */
7    data class Term(val text: String) {
8
9        fun permutations(): Set<Term> {
10            val result = mutableSetOf<Term>()
11            return result
12        }
13   }
```

There are a couple of things here that we haven't seen before. Notice, in the middle of line 7, that the constructor is

```
val text: String
```

The constructor parameter is labeled val, and there is no explicit init block. This is Kotlin shorthand for there being a field called text, which is of type String and which is set to be the value passed in to the constructor.

Notice too that line 7 starts with the keyword data. This makes Term a so-called *data class*, and Kotlin adds code automatically that allows us to compare Terms using the == operator.

PROJECT STEP 11.7

To see this in action, open the class TermTest and add the following:

```
1    @Test
2    fun equalsTest() {
```

```
3        val cat = Term("cat")
4        val feline = Term("cat")
5        val dog = Term("dog")
6        Assert.assertTrue(cat == feline)
7        Assert.assertFalse(cat == dog)
8   }
```

On lines 3 and 4, we declare Term instances, called cat and feline, respectively, that both have the String "cat" as their word. On line 6, we compare these using the == operator and expect the comparison to be true.

Check that this test passes.

Confirm that if you remove the data keyword from the declaration of the Term class, the test fails.

Make sure that you put the data keyword back!

11.4 Permutations

Permutations are rearrangements. We can permute the Chars in a String to produce other Strings. For example, from "ab", we can get "ab" itself and also "ba". From "abc", we can get six permutations: "abc", "acb", "bca", "bac", "cab", and "cba". If a String contains repeated Chars, then some rearrangements will be equal to others. We are only interested in the distinct permutations. So from "aab", we get "aab", "aba", and "baa".

By the permutations of a Term, we mean the Set of Terms built from rearrangements of its text.

11.5 The permutations Function

The Term class comes prebuilt with a stub for the permutations function. This means that we can get straight down to writing the unit tests that will help us to implement it correctly. (We need the function stub in order for the unit tests to be able to be written. It's a pain writing tests for a nonexistent function, as IntelliJ shows lots of errors. However, there are some programmers who write unit tests even before they write the function stubs.)

PROJECT STEP 11.8

As we have seen, there are two permutations of "ab". Here's a test function that checks the Set<Term> returned by calling the permutations function on the Term constructed from "ab":

```
@Test
fun permutationsAB() {
    val ab = Term("ab")
    val permutations = ab.permutations()
    Assert.assertEquals(2, permutations.size)
    Assert.assertTrue(permutations.contains(Term("ab")))
    Assert.assertTrue(permutations.contains(Term("ba")))
}
```

Copy this code into TermTest. Run it and check that it fails.

PROJECT STEP 11.9

Based on the test for "ab", write a test that checks the permutations returned by Term("abc").

PROJECT STEP 11.10

It will be good to have a test for permutations for a Term constructed from a String with repeated Chars.

Can you write a test that checks the permutations returned by Term("aab")?

PROJECT STEP 11.11

We should make sure that our permutations function (when it is implemented!) handles short Strings.

Copy this function into `TermTest`:

```
@Test
fun permutationsA() {
    val ab = Term("a")
    val permutations = ab.permutations()
    Assert.assertEquals(1, permutations.size)
    Assert.assertTrue(permutations.contains(Term("a")))
}
```

PROJECT STEP 11.12

Cases like getting the `permutations` for a single-`Char` `Term` are called *edge cases.* A more extreme edge case is to get the `permutations` from the `Term` constructed with the empty `String`. There is only one permutation of the empty `String`, which is the empty `String` itself.

Copy the following code into `TermTest`:

```
@Test fun permutationsWhenEmpty() {
    val empty = Term("")
    val permutations = empty.permutations()
    Assert.assertEquals(1, permutations.size)
    Assert.assertTrue(permutations.contains(Term("")))
}
```

The tests written in these project steps form a really solid foundation for implementing the permutations function. Including the equalsTest created earlier, our TermTest class should now be something like this:

```
package lpk.anagrams.test

import org.junit.Assert
import org.junit.Test
import lpk.anagrams.Term
```

```kotlin
class TermTest {
    @Test
    fun equalsTest() {
        val cat = Term("cat")
        val feline = Term("cat")
        val dog = Term("dog")
        Assert.assertTrue(cat == feline)
        Assert.assertFalse(cat == dog)
    }

    @Test fun permutationsWhenEmpty() {
        val empty = Term("")
        val permutations = empty.permutations()
        Assert.assertEquals(1, permutations.size)
        Assert.assertTrue(permutations.contains(Term("")))
    }

    @Test
    fun permutationsA() {
        val ab = Term("a")
        val permutations = ab.permutations()
        Assert.assertEquals(1, permutations.size)
        Assert.assertTrue(permutations.contains(Term("a")))
    }

    @Test
    fun permutationsAB() {
        val ab = Term("ab")
        val permutations = ab.permutations()
        Assert.assertEquals(2, permutations.size)
        Assert.assertTrue(permutations.contains(Term("ab")))
        Assert.assertTrue(permutations.contains(Term("ba")))
    }

    @Test
    fun permutationsABC() {
        val ab = Term("abc")
        val permutations = ab.permutations()
```

```
        Assert.assertEquals(6, permutations.size)
        Assert.assertTrue(permutations.contains(Term("abc")))
        Assert.assertTrue(permutations.contains(Term("acb")))
        Assert.assertTrue(permutations.contains(Term("bac")))
        Assert.assertTrue(permutations.contains(Term("bca")))
        Assert.assertTrue(permutations.contains(Term("cab")))
        Assert.assertTrue(permutations.contains(Term("cba")))
    }

    @Test
    fun permutationsAAB() {
        val ab = Term("aab")
        val permutations = ab.permutations()
        Assert.assertEquals(3, permutations.size)
        Assert.assertTrue(permutations.contains(Term("aab")))
        Assert.assertTrue(permutations.contains(Term("aba")))
        Assert.assertTrue(permutations.contains(Term("baa")))
    }
}
```

11.6 Generating the Permutations of a Term

As a starting point for implementing the permutations function of Term, let's think about how we might find the possible permutations of "abc".

Some of the rearrangements will have the Char a in the first position. How many, and what are they? Well, with a already used, we have b and c left. There are just two ways of arranging these letters: "bc" and "cb". It follows that there are exactly two permutations of "abc" in which a is in the first place: "abc" and "acb".

What about the permutations with a in second place? These are produced from permutations of "bc" by inserting an a between the first and second letters of the permutation. This gives "bac" and "cab".

Finally, the permutations of "abc" in which the a appears in the third position are obtained by generating the two permutations of "bc" and adding a onto the end, which gives "bca" and "cba".

```
┌──────────────────────────────────────────────────────────────┐
│                     PROJECT STEP 11.13                         │
└──────────────────────────────────────────────────────────────┘
```

Let's calculate the permutations of "xabc". It's best to do this in a text editor using a font in which all characters have the same width, so that columns of text will line up.

Write out the permutations of "abc" in a single line. There should be six of these.

Now copy this list three times to give four identical lines that each contain the six permutations of "abc".

For each of the terms in the first line, add an x to the start.

For each of the terms in the second line, insert an x between the first and second letters.

For the third line, insert an x between the second and third letters of each term.

For the last line, add an x to the end of each term.

There should now be the 24 distinct permutations of "xabc", written over four lines.

Here is our algorithm for calculating the permutations of a Term:

- If the Term has only one character, then there is only one permutation, which is the Term itself, so just return a Set containing the original Term.

- For Terms of length greater than one, remove the first letter. The resulting Term has one letter fewer than the original. Calculate the permutations of the trimmed Term.

- For each of these, create new Terms by inserting the first letter of the original Term at each possible position within that Term.

The second step of this algorithm actually invokes the algorithm itself. This is called *recursion* and is an extremely important technique in programming.

How do we know that this algorithm eventually stops? Well

- The recursive call uses a shorter input than the original.

- For input of length 1, we do not make a recursive call, but just return a result.

To implement this algorithm, we will need two "helper" functions. The first is to create a new Term from an existing one by removing its first letter. We will call this function tail. As usual, our procedure is to provide a stub, then write tests, and then do the implementation. Here is a stub for the function:

```
fun tail(): Term {
    return Term("")
}
```

PROJECT STEP 11.14

Copy this function into Term.

The function is pretty straightforward, but there are a couple of corner cases to test carefully.

PROJECT STEP 11.15

It's not clear how we should take the tail of an empty Term. Let's just decide to return the Term itself. To lock in this behavior, add the following to TermTest:

```
@Test
fun tailEmpty() {
    val empty = Term("")
    Assert.assertEquals(empty, empty.tail())
}
```

The second corner case is dealing with a Term that has length one.

PROJECT STEP 11.16

Copy this code into TermTest:

```
@Test
fun tailOne() {
    val a = Term("a")
    Assert.assertEquals(Term(""), a.tail())
}
```

We should also have a test for a more normal Term.

PROJECT STEP 11.17

Add this unit test:

```
@Test
fun tailTest() {
    val anaconda = Term("anaconda")
    Assert.assertEquals(Term("naconda"), anaconda.tail())
}
```

The String data type has functions for creating a new String from part of an existing one. One of these, called substring, takes an Int parameter which marks the position at which the String is to be cut. The returned String is the part of the original one after, and including, the indexed Char. (And remember that String indexes start at 0.) We can use substring to implement tail.

PROJECT STEP 11.18

Replace the stub implementation of tail with this code:

```
fun tail(): Term {
    if (text == "") {
        return Term("")
    }
```

```
    return Term(text.substring(1))
}
```

Check that the three tests for `tail` now pass.

The second helper function that we need is one that will insert a Char into a Term, at a given position, and so produce a new Term. For example, if we start with "xyz" and call insert(a, 1), we should get "xayz".

PROJECT STEP 11.19

Add the following stubbed function to Term:

```
fun insert(newChar: Char, position: Int): Term {
    return Term("")
}
```

As with the `tail` function, there are three tests that we should implement: two corner cases for short Terms and a straightforward example.

PROJECT STEP 11.20

If we start with an empty Term, there is only one location at which it makes sense to do an insertion: 0. The resulting Term should just consist of the inserted Char.

Copy the following test for this "empty" scenario into TermTest:

```
@Test
fun insertIntoEmpty() {
    val empty = Term("")
    Assert.assertEquals(Term("a"), empty.insert('a', 0))
}
```

PROJECT STEP 11.21

For a Term of length one, we can insert a Char either at position 0 or at position 1. Here's a test for these options:

```
@Test
fun insertIntoLengthOneTerm() {
    val x = Term("x")
    Assert.assertEquals(Term("ax"), x.insert('a', 0))
    Assert.assertEquals(Term("xa"), x.insert('a', 1))
}
```

Copy it into TermTest.

PROJECT STEP 11.22

Here's a test using a longer Term:

```
@Test
fun insertTest() {
    val x = Term("xy")
    Assert.assertEquals(Term("axy"), x.insert('a', 0))
    Assert.assertEquals(Term("xay"), x.insert('a', 1))
    Assert.assertEquals(Term("xya"), x.insert('a', 2))
}
```

Add it to TermTest.

The substring function of String that we used earlier actually comes in two forms. We've already used the single parameter version, but there is also a version that takes two Int parameters. The String returned by this function contains the text between the positions indicated by these parameters. We can implement insert by using these two versions of substring.

PROJECT STEP 11.23

Replace the stub implementation of `insert` with this code:

```
fun insert(newChar: Char, position: Int): Term {
    val before = text.substring(0, position)
    val after = text.substring(position)
    return Term(before + newChar + after)
}
```

Check that the tests for this function now pass.

With these two helper functions in place, we can finally implement `permutations`. First, let's replace our stub implementation by one in which the algorithm is sketched out using comments:

```
1    fun permutations(): Set<Term> {
2        //Create a result set to which the permutations will be added.
3
4        //If the Term has length 0 or 1, then the Term itself is
5        //the only permutation,
6        //so add it to the result and return.
7
8        //At this point we know that the length is at least two.
9        //Break the Term into a single Char, the head,
10       //and a Term that is one Char shorter, the tail.
11
12       //Apply recursion to get the permutations of the tail.
13
14       //For each possible insertion position,
15
16       //for each Term in the permutations of the tail,
17
18       //create a new Term by inserting
19       //the head Char at the position,
20
```

```
21        //and add this to the result.
22
23        //Return the result.
24    }
```

PROJECT STEP 11.24

Copy this into Term as the new implementation of permutations (so replace the existing code with this).

PROJECT STEP 11.25

On line 3, add a val called result that is initialized using a mutableSetOf<Term>() function call.

Add code after line 23 to return this result.

PROJECT STEP 11.26

We can tell if the Term in which this function is being called has length 0 or 1 using an if block:

```
if (text.length <= 1) {

}
```

Put a block like this at line 7. Within the if block that we've just added, we are handling the situation where the Term we are working with is empty or has just a single Char. We know from our unit tests that such Terms have just a single permutation, which is exactly the same as the Term itself. So we want to add the Term on which the permutation function has been called to result. There is a special keyword for talking about the current object, which is this. Add the following lines inside the if block:

```
result.add(this)
return result
```

Once this is done, the unit tests dealing with one-Char and empty Terms should pass.

PROJECT STEP 11.27

At line 11, create a val called head that is initialized to the first Char in text.

PROJECT STEP 11.28

After the line just added, create a val called tail that is initialized to the result of calling the tail function.

PROJECT STEP 11.29

The val we just created is a Term, so we can call permutations on it. At line 13, create a val called tailPermutations that is initialized to the return value of permutations called on tail.

We have just implemented the recursive step of the algorithm. At this point, our code should look something like this:

```
1    fun permutations(): Set<Term> {
2        //Create a result set to which the permutations will be added.
3        val result = mutableSetOf<Term>()
4        //If the Term has length 0 or 1, then the Term itself is
5        //the only permutation,
6        //so add it to the result and return.
7        if (text.length <= 1) {
8            result.add(this)
9            return result
10       }
11       //At this point we know that the length is at least two.
12       //Break the Term into a single Char, the head,
13       //and a Term that is one Char shorter, the tail.
14       val head = text[0]
```

```
15        val tail = tail()
16        //Apply recursion to get the permutations of the tail.
17        val tailPermuations = tail.permutations()
18        //For each possible insertion position,
19
20        //for each Term in the permutations of the tail,
21
22        //create a new Term by inserting
23        //the head Char at the position,
24
25        //and add this to the result.
26
27        //Return the result.
28        return result
29    }
```

The last pieces of the function are to create new words from head and the Terms in tailPermutations. Each of the elements of tailPermutations is of length

```
text.length - 1
```

so the possible insertion positions are 0, 1, and so on.

PROJECT STEP 11.30

Paste this loop code:

```
for (i in 0..text.length - 1) {
```

at line 19 and place a closing brace at line 26. When you do this, IntelliJ will probably indent the intervening lines.

PROJECT STEP 11.31

We can use a for-loop at line 21.

Copy this code into that location:

for (tailPermutation in tailPermuations) {

and again add a closing brace at line 26.

With these loops in place, our function should look like this:

```
1    fun permutations(): Set<Term> {
2        //Create a result set to which the permutations will be added.
3        val result = mutableSetOf<Term>()
4        //If the Term has length 0 or 1, then the Term itself is
5        //the only permutation,
6        //so add it to the result and return.
7        if (text.length <= 1) {
8            result.add(this)
9            return result
10       }
11       //At this point we know that the length is at least two.
12       //Break the Term into a single Char, the head,
13       //and a Term that is one Char shorter, the tail.
14       val head = text[0]
15       val tail = tail()
16       //Apply recursion to get the permutations of the tail.
17       val tailPermuations = tail.permutations()
18       //For each possible insertion position,
19       for (i in 0..text.length - 1) {
20           //for each Term in the permutations of the tail,
21           for (tailPermutation in tailPermuations) {
22               //create a new Term by inserting
23               //the head Char at the position,
24
```

```
25                     //and add this to the result.
26
27              }
28          }
29       //Return the result.
30       return result
31   }
```

At line 24 in the preceding code listing, we have an insertion location, i, and a Term, tailPermutation, into which to insert the Char head.

PROJECT STEP 11.32

At line 24, write code that creates a val called newTerm.

This should use tailPermutation, head, and i.

Then at line 26, write a line of code that adds newTerm to result.

This completes the implementation of permutations. All of the tests should now pass.

11.7 Putting It All Together

With Dictionary and Term now implemented, we can return to the main function in AnagramFinder. Here's the stub of this file:

```
1    package lpk.anagrams
2
3    import java.nio.file.Paths
4
5    /**
6      * Finds and prints the anagrams of a word.
7      */
8    fun main() {
9        //Create a dictionary from "english.txt" in resources/books
10
```

```
11          //Create a Term from our initial English word.
12
13          //Get all rearrangements of the letters in this word.
14
15          //For each of these,
16
17          //...if it is in the dictionary
18
19          //...print it.
20     }
```

PROJECT STEP 11.33

Add these lines at line 10:

```
val path = Paths.get("src/main/resources/books/english.txt")
val dictionary = Dictionary(path)
```

PROJECT STEP 11.34

Let's find the anagrams of "regal". Add this code at line 12:

```
val word = Term("regal")
```

PROJECT STEP 11.35

The next comment asks for the permutations of word and is easily implemented:

```
val anagrams = word.permutations()
```

```
                    PROJECT STEP 11.36
```

The comment "For each of these," is translated into a for-loop:

```
for (w in anagrams) {
```

Paste this code into line 16 and add a closing brace just after line 19.

```
                    PROJECT STEP 11.37
```

To test if a Term w represents a word in the dictionary, we can use

```
if (dictionary.contains(w.text)) {
```

Add this line and then add a closing brace just after line 19.

```
                    PROJECT STEP 11.38
```

Finally, add a print statement on line 18.

The finished code should be as follows:

```kotlin
package lpk.anagrams

import java.nio.file.Paths

/**
 * Finds and prints the anagrams of a word.
 */
fun main(args: Array<String>) {
    //Create a dictionary from "english.txt" in resources/books
    val path = Paths.get("src/main/resources/books/english.txt")
    val dictionary = Dictionary(path)
    //Create a Term from our initial English word.
    val word = Term("regal")
```

```
//Get all rearrangements of the letters in this word.
val anagrams = word.permutations()
//For each of these,
for (w in anagrams) {
    //...if it is in the dictionary
    if (dictionary.contains(w.text)) {
        //...print it.
        println(w)
    }
}
}
```

Run the code. There should be five anagrams:

`large, glare, ergal, regal, lager`

The words might appear in a different order, since they were put in a Set, which is an unordered collection.

11.8 Summary

In this project, we have used recursion, which is one of the most interesting and conceptually difficult ideas in programming. We also continued to improve our skills in object-oriented design and testing and solved a very interesting linguistic problem.

The completed code for this chapter is available from `https://github.com/Apress/learn-to-program-w-kotlin-anagrams-complete.git`.

CHAPTER 12

Palindromes

A palindrome is a word that is the same whether written forward or backward, for example, "kayak." In this chapter, we will find all English words that are palindromes. This will give us further practice with object-oriented programming, unit testing, and recursion.

The classes we developed in the previous chapter are a great starting point for this project. Our implementation strategy will be based on adding an isPalindrome function to the Term class. We will then write a main function that loops through the words in the dictionary, creates Terms from them, and then filters these using isPalindrome.

To get started, use IntelliJ to check out the completed code from Chapter 11, which is available from https://github.com/Apress/learn-to-program-w-kotlin-anagrams-complete.git.

12.1 Reversing a Term

To implement isPalindrome, we will need code to reverse a Term. As usual, we will add a stub of the function, write a test, and then go back and implement it properly.

PROJECT STEP 12.1

Copy this stub code into Term:

```
fun reverse() : Term {
    returnTerm("")
}
```

© Tim Lavers 2021
T. Lavers, *Learn to Program with Kotlin*, https://doi.org/10.1007/978-1-4842-6815-5_12

PROJECT STEP 12.2

The following test checks that if we apply reverse to "ab", we get "ba" as the result:

```
@Test
fun reverseTest() {
    Assert.assertEquals(Term("ba"), Term("ab").reverse())
}
```

This is a good start for a unit test, but we should also add lines to check the results when we reverse

- An empty Term

- A Term with just one letter

- Terms with three or four letters

- A Term that has some repeated letters.

See if you can add lines for these tests.

After this step, TermTest should include a test function along the lines of

```
@Test
fun reverseTest() {
    Assert.assertEquals(Term(""), Term("").reverse())
    Assert.assertEquals(Term("a"), Term("a").reverse())
    Assert.assertEquals(Term("ba"), Term("ab").reverse())
    Assert.assertEquals(Term("cba"), Term("abc").reverse())
    Assert.assertEquals(Term("aabb"), Term("bbaa").reverse())
}
```

Of course, you may have made separate tests for each of these assertions or have other differences.

One of the programming challenges in Chapter 7 was to reverse a String, and we can use that code to implement reverse:

```
fun reverse() : Term {
    var result =""
```

```
for (c in text) {
    result = c + result
}
returnTerm(result)
}
```

PROJECT STEP 12.3

Replace the stub implementation with that shown earlier. Check that with this change, the unit test passes.

PROJECT STEP 12.4

There's actually a library function for String reversal. Replace your implementation of reverse with this:

```
fun reverse() : Term {
    returnTerm(text.reversed())
}
```

Check that the unit test still passes.

We already have two different implementations of reverse; now we'll look at a recursive implementation, as it is good practice in this essential programming technique.

A recursive approach to Term reversal begins with two basis steps:

- The reverse of the empty Term is itself.

- The reverse of a Term with just one letter is itself.

These steps are in fact checked in our unit test. Now consider a longer word, such as "abcde". This word can be broken into three parts:

- The first Char, which is a

- The last Char, which is e

- A word of length three in the middle, which is "bcd"

To form the reverse, we start with e, then add the reverse of the middle section, then add a. How do we get the reverse of the middle section? By applying recursion!

PROJECT STEP 12.5

Replace the current version of reverse with this:

```
1   fun reverse() : Term {
2       val length = text.length
3       //If the word is empty or just one letter,
4       //it is its own reverse.
5       if (length < 2) {
6           return this
7       }
8       //Get the first and last characters and the
9       //inner word formed by the letters in between.
10      val first = text[0]
11      val last = text[length - 1]
12      val inner = Term(text.substring(1, length - 1))
13      //Use recursion to get the reverse of the inner word.
14      val reverseOfInner = inner.reverse().text
15      //Put the three pieces together to form the result.
16      val newText = last + reverseOfInner + first
17      return Term(newText)
18  }
```

Check that the unit tests still pass.

There are a couple of points worth noting about this code. First, on line 2, we have introduced a val, called length, which stores the length of the Term's text. This is a convenience so that we don't need to call text.length on lines 4, 10, and 11. Second, on line 11, we have used the substring function of String to get the inner part of the text.

PROJECT STEP 12.6

To see the recursion in action, add the following printout as the first line of `reverse`:

```
println(text)
```

Now add a new test function:

```
@Test
fun abcdeTest() {
    Assert.assertEquals(Term("edcba"), Term("abcde").reverse())
}
```

When you run this test, you should get the following printout:

```
text = 'abcde'
text = 'bcd'
text = 'c'
```

The first printout is from the initial call to `reverse`, and then there are printouts for two recursive calls. The call to `reverse` for the Term "c" does not result in a further recursive call because this word has just one letter.

Now make a test using the input "abcdef". What printouts do you expect to see? How does the recursion end with this input?

Make sure you remove the printout after running these tests!

12.2 Detecting Palindromes

With the `reverse` function at our disposal, it is very simple to add a function that returns `true` if and only if a Term is palindromic. In fact, it's so simple that we implement it immediately:

```
fun isPalindrome(): Boolean {
    returnequals(reverse())
}
```

PROJECT STEP 12.7

Add this function to Term.

PROJECT STEP 12.8

Even a simple function should have a test. Add the following to TermTest:

```
@Test
fun isPalindromeTest() {
    Assert.assertTrue(Term("").isPalindrome())
    Assert.assertTrue(Term("a").isPalindrome())
    Assert.assertTrue(Term("aa").isPalindrome())
    Assert.assertTrue(Term("aaa").isPalindrome())
    Assert.assertTrue(Term("madam").isPalindrome())
    Assert.assertFalse(Term("ab").isPalindrome())
}
```

This completes the changes to Term that we need. You can either leave the recursive version of reverse (but make sure that you have deleted the printout) or change it back to one of the other implementations. The fact that we can have different implementations of a function is one of the key features of object-oriented programming. The implementation details are hidden within the method itself, so we are free to change our approach without any unexpected effects in classes that use the function.

12.3 Putting It All Together

We now have the tools necessary to achieve our goal of finding all of the palindromes in english.txt in the resources directory. We've already got a program that reads this file and creates a Dictionary from it, so let's copy that program.

In the project tree, right-click the file AnagramFinder.kt. From the menu that pops up, select Refactor ➤ Copy, as in Figure 12-1. A dialog box will show, asking you for the name of the new file. Set this to be PalindromeFinder.kt. Once this is done, IntelliJ will open the new file.

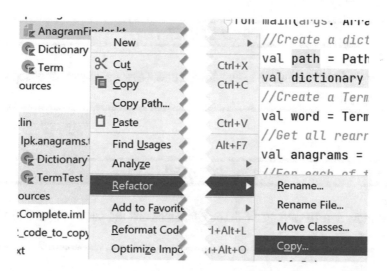

Figure 12-1. *Using the right-click menu to copy AnagramFinder.kt*

PROJECT STEP 12.9

Edit the `main` function to be as follows:

```
1    fun main() {
2        //Create a dictionary from "english.txt" in resources/books
3        val path = Paths.get("src/main/resources/books/english.txt")
4        val dictionary = Dictionary(path)
5        //For each string in the dictionary...
6
7            //...create a Term from the string
8
9            //...test to see if the word is a palindrome...
10
11               //...if it is, print it.
12   }
```

PROJECT STEP 12.10

Replace the empty line 6 with a for-loop that iterates over `dictionary.allWords`. Call the loop variable `"str"`. The loop body should include lines 7 to 11.

PROJECT STEP 12.11

Replace the empty line 8 with code to construct a new Term using `str` (the loop `val`). Call the new variable "word".

PROJECT STEP 12.12

Replace the empty line 10 with an `if`-block that includes the comment on line 11. The `if` should check `if word` is a palindrome.

PROJECT STEP 12.13

Add a statement just after line 11 that prints out `word`.

At this point, you should be able to run the program. If not, check your version of `PalindromeFinder.kt` with this:

```kotlin
package lpk.anagrams

import java.nio.file.Paths

/**
 * Finds and prints out English palindromes.
 */
fun main() {
    //Create a dictionary from "english.txt" in resources/books
    val path = Paths.get("src/main/resources/books/english.txt")
    val dictionary = Dictionary(path)
    //For each string in the dictionary...
    for (str in dictionary.words) {
        //...create a Term from the string
        val word = Term(str)
        //...test to see if the word is a palindrome...
```

```
    if (word.isPalindrome()) {
        //...if it is, print it.
        println(word)
    }
  }
}
```

The list of words printed out should include all of the letters, plus some two- and three-letter words, and then some more interesting ones. My personal favorites are "rotator" because it is self-describing and "malayalam" for its length.

If you want to take things a bit further, you might change the code to eliminate the short words.

12.4 Summary

By building on our previous work in the Anagrams project, we have been able to find all of palindromes listed in the 1913 edition of Webster's dictionary. This short project gave us more practice in object-oriented programming and unit testing and in working with recursive algorithms.

The completed code for this chapter is available from https://github.com/Apress/ learn-to-program-w-kotlin-palindromes-complete.git.

CHAPTER 13

Word Switch

How can one turn "cave" into "home"? Here's one way:

cave → came → come → home.

This is the *word switch* game: choose two words and then see if one can be transformed into the other by changing one letter at a time, such that a valid word is produced by each change.

In this chapter, we will write software that solves the word switch problem for any two words—if there is a solution—and lets us know if there is not. As well as being an interesting problem, this will give us yet more practice with object-oriented programming and unit testing, and we will also build a new kind of data structure, which is in fact recursive.

13.1 The Algorithm

One approach to solving this problem is to create "generations" of words, with each generation created from the previous one by single-letter substitutions, taking care to remember the words that have already been generated. When a generation is found that contains the target word, the process finishes with success. When a generation contains only words that were found in previous generations, the process finishes with failure. It's best to look at this using an example. Suppose that the start word is fight and the target is argue.

13.1.1 Generation 1

The words that can be derived from fight by changing just any one letter are

bight, dight, eight, hight, light, might,
night, pight, right, sight, tight, wight

© Tim Lavers 2021

T. Lavers, *Learn to Program with Kotlin*, https://doi.org/10.1007/978-1-4842-6815-5_13

These are all new, but none of them is the target, so we use them to build a new generation.

13.1.2 Generation 2

Each of the words from Generation 1 can be changed to `fight`, but that was our starting word, so has already been seen. Apart from that:

- From `bight`, we get `bigot` and `bigha`.

- From `dight`, we get `digit`.

- From `eyght`, we get `eight`.

- `night` generates `noght`.

- `tight` generates `toght`.

So the new words in Generation 2 are

`bigot, bigha, digit, eyght, noght, toght`

13.1.3 Generation 3

Of the words created in Generation 2, only two new words can be created: `bigot` begets `begot`, and `digit` can be changed to `dimit`.

13.1.4 Generation 4

From the words that were new in Generation 3, we get `besot`, `beget`, and `begod` from `begot`, and we get `limit` and `demit` from `dimit`.

13.1.5 Algorithm Termination with Success

After many generations, the target word, `argue`, is found. The word that gave rise to it was `argus`. The word that gave rise to `argus` was `argas`, and so on, backward, until we get to `bigot` and then `bight` and, finally, the start word, `fight`. The complete chain of words is

```
fight, bight, bigot, begot, beget, reget, revet, levet,
lever, laver, lager, eager, egger, agger, anger, angor,
algor, algol, argol, argal, argas, argus, argue
```

13.1.6 Algorithm Termination with Failure

It's also worth looking at an example where the algorithm terminates without finding the target word. Suppose that our start word is viola and our target is cello. The first generation contains just two new words: villa and viole. From villa, we can get viola (of course) plus the new words zilla and villi, but viole cannot be changed into a new word. So we have

```
Start word: viola
Generation 1: villa, viole
Generation 2: zilla, villi
```

However, neither zilla nor villi can be changed into new words, so Generation 3 is empty and the algorithm terminates.

13.2 Main Classes and Project Setup

As the examples have shown, there are three key processes in our algorithm. First, there is the task of generating new words from existing ones. We will have a class called WordNode to do this. Second, words created by WordNode need to be checked to see if they are valid and if they have previously been seen. This job will be done by a class called WordChecker. Finally, if the target word is found, we need to build the "path" of words from the starting word to the target. Our WordNode class will do this job, in addition to creating new words.

Two more classes are needed. The Dictionary from previous chapters will be used by the WordChecker to test the validity of potential new words. Finally, a class called WordSwitch will provide a main function and implement the word switch algorithm.

Stubs for WordChecker, WordNode, and WordSwitch and their unit tests have already been created, and we are using the same Dictionary class and test as in previous chapters. To get started, open the project https://github.com/Apress/learn-to-program-w-kotlin-wordswitch.git.

13.3 The WordChecker Class

When the project is first opened, the WordChecker class should look like this:

```
1    package lpk.words
2
3    /**
4     * Checks that potential new words are in the dictionary
5     * and have not previously been seen.
6     */
7    class WordChecker(val dictionary: Dictionary) {
8
9        val wordsSoFar = mutableSetOf<String>()
10
11       fun isPreviouslyUnseenValidWord(string: String): Boolean {
12           return false
13       }
14   }
```

As can be seen from line 7, WordChecker has a Dictionary as a field, which is passed into the constructor.

There is currently just a single function, isPreviouslyUnseenValidWord, and it is given a stub implementation that always returns false. Our first programming task will be to write a unit test for this function, so that we can safely replace the stub with a correct implementation. A couple of test cases spring to mind:

- If a String is not in the Dictionary, the function should return false.

- For a String that is in the Dictionary, the first time the word is seen, the function should return true, but subsequent calls should all return false.

In writing the unit test, we can create a five-word dictionary, as we did in the previous project, and then create a WordChecker from this.

PROJECT STEP 13.1

Open WordCheckerTest in IntelliJ and copy this partially implemented test function into the class:

```
@Test
fun notInDictionaryTest() {
    val path = Paths.get("src/test/resources/books/FiveWords.txt")
    val dictionary = Dictionary(path)
    val checker = WordChecker(dictionary)

}
```

Add a line to this function that checks that the word "aardwolf" is not a previously unseen valid word.

Do you expect this test to pass or fail, given the stub implementation of isPreviouslyUnseenValidWord?

Tip   The solution to this and other project steps is at the end of this chapter.

After implementing this project step, WordCheckerTest should look something like this:

```
package lpk.words.test

import org.junit.Assert
import org.junit.Test
import lpk.words.Dictionary
import lpk.words.WordChecker
import java.nio.file.Paths

class WordCheckerTest {
    @Test
    fun notInDictionaryTest() {
        val path = Paths.get("src/test/resources/books/FiveWords.txt")
        val dictionary = Dictionary(path)
```

```
        val checker = WordChecker(dictionary)
        Assert.assertFalse(checker.isPreviouslyUnseenValidWord("aardworlff"))
    }
}
```

Note that your import statements might be slightly different, but as long as there are no error indications, that is no problem. Let's now implement the second test scenario.

PROJECT STEP 13.2

Add this partial test function to WordCheckerTest:

```
@Test
fun validWordTest() {
    val path = Paths.get("src/test/resources/books/FiveWords.txt")
    val dictionary = Dictionary(path)
    val checker = WordChecker(dictionary)

}
```

Add an assertion that "bat" is a previously unseen valid word.

Then add an assertion that it is not (because the word was seen in the first line you added).

As the tests imply, the implementation of isPreviouslyUnseenValidWord should

- Return false if the word is not in the dictionary, and not bother recording it

- Record a new valid word and then return true

- Return false if the word has already been recorded

PROJECT STEP 13.3

Notice that the stub for WordChecker already has a Dictionary and a Set<String>.
Using these, implement the function, and then check that the tests pass.

13.4 The `WordNode` Class

A `WordNode` will be created from a `String` and will have a function to generate the valid one-letter variants of it. The downloaded project files should include the following stub for `WordNode`:

```
package lpk.words

/**
 * Generates one-letter variants of a word.
 */
data class WordNode(val text: String) {
    fun variantsByOneLetter(checker: WordChecker): List<WordNode> {
        val result = mutableListOf<WordNode>()
        return result
    }
}
```

The `variantsByOneLetter` function is what our algorithm will use to generate new words. As usual, it's very useful to think about how this function will work in some simple cases.

- If we start with an empty word, no variations get generated.

- From a one-letter word, we get every other possible one-letter word that is in the dictionary.

- From the word ab, we can get every word of the form a_, where _ represents any letter apart from b, that is in the dictionary, plus every word of the form _b that is in the dictionary, where now _ represents any letter apart from a.

In turning these scenarios into unit tests, we are faced with the problem of not actually knowing what words are in the dictionary. For the one-letter words, this would not be too hard to discover. However, for the two-letter words, it would be a real challenge. We would have to write a program to search the dictionary for them, which would be a lot of work. Given that we will probably also want tests involving three- and four-letter words at some stage, we need to find another approach.

What we can do is create another dictionary that contains just a small number of words and create the `WordChecker` used in our tests from this restricted dictionary.

In fact, such a dictionary file, called `abcd.txt`, has already been created and is in the test resources for the project, as shown in Figure 13-1. This file contains just the following entries:

Figure 13-1. *The dictionary file* `abcd.txt`

```
a, b, c, d, aa, ab, ac, ad, ba, bb, bc,
bd, ca, cb, cc, cd, da, db, dc, dd
```

PROJECT STEP 13.4

There is already an empty unit test class for `WordNode`. Copy the following code into it:

```kotlin
@Test
fun testEmpty() {
    val path = Paths.get("src/test/resources/books/abcd.txt")
    val dictionary = Dictionary(path)
```

```
    val checker = WordChecker(dictionary)
    val wordNode = WordNode("")
}
```

Add a line to the test that checks that `variantsByOneLetter` returns an empty list. Given our stub implementation for the function, do you expect this test to pass or fail?

PROJECT STEP 13.5

Let's now consider the length-one word scenario. Add this partially implemented test function to WordNodeTest:

```
@Test
fun testOneLetterWord() {
    val path = Paths.get("src/test/resources/books/abcd.txt")
    val dictionary = Dictionary(path)
    val checker = WordChecker(dictionary)
    val nodeA = WordNode("a")
    val generated = nodeA.variantsByOneLetter(checker)
}
```

According to our preceding analysis, the val `generated` should contain three words. What are they?

Can you add assertions that check this?

13.5 Refactoring WordNodeTest

The two test functions in WordNodeTest contain several lines of code that are identical. It would be best if we could avoid this duplication, as it is visual clutter that makes the tests hard to read. Also, if we make any changes to the way the WordChecker is created, then the corresponding changes will need to be made in two places. To fix this problem, we can extract the common code as a function that is called instead of the repeated code. IntelliJ has great support for this. To begin, highlight the first three lines of testEmpty, as showin in Figure 13-2.

```
class WordNodeTest {
    @Test
    fun testEmpty() {
        val path = Paths.get( first: "src/      bcd.txt")
        val dictionary = Dictionary(pa
        val checker = WordChecker(dict.
        val wordNode = WordNode( text: ""
        Assert.assertTrue(wordNode.var      .r).isEmpty())
    }
```

Figure 13-2. *To begin fixing the problem of duplicated code, highlight one of the duplicate code blocks*

With the code block highlighted, choose the menu **Refactor** and then the submenu `Refactor This...`, as shown in Figure 13-3.

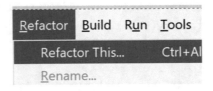

Figure 13-3. *The refactor menu*

A small window will appear with a number of options, as shown in Figure 13-4. From these options, choose `Function`. A fairly complex dialog with various options, plus a preview of the changes, will be shown, as in Figure 13-5. Just press **OK**.

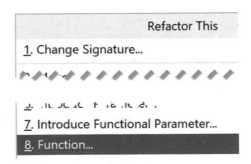

Figure 13-4. *The refactoring tools dialog*

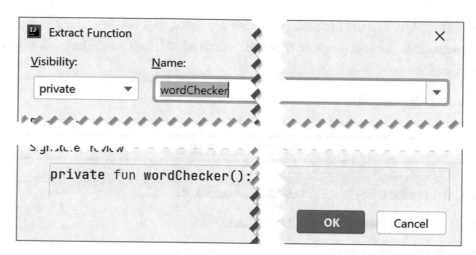

Figure 13-5. *The function extraction tool*

IntelliJ will now throw up an option to refactor the second code block, as shown in Figure 13-6. Click **Yes**. The test functions should now be refactored to call the wordChecker function in place of the duplicated code blocks. For now, the savings in space and complexity are not huge, but as we add more functions, the work that we have just done (or had IntelliJ do for us!) will definitely pay off.

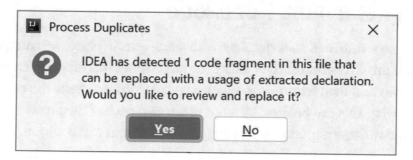

Figure 13-6. *IntelliJ offers to refactor other matching code blocks*

13.6 Further Tests of WordNode

With our code now simplified, we can go back to our test scenarios and implement those that involved generating new words from a two-letter word. If we start with the word ab, then by changing the first letter, we can get bb, cb, db, eb, fb, and so on. Of these, just the first three are in the dictionary that we are using in these tests. By changing the second letter of ab, we can produce the valid words aa, ac, and ad. So in total we have six variants:

aa, ac, ad, bb, cb, db

PROJECT STEP 13.6

Copy and paste the entire function testOneLetterWord.

Rename the copied function to testTwoLetterWord.

Then modify the body as follows:

- Instead of creating a WordNode from "a", create it from "ab".

- Add an assertion that generated has six elements.

- Instead of asserting that generated contains WordNode("b") and so on, check that it contains the elements listed earlier.

13.7 Implementing WordNode

We already have a stub for WordNode. Now, with some tests in place, we can fill in the details of variantsByOneLetter. Our stub code already has this function creating a List<WordNode> and then returning it. What we need to do is to write the code that populates this list. This can be done by looping through each of the positions in the word and adding the variations produced by changing the letter at that position.

PROJECT STEP 13.7

Replace variantsByOneLetter with this code:

```
1    fun variantsByOneLetter(checker: WordChecker): List<WordNode> {
2        val result = mutableListOf<WordNode>()
3        //For each position in the word...
4        for (i in 0..text.length - 1) {
5            //...add the variants made by changing
```

```
6              //just the letter at that position.
7
8        }
9        return result
10   }
```

Line 7 in this code, currently blank, requires some thought. At this point, the objects in scope are result, to which new variations need to be added, checker for testing possible words, the letter position i, and of course the field word, which is declared in the class constructor.

In developing an algorithm for this kind of tricky problem, it is very useful to think of a particular example. So suppose that our WordNode is for "bolt" and that i is 2. We want to know what words can be obtained by replacing the "l". Before the "l", we have "bo", and after it we have "t". These pieces create a template, "bo_t". For each letter in the alphabet, we can replace the underscore character with that letter and test the resulting String using the checker. So we ask:

- is "boat" ok,

- is "bobt" ok,

- is "boct" ok,

- and so on, to

- is "bozt" ok?

The exception is that we do not bother asking about "bolt" because that is the word that we are working on. As an algorithm, this is

- Get the text before the position

- Get the text after the position

- For each letter in the alphabet

  - If the letter is not the same as from our word, create a new word using it.

  - If the new word is ok, add it.

Because this logic is very complex, we will put it into a dedicated function and use it on line 7 of variantsByOneLetter.

PROJECT STEP 13.8

Copy this function into WordNode:

```
private fun addVariantsAtPosition(position: Int, nodes:
MutableList<WordNode>, checker: WordChecker) {
    val textBeforePosition = text.substring(0, position)
    val textAfterPosition = if (text.length > 1) text.substring(position + 1,
    text.length) else ""
    val originalLetter = text[position]
    for (fromAlphabet in "abcdefghijklmnopqrstuvwxyz") {
        if (originalLetter != fromAlphabet) {
            val variant = textBeforePosition + fromAlphabet +
            textAfterPosition
            if (checker.isPreviouslyUnseenValidWord(variant)) {
                nodes.add(WordNode(variant))
            }
        }
    }
}
```

Compare the lines of code in the function with the steps of the algorithm given earlier.

Then replace the empty line 7 in Project Step 13.7 with this call to the new function:

```
addVariantsAtPosition(i, result, checker)
```

Check that, with these changes, the tests now pass.

13.8 The WordSwitch Class

Our WordChecker and WordNode classes implement key parts of the word switch algorithm. To coordinate the activities of these two classes, we will use a third class, called WordSwitch. This class has already been partially implemented. If you open it in IntelliJ, you should see this code:

```
1    package lpk.words
2
```

```
3    import java.nio.file.Paths
4
5    /**
6     * Implements the Word Switch algorithm.
7     */
8    class WordSwitch(dictionary: Dictionary, start: String, val target:
     String) {
9
10       val startNode: WordNode
11       val checker: WordChecker
12
13       init {
14           startNode = WordNode(start)
15           checker = WordChecker(dictionary)
16       }
17
18       fun lookForTarget(): WordNode? {
19           //Declare a variable to hold the new words that get created
20           //in each generation. Initialise it with the words generated
21           //by the start word.
22
23           //Have a loop to create new generations so long as these
24           //contain new words and the target is not found.
25
26           return null
27       }
28   }
```

The constructor on line 8 shows that there is a field, called target, which is a String. The other two constructor parameters are a Dictionary and a String, from which the search starts. These two parameters are used in the init block to initialize two fields. These fields are a WordNode from which the search algorithm is launched and a WordChecker.

Line 18 introduces a function, lookForTarget, that will actually do the searching. This function will return a WordNode holding the destination, if it can be reached, else will return null, the "nothing" object. The possibility of a null means that the return type is WordNode? rather than WordNode.

We will of course write unit tests before attempting to fill out the details of this function. In these unit tests, we will reuse the "abcd" dictionary from WordCheckerTest. Here are some possible test cases:

- If the start word is ab and the destination is abc, then the destination will not be reached, as it is of a different length from the starting word.

- The word ae is unreachable because it is not in the dictionary.

- The word b should be reachable from a, bb should be reachable from aa, bbb from aaa, and so on.

PROJECT STEP 13.9

Open WordSwitchTest and copy these two test functions into the body of the class:

```
@Test
fun noPathDifferentLengths() {
    val path = Paths.get("src/test/resources/books/abcd.txt")
    val dictionary = Dictionary(path)
    val wordSwitch = WordSwitch(dictionary, "ab", "abc")
    Assert.assertNull(wordSwitch.lookForTarget())
}

@Test
fun noPathTargetNotInDictionary() {
    val path = Paths.get("src/test/resources/books/abcd.txt")
    val dictionary = Dictionary(path)
    val wordSwitch = WordSwitch(dictionary, "aa", "ae")
    Assert.assertNull(wordSwitch.lookForTarget())
}
```

Run these tests. Why do they pass?

PROJECT STEP 13.10

Notice that both test functions start with the same first two lines. Can you get IntelliJ to refactor this duplicated code?

PROJECT STEP 13.11

After refactoring, your code should look something like that in the solution to Project Step 13.8. In this code, the two test functions each declare and create a `Dictionary` that is used only in the next line as a parameter to the `WordSwitch` constructor call, for example:

```
1   @Test
2   fun noPathDifferentLengths() {
3       val dictionary = dictionary()
4       val wordSwitch = WordSwitch(dictionary, "ab", "abc")
5       Assert.assertNull(wordSwitch.lookForTarget())
6   }
```

This can be simplified further by replacing the `dictionary` parameter used in the `WordSwitch` constructor on line 4 with a call to `dictionary()` and then deleting line 3:

```
@Test
fun noPathDifferentLengths() {
    val wordSwitch = WordSwitch(dictionary(), "ab", "abc")
    Assert.assertNull(wordSwitch.lookForTarget())
}
```

Perform the same refactoring on the other test function. This kind of refactoring is called *inlining*.

Now that the test code has been cleaned up a bit, let's look at some of the other test scenarios. One test that we want to implement is that if we start with a, then we can get to b. We start a test for this by creating a `WordNode` from a:

```
val wordSwitch = WordSwitch(dictionary(), "a", "b")
```

Then run `lookForTarget` and assign the result to a `val`:

```
val result = wordSwitch.lookForTarget()
```

Now we need to check that the `text` inside `result` is equal to b. That is, we would like to make a call such as

```
Assert.assertEquals("b", result.text)
```

However, this code is wrong because `result` is not of type `WordNode`; it is of type `WordNode?`. That is, it may be `null`. This is very inconvenient, because we know that it should not be `null`: it should be a `WordNode` that has `text` equal to "b". Fortunately, Kotlin has a way around the problem. A special operator, called the *non-null assertion*, and written `!!` can be added, and then we can treat `result` as if it truly is a `WordNode`:

```
Assert.assertEquals("b", result!!.text)
```

We now have the pieces we need in order to test that we can get from a to b.

PROJECT STEP 13.12

Create a function in `WordSwitchTest` that tests that "a" can be transformed to "b". Call the function a_to_b.

PROJECT STEP 13.13

Copy the test function a_to_b and modify it to check that the word "ab" can be transformed to "ba".

13.9 The Implementation of `lookForTarget`

We already have a commented stub for `lookForTarget`. We also have some tests in place that can guide us in our implementation and let us know if it is correct. Let's now start filling in the blanks. Referring back to the code listing for `WordSwitch` on page 209, the first thing that we need is a var to hold newly generated words, initialized with those derived from the startNode:

```
var currentGeneration = startNode.variantsByOneLetter(checker)
```

The next part of the code requires a variable to hold the target. This is initially null. Now, normally, Kotlin is able to deduce the type of a var from its declaration, but if it is initially null, then this is not possible. The type could be String?, or Int?, or something else. In this situation, we have to help Kotlin by including the type in the declaration:

```
var targetNode : WordNode? = null
```

Our code will repeatedly create new generations of words from the current generation. We need to keep searching so long as it is possible to create new words and we have not yet found the target. This can be expressed with a construction called a while loop:

```
while (currentGeneration.isNotEmpty() && targetNode == null) {
    //This is the loop body.
    //Calculations go here.
}
```

We have previously seen loops over the elements of a list or array. while loops work differently. The code in the loop body is executed repeatedly, stopping only when the loop conditions are false. Our loop conditions are that the currentGeneration is not empty and targetNode is not null. In other words, our loop will stop if targetNode is assigned a non-null value or if currentGeneration is empty.

Within the loop body, we create a variable to hold the words generated from currentGeneration:

```
val nextGeneration = mutableListOf<WordNode>()
```

To actually generate the new words, we will need to loop through each of the words in currentGeneration:

```
for (wordNode in currentGeneration) {
    //Process this wordNode.
}
```

The loop val `wordNode` represents a word within the current generation. It may actually be the target. Let's check this possibility:

```
if (wordNode.text == target) {
    targetNode = wordNode
}
```

Also within the loop, we need to generate new words from `wordNode` and add them to the next generation:

```
nextGeneration.addAll(wordNode.variantsByOneLetter(checker))
```

Once all of the words in `currentGeneration` have been used to generate new words, the `currentGeneration` needs to be replaced by the `nextGeneration`:

```
currentGeneration = nextGeneration
```

Putting this all together, we have implemented the main search algorithm:

```
fun lookForTarget(): WordNode? {
    //Declare a variable to hold the new words that get created
    //in each generation. Initialise it with the words generated
    //by the start word.
    var currentGeneration = startNode.variantsByOneLetter(checker)
    //Have a loop to create new generations so long as these
    //contain new words and the target is not found.
    var targetNode: WordNode? = null
    while (currentGeneration.isNotEmpty() && targetNode == null) {
        //Create a val to hold the words that will be generated.
        val nextGeneration = mutableListOf<WordNode>()
        //For each word in the current generation...
        for (wordNode in currentGeneration) {
            //...check to see if it is the target...
            if (wordNode.text == target) {
                targetNode = wordNode
            }
            //...and generate all new words from it.
            nextGeneration.addAll(wordNode.variantsByOneLetter(checker))
        }
```

```
        //Having dealt with the current generation,
        //replace it by the words it generated.
        currentGeneration = nextGeneration
    }
    return targetNode
}
```

PROJECT STEP 13.14

Replace the existing code for lookForTarget with the preceding code, and then check that the tests pass.

This is a *super-difficult* algorithm, with nested loops, so as usual don't be concerned about understanding it all in one go. In fact, this is the hardest part of the book.

13.10 Finding the Path

At this point, our WordSwitch program can tell us if one word can be transformed into another, but it does not tell us the sequence of words in the transformation. To retrieve this information, we will supply each WordNode with the WordNode from which it was derived. Then we can work backward from the target WordNode to the original, which will give us the sequence of transitions in reverse.

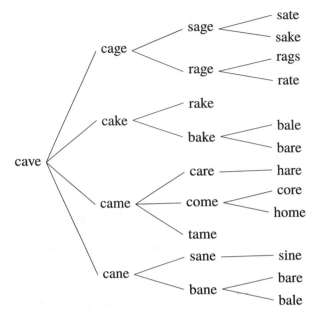

Figure 13-7. *Part of the tree of* WordNodes *deriving from* cave

For example, consider the transition from cave to home. Our starting WordNode is cave. It has no precursor, because it is the start. The variants of cave are cage, cake, came, cane, and so on. For each of these WordNodes, we set cave as the parent. In the next generation, we can derive bake and rake with cake as parent, rage and sage with cage as parent, and so on. In this way, we can form a tree-like structure of WordNodes, with cave as the *root* of the tree.

In order to represent this structure in software, we simply need to add a new instance variable, which we may as well call parent, to WordNode. We will change the constructor to set the variable.

PROJECT STEP 13.15

Change the declaration of WordNode to

```
data class WordNode(val text: String, val parent: WordNode? = null)
```

The new part of this constructor is

```
val parent: WordNode? = null
```

This code means

- There is a field called `parent`.

- It is a `val` (not a `var`).

- It is of type `WordNode?`.

- When calling the constructor, `parent` can be left out, in which case it will be `null`.

This last property, that the parameter can be omitted, is a really handy feature of Kotlin. We call this an *optional parameter*.

When a `WordNode` is created as a variant of an existing `WordNode`, the new one should have the old as parent. Let's test this. In `WordNodeTest`, we currently have this test function:

```
1   @Test
2   fun testOneLetterWord() {
3       val path = Paths.get("src/test/resources/books/abcd.txt")
4       val dictionary = Dictionary(path)
5       val checker = WordChecker(dictionary)
6       val nodeA = WordNode("a")
7       val generated = nodeA.variantsByOneLetter(checker)
8       Assert.assertEquals(3, generated.size)
9       Assert.assertTrue(generated.contains(WordNode("b")))
10      Assert.assertTrue(generated.contains(WordNode("c")))
11      Assert.assertTrue(generated.contains(WordNode("d")))
12  }
```

This test needs to be changed to check that the `WordNode`s on lines 9, 10, and 11 have `nodeA` as parent.

PROJECT STEP 13.16

Change lines 9–11 to be

```
Assert.assertTrue(generated.contains(WordNode("b", nodeA)))
Assert.assertTrue(generated.contains(WordNode("c", nodeA)))
Assert.assertTrue(generated.contains(WordNode("d", nodeA)))
```

Then make the equivalent changes to `testTwoLetterWord`.

These changed tests should fail because we are not adding a WordNode as parent to its variants when they are created in the addVariantsAtPosition function. On line 26 of this function, as listed on page 207, we have WordNode variants being created:

```
nodes.add(WordNode(variant))
```

The constructor calls must be modified to include a reference to the WordNode in which the function is running. Recall that there is a keyword, this, that refers to the current object.

PROJECT STEP 13.17

Change the line of code to

```
nodes.add(WordNode(variant, this))
```

Check that all of the tests in WordNodeTest now pass.

This variable will allow us to calculate the sequence of WordNodes from any WordNode back to the original WordNode. This sequence is called the *path* to the root.

PROJECT STEP 13.18

Add this stub function to WordNode:

```
fun rootPath() : List<WordNode> {
    val result = mutableListOf<WordNode>()
    return result
}
```

Here are some test cases for this function:

- If we create a WordNode with a null parent, it is assumed to be the root, so the function should return a list consisting of just that WordNode.

- If we create a WordNode called a with a null parent, and then use it as the parent in creating a second node b, then the path from b to the root contains b and a.

- Continuing the preceding example, if we create a WordNode with c having b as a parent, then the path to the root from c would be c, b, a.

PROJECT STEP 13.19

Copy this code into WordNodeTest:

```
@Test
fun testPathFromRootWithNullParent() {
    val a = WordNode("a", null)
    val path = a.rootPath()
    Assert.assertEquals(1, path.size)
    Assert.assertEquals(a, path.get(0))
}
```

Check that the test fails.

PROJECT STEP 13.20

Here's the second scenario as a test function:

```
@Test
fun testPathFromRootLengthTwo() {
    val a = WordNode("a", null)
    val b = WordNode("b", a)
    val path = b.rootPath()
```

```
Assert.assertEquals(2, path.size)
Assert.assertEquals(a, path.get(0))
Assert.assertEquals(b, path.get(1))
}
```

Copy this into WordNodeTest and check that the test fails.

PROJECT STEP 13.21

Can you add a test for the third scenario?

The implementation of rootPath is very simple. Start off with an empty list. Then, if the WordNode has a parent, add the parent's path. Finally, add the WordNode itself. This algorithm, expressed as code, is given as follows. Note that on line 5 we are using the addAll function that inserts all of the elements of one List into another.

```
1    fun rootPath() : List<WordNode> {
2        val result = mutableListOf<WordNode>()
3        if (parent != null) {
4            val parentRootPath = parent.rootPath()
5            result.addAll(parentRootPath)
6        }
7        result.add(this)
8        return result
9    }
```

PROJECT STEP 13.22

Replace the stub implementation of rootPath with the preceding code.

Check that the tests now pass.

The fact that a WordNode contains another WordNode makes it a *recursive data structure*. The rootPath function is effectively recursive because of the parent.rootPath call on line 4 earlier.

13.11 Putting It All Together

We now have all of the pieces we need in order to solve our word switching problem. The WordSwitch class has a function for finding a target WordNode from an original word, by one-letter transitions through real words, when this is possible. The target WordNode, if it is not null, can then give us the list of words in the transition.

PROJECT STEP 13.23

Add the following main function to the WordSwitch.kt file, above the declaration of the class:

```kotlin
fun main() {
    //Load the dictionary.
    val path = Paths.get("src/main/resources/books/english.txt")
    val dictionary = Dictionary(path)
    //Create a WordSwitch to look for
    //a path from "swine" to "whale".
    val wordSwitch = WordSwitch(dictionary, "swine", "whale")
    //Calculate the target node.
    val target = wordSwitch.lookForTarget()
    if (target == null) {
        //If the target is null, print out that the word
        //could not be reached.
        println("Could not reach target.")
    } else {
        //Else retrieve the path from the root to the
        //target and print it out.
        val fromRoot = target.rootPath()
        for (wordNode in fromRoot) {
            println(wordNode.text)
        }
    }
}
```

Run the `main` function by clicking the green triangle that appears beside the `main` function. The output should show

swine, shine, whine, while, whale

To calculate different word searches, just change "swine" and "whale" to whatever you want.

13.12 Summary and Step Details

We have built a recursive data structure to solve a hard problem. This is actually pretty sophisticated programming, so well done if you followed most of the code, and don't worry if you got a bit lost—this is very advanced coding, and it might take a while to sink in. The decomposition of the problem into various classes gave us more practice at object-oriented programming. As usual, we had a strong emphasis on unit tests. There was also some new syntax: we learned about `while` loops. Finally, we did some refactoring to reduce code duplication, which is a really important programming skill.

This really has been a huge chapter. Things will get simpler (and more colorful!) going forward.

13.12.1 Details of Project Step 13.1

The test passes because it is checking that `false` is returned, which it always is in our stub of the function. The reason that we have the test is to protect us from future mistakes.

13.12.2 Details of Project Step 13.2

Here's the fully implemented test:

```
@Test
fun validWordTest() {
    val path = Paths.get("src/test/resources/books/FiveWords.txt")
    val dictionary = Dictionary(path)
    val checker = WordChecker(dictionary)
    Assert.assertTrue(checker.isPreviouslyUnseenValidWord("bat"))
    Assert.assertFalse(checker.isPreviouslyUnseenValidWord("bat"))
}
```

13.12.3 Details of Project Step 13.3

A possible implementation of the function is as follows:

```
fun isPreviouslyUnseenValidWord(string: String): Boolean {
    if (!dictionary.contains(string)) {
        return false
    }
    if (wordsSoFar.contains(string)) {
        return false
    }
    wordsSoFar.add(string)
    return true
}
```

13.12.4 Details of Project Step 13.4

Here's the complete test function:

```
@Test
fun testEmpty() {
    val path = Paths.get("src/test/resources/books/abcd.txt")
    val dictionary = Dictionary(path)
    val checker = WordChecker(dictionary)
    val wordNode = WordNode("")
    Assert.assertTrue(wordNode.variantsByOneLetter(checker).isEmpty())
}
```

This passes even with our stub implementation, because it always returns an empty list. Even though it may seem pointless having such a test, it insures us against future code changes that might contain bugs.

13.12.5 Details of Project Step 13.5

The completed test is

```
@Test
fun testOneLetterWord() {
    val path = Paths.get("src/test/resources/books/abcd.txt")
    val dictionary = Dictionary(path)
    val checker = WordChecker(dictionary)
    val nodeA = WordNode("a")
    val generated = nodeA.variantsByOneLetter(checker)
    Assert.assertEquals(3, generated.size)
    Assert.assertTrue(generated.contains(WordNode("b")))
    Assert.assertTrue(generated.contains(WordNode("c")))
    Assert.assertTrue(generated.contains(WordNode("d")))
}
```

Note that generated is a List<WordNode>, *not* a List<String>, which is why we have

```
Assert.assertTrue(generated.contains(WordNode("b")))
```

not

```
Assert.assertTrue(generated.contains("b"))
```

Note also that we are checking that generated contains three particular WordNodes and that it has size three. The size check ensures that there are no WordNodes in generated other than those that we have checked.

13.12.6 Details of Project Step 13.6

Here's the test:

```
@Test
fun testTwoLetterWord() {
    val checker = wordChecker()
    val nodeAB = WordNode("ab")
    val generated = nodeAB.variantsByOneLetter(checker)
    Assert.assertEquals(6, generated.size)
```

```
Assert.assertTrue(generated.contains(WordNode("aa")))
Assert.assertTrue(generated.contains(WordNode("ac")))
Assert.assertTrue(generated.contains(WordNode("ad")))
Assert.assertTrue(generated.contains(WordNode("bb")))
Assert.assertTrue(generated.contains(WordNode("cb")))
Assert.assertTrue(generated.contains(WordNode("db")))
}
```

13.12.7 Details of Project Step 13.9

The tests pass because they are testing `null` is returned, and that is precisely what the stub implementation does. As usual, the tests are to make sure that this still happens after we write the function body.

Actually, the tests also serve a documentation purpose, making it much easier for other programmers to understand the class. In the last 10 years or so, there has been a tendency to use unit tests as documentation for class behavior. Because the tests are actually executable, they are guaranteed to be up to date, whereas other kinds of documentation, such as code comments, tend to get stale quickly. Most software developers hate writing documentation.

13.12.8 Details of Project Step 13.10

Here is the refactored code, with the extracted function moved to the end of the file:

```
1   class WordSwitchTest {
2       @Test
3       fun noPathDifferentLengths() {
4           val dictionary = dictionary()
5           val wordSwitch = WordSwitch(dictionary, "ab", "abc")
6           Assert.assertNull(wordSwitch.lookForTarget())
7       }
8
9       @Test
10      fun noPathTargetNotInDictionary() {
11          val dictionary = dictionary()
12          val wordSwitch = WordSwitch(dictionary, "aa", "ae")
```

```
13              Assert.assertNull(wordSwitch.lookForTarget())
14          }
15
16      private fun dictionary(): Dictionary {
17          val path = Paths.get("src/test/resources/books/abcd.txt")
18          val dictionary = Dictionary(path)
19          return dictionary
20      }
21   }
```

Notice that lines 4 and 11 are a little bit confusing because they both declare a val called dictionary and set it to contain the return of the *function* also called dictionary, but with brackets used to denote the function call. This confusion is eliminated by inlining the code, which is done later in the chapter.

13.12.9 Details of Project Step 13.12

The test is

```
@Test
fun a_to_b() {
    val wordSwitch = WordSwitch(dictionary(), "a", "b")
    val result = wordSwitch.lookForTarget()
    Assert.assertEquals("b", result!!.text)
}
```

13.12.10 Details of Project Step 13.13

The test is

```
@Test
fun ab_to_ba() {
    val wordSwitch = WordSwitch(dictionary(), "ab", "ba")
    val result = wordSwitch.lookForTarget()
    Assert.assertEquals("ba", result!!.text)
}
```

13.12.11 Details of Project Step 13.16

Here are the details:

```
@Test
fun testTwoLetterWord() {
    val checker = wordChecker()
    val nodeAB = WordNode("ab")
    val generated = nodeAB.variantsByOneLetter(checker)
    Assert.assertEquals(6, generated.size)
    Assert.assertTrue(generated.contains(WordNode("aa", nodeAB)))
    Assert.assertTrue(generated.contains(WordNode("ac", nodeAB)))
    Assert.assertTrue(generated.contains(WordNode("ad", nodeAB)))
    Assert.assertTrue(generated.contains(WordNode("bb", nodeAB)))
    Assert.assertTrue(generated.contains(WordNode("cb", nodeAB)))
    Assert.assertTrue(generated.contains(WordNode("db", nodeAB)))
}
```

13.12.12 Details of Project Step 13.21

The test function is

```
@Test
fun testPathFromRootLengthThree() {
    val a = WordNode("a", null)
    val b = WordNode("b", a)
    val c = WordNode("c", b)
    val path = c.rootPath()
    Assert.assertEquals(3, path.size)
    Assert.assertEquals(a, path.get(0))
    Assert.assertEquals(b, path.get(1))
    Assert.assertEquals(c, path.get(2))
}
```

PART III

Images

In Part III, we learn the fundamentals of Functional Programming by writing software that manipulates images.

CHAPTER 14

Color Pictures

In this chapter, we will return to programs that display images. We will begin by showing simple color patterns such as national flags. Then we will see how to load image files such as photographs. Finally, we will write code that does simple image manipulations, such as flipping them in the vertical axis.

14.1 Modeling Color

Computer screens display images by producing huge numbers of tiny colored dots called *pixels*. (The word "pixels" is short for "picture cells.") On many modern screens, these dots are too small to be seen with the naked eye, but they are generally visible on large television screens.

If you do get a look at a screen that has relatively large pixels, you might see that each pixel itself consists of tiny red, green, and blue subpixels. (You can see the subpixels on some phone screens if a raindrop is on the screen, acting as a magnifier.) Because these screens emit light, they can produce any color by combining red, green, and blue values at different intensities. In Figure 14-1, on the following page, Figure 14-1a is pure red at a low intensity, whereas Figure 14-1b is a mixture of equal parts green and blue, both at high intensity.

PROGRAMMING CHALLENGE 14.1

For each of the following squares, give a rough indication (low, medium, or high) of the intensity of red, green, and blue used.

© Tim Lavers 2021
T. Lavers, *Learn to Program with Kotlin*, https://doi.org/10.1007/978-1-4842-6815-5_14

To model real-world colors, we will be using a class called `java.awt.Color`. In this model, a color is represented as a trio of Ints between 0 and 255, one each for the red, green, and blue components. In the rust-colored image shown in Figure 14-1a, red has a value of 127, and both green and blue have value 0. The turquoise image has a red value of 0 and green and blue values of 255. We can construct `Color` objects by passing in the respective red, green, and blue components. For example, the rusty red is `Color(127, 0, 0)`, and the turquoise is `Color(0, 255, 255)`. If the red, green, and blue values are the same, we get a shade of gray. At one extreme, with all values 0, this is black. White is `Color(255, 255, 255)`.

(a) Medium intensity red.

(b) Mixture of green and blue.

Figure 14-1. *Combining red, green, and blue to create different colors*

By the way, there are two "Color" classes in the standard Java libraries: `java.awt.Color` and `javafx.scene.paint.Color`. Package names really are important, and if your programs won't compile, there is a chance that it is because the `import` statements are bringing the wrong `Color` class in.

14.2 Modeling Pictures

We will model a picture as an array of rows of pixels, and each row of pixels will be modeled as an array of `Colors`. This gives an array of arrays, that is, a double array, of `Colors`. In code, this is

```
1    package lpk.imaging
2
3    import java.awt.Color
4
5    class Picture(val pixels: Array<Array<Color>>) {
6        fun height(): Int {
7            return pixels.size
8        }
9
```

```
10        fun width(): Int {
11            return pixels[0].size
12        }
13
14        fun pixelByRowColumn(row: Int, column: Int): Color {
15            return pixels[row][column]
16        }
17    }
```

Line 5 shows that a Picture is constructed from the double array of Colors and that the double array passed into the constructor is available within the class. That is, it is a field. The height function returns the number of elements in the double array, which is the number of arrays of Colors that are the rows. The width function returns the number of Color objects in the first row. (We are assuming that all rows have the same number of pixels.) The pixelByRowColumn function gives us access to any particular pixel in the image.

To get started with the code, use IntelliJ to download the project https://github. com/Apress/learn-to-program-w-kotlin-ch14.git. The checked out project should have a structure that is by now familiar, with main and test directories. As well as Picture.kt, there are files PicturePanel.kt, Flag.kt, PhotoDisplayer.kt, and PictureDisplayer.kt. The Flag class will be used to create and display Pictures that represent national flags—producing these is a very good exercise in array manipulation. PhotoDisplayer is currently mostly empty. We will work with it toward the end of this chapter.

The Flag.kt file contains the following code:

```
1    package lpk.imaging
2
3    import java.awt.Color
4
5    fun main() {
6        Flag().show()
7    }
8
```

```
 9   class Flag : PictureDisplayer() {
10
11       fun createPictureOfFlag(): Picture {
12           val height = 300
13           val width = 450
14
15           val pixels = Array(height) {
16               Array(width) { Color(255, 255, 255) }
17           }
18           for (row in 0..height - 1) {
19               for (column in 0..width - 1) {
20                   if (row < height / 2) {
21                       pixels[row][column] = Color(255, 0, 0)
22                   } else {
23                       pixels[row][column] = Color(255, 255, 255)
24                   }
25               }
26           }
27           return Picture(pixels)
28       }
29
30       //Don't change anything below here.
31       override fun createPicture(): Picture {
32           return createPictureOfFlag()
33       }
34
35       fun show() {
36           doLaunch()
37       }
38   }
```

The important points of this are as follows:

- The first line is a declaration of the package in which the code belongs.

- Line 3 imports the java.awt.Color class, which is what we use to represent pixels.

- On line 5, there is the declaration of a main function, which we will run later.

- Line 9 is the declaration of the Flag class. The part " : PictureDisplayer()" means that a Flag is a kind of PictureDisplayer. Effectively, this gives Flag the properties of PictureDisplayer, such as the ability to display itself. This is called *inheritance* and is an important aspect of object-oriented programming, though not one that we will spend much time on in this book.

- At line 11, we have a function that creates a Picture. We will return to this.

- The rest of the code supports the inheritance of Flag from PictureDisplayer.

The section of code that is of interest to us is that which creates the Picture:

```
1    fun createPictureOfFlag(): Picture {
2        val height = 300
3        val width = 450
4
5        val pixels = Array(height) {
6            Array(width) { Color(255, 255, 255) }
7        }
8        for (row in 0..height - 1) {
9            for (column in 0..width - 1) {
10               if (row < height / 2) {
11                   pixels[row][column] = Color(255, 0, 0)
12               } else {
13                   pixels[row][column] = Color(255, 255, 255)
14               }
15           }
16       }
17       return Picture(pixels)
18   }
```

Some of this should be quite familiar from Chapter 3. Lines 5 to 7 define a double array of Colors and initialize every element to be Color(255, 255, 255), which is white. The for-loop on line 8 iterates through the rows. An inner, or nested, loop on line 9 iterates through the pixels in the current row. Within the inner loop (lines 10 to 14), the elements of the row are set to be either Color(255, 255, 255) or Color(255, 0, 0) depending on whether they are in the upper or lower half of the Picture. If you run the main function (there should be a green arrow that you can click), you should see an image of the Indonesian flag, as shown in Figure 14-2. To stop the program, click the red square button in the IntelliJ run pane, shown in Figure 14-3.

Figure 14-2. *The code should show an approximation of the Indonesian flag. Here, it has been shown against a black background, which gives the appearance of a border*

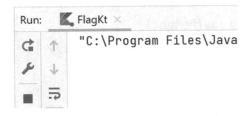

Figure 14-3. *The* Flag *program can be stopped by clicking the red button*

The code to build the pixels double array has two parts: first, we set up the array and fill it with the value Color(255, 255, 255), and then we adjust the values by looping through them and applying a condition that depends on the row. These two operations can in fact be combined as in the following rewritten version of the function:

```
1    fun createPictureOfFlag(): Picture {
2        val height = 300
3        val width = 450
4
```

```
 5        val pixels = Array(height) { row ->
 6            if (row < height / 2) {
 7                Array(width) { column -> Color(255, 0, 0) }
 8            } else {
 9                Array(width) { column -> Color(255, 255, 255) }
10            }
11        }
12        return Picture(pixels)
13    }
```

Change Flag to use the new version of the function and check that the correct image still shows.

This new code works as follows. On line 4, the val pixels is created as an array with height rows. Line 5 has the syntax "row ->", which is Kotlin shorthand for "consider a particular row." The code that follows this specifies what to do at that row. If the row is in the top half, we apply the code:

```
Array(width) { column -> Color(255, 0, 0) }
```

This line creates an array of Colors with width elements and then applies the rule:

```
column -> Color(255, 0, 0)
```

which means "for any column, use Color(255, 0, 0)". It takes some practice to get used to this new syntax, but we will use it a great deal in the rest of this book.

PROGRAMMING CHALLENGE 14.2

The Ukraine flag has the same proportions as the Indonesian flag but has blue in the upper half and yellow below. The blue is approximately Color(51, 102, 255), and the yellow is approximately Color(254, 203, 0). Change createPictureOfFlag so that the Ukraine flag shows.

PROGRAMMING CHALLENGE 14.3

The German flag has a height to width ratio of 3:5 and has three equally broad bands of color, which are black, red, and gold, going from top to bottom.

If we draw a flag that has 300 rows, how many columns should each row have?

Can you modify `createPictureOfFlag` to produce an image of the German flag? Hint: Use `Color(255, 212, 0)` for the gold color.

The Dubai flag has a white vertical stripe closest to the flag pole, and the rest of the flag is red. The proportions are rather unusual: the width to height ratio is 17:8. The white stripe is five seventeenths of the width of the flag. The flag is shown against a black background in Figure 14-4.

Figure 14-4. *The Dubai flag, against a black background, which acts as a border*

Here is a version of `createPictureOfFlag` that produces this flag:

```
1    fun createPictureOfFlag(): Picture {
2        val height = 160
3        val width = 340
4        val pixels = Array(height) {
5                row ->
6            Array(width) {
7                    column ->
8                if (column < 100) {
9                    Color(255, 255, 255)
```

```
10                  } else {
11                      Color(255, 0, 0)
12                  }
13              }
14          }
15      return Picture(pixels)
16  }
```

Remember that line 5 means "for any row, apply the following code." Line 6 creates an array for the row, and then line 7 means "for any column, apply the following code." The code that does follow, lines 8 to 12, creates either a red or white pixel, depending on how close to the left edge the pixel is.

PROGRAMMING CHALLENGE 14.4

The Italian flag has width to height ratio of 3:2 and has three vertical stripes, which are dark green, white, and medium red, from left to right. Can you modify `createPictureOfFlag` to produce an image of this flag? For the green, use `Color(0, 145, 69)`, and for the red use `Color(207, 43, 56)`.

Suppose now that we'd like to produce a square with sides 400, that has red borders, of thickness 80, and is white in the center, such as is shown in Figure 14-5. For starters, let's just see if we can produce the top border. This consists of all pixels for which the row is less than 80. So code like this will work:

Figure 14-5. *Red box with white center. We will modify this to produce the Swiss flag*

```
fun createPictureOfFlag(): Picture {
    val height = 400
    val width = 400
    val pixels = Array(height) {
            row ->
        if (row < 80) {
            Array(width) {
                    column ->
                Color(255, 0, 0)
            }
        } else {
            Array(width) {
                    column ->
                Color(255, 255, 255)
            }
        }
    }
    return Picture(pixels)
}
```

Check that this code does produce a white square with a red top border. Now let's get the left-hand border in. We can do this by altering the else block to decide to return a red or white pixel, depending on the value of column. If column < 80, the pixel should be red, else it should be white. So our code becomes

```
1   fun createPictureOfFlag(): Picture {
2       val height = 400
3       val width = 400
4       val pixels = Array(height) {
5               row ->
6           if (row < 80) {
7               Array(width) {
8                       column ->
9                   Color(255, 0, 0)
10              }
```

```
11              } else {
12                  Array(width) {
13                          column ->
14                      if (column < 80) {
15                          Color(255, 0, 0)
16                      } else {
17                          Color(255, 255, 255)
18                      }
19                  }
20              }
21          }
22      return Picture(pixels)
23  }
```

This code works (run it to confirm), but it is getting very messy. One of the problems is that we have the same code for constructing a red pixel on lines 9 and 15. This can be fixed by extracting the Colors we need as fields of Flag. A second problem is that we have complex code for iterating through the double array, and into this we mix the logic for deciding the color of the array entry. We can pull the color-choice logic out of the loops as follows:

```
1   val white = Color(255, 255, 255)
2   val red = Color(255, 0, 0)
3
4   fun createPictureOfFlag(): Picture {
5       val height = 400
6       val width = 400
7       val pixels = Array(height) {
8               row ->
9           Array(width) {
10                  column ->
11              colorForLocation(row, column)
12          }
13      }
14      return Picture(pixels)
15  }
16
```

```
17   fun colorForLocation(row: Int, column: Int): Color {
18       if (row < 80) {//top
19           return red
20       } else {
21           if (column < 80) {//left
22               return red
23           } else {
24               return white
25           }
26       }
27   }
```

This is an improvement, but the colorForLocation function can actually be neatened up:

```
fun colorForLocation(row: Int, column: Int): Color {
    if (row < 80) return red//top
    if (column < 80) return red//left
    return white//anything else
}
```

This is because, in Kotlin, a single-line block inside an if statement can be put on the same line as the 'if'. With the code in this format, it's easy to change to add the bottom and right borders:

```
fun colorForLocation(c: Int, r: Int): Color {
    if (r < 80) return red//top
    if (r > 320) return red//bottom
    if (c < 80) return red//left
    if (c > 320) return red//right
    return white//anything else
}
```

PROGRAMMING CHALLENGE 14.5

Check that with these changes, the red box is produced.

The complete code for Flag.kt at this point is given in the solution to the challenge, so if you made an editing mistake, you can look there for help.

Figure 14-6. *The Swiss flag*

PROGRAMMING CHALLENGE 14.6

By modifying colorForLocation, can you produce an image of the Swiss flag, shown in Figure 14-6?

Hint Any pixel that was red in the red box code should still be red, and there are four new red regions. Try first to get the box with just one of these regions, as shown in Figure 14-7.

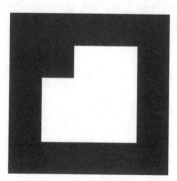

Figure 14-7. *A first step in converting the red box into the Swiss flag*

14.3 Photographs

There are several file formats for storing images on computers. JPEG and PNG are the most commonly used. Given a file in one of these formats, how can we turn it into a Picture? Image processing is such an important task that there are library classes that can help. In fact, there is a class called javax.imageio.ImageIO which can do most of the work for us. Replace all of the code in Picture.kt with

```kotlin
package lpk.imaging

import java.awt.Color
import java.io.File
import javax.imageio.ImageIO

fun loadPictureFromFile(imageFile: File): Picture {
    val image = ImageIO.read(imageFile)
    val width = image.width
    val height = image.height
    val pixels = Array(height) { row ->
        Array(width) { column ->
            Color(image.getRGB(column, row))
        }
    }
    return Picture(pixels)
}

class Picture(val pixels: Array<Array<Color>>) {
    fun height(): Int {
        return pixels.size
    }

    fun width(): Int {
        return pixels[0].size
    }

    fun pixelByRowColumn(row: Int, column: Int): Color {
        return pixels[row][column]
    }
}
```

This new version of the file imports the libraries needed for reading image files. Then there is a loadPictureFromFile function, which works as follows. The single parameter to the function is a File containing the image data. The first line of the function reads the file into a val called image. This val can give us the height and width of the image, and these are used in creating a double array of pixels. We are able to get the pixel at a particular location using the getRGB function, which is used in initializing the double array.

It's important not to get too bogged down in the details of this function. The array initialization code should look familiar after all of the hard work we have done writing similar code to produce flags. However, we should satisfy ourselves that the code is correct by writing a test. The project we are working on already contains an almost empty PictureTest class, and there are some image files we can use as test data, as shown in Figure 14-8.

Figure 14-8. *The* resources *subdirectory of the* test *directory has simple images that we can use for tests*

The file green_h50_w100.png in the images directory is a green rectangle with 50 rows and 100 columns. Let's write a test that uses loadPictureFromFile to create an image from this file and then checks that

- The Picture has 50 rows.

- It has 100 columns.

- Each pixel is green.

Replace the current contents of `PictureTest.kt` with the following code:

```
1    package lpk.imaging.test
2
3    import org.junit.Assert
4    import org.junit.Test
5    import lpk.imaging.Picture
6    import lpk.imaging.loadPictureFromFile
7    import java.awt.Color
8    import java.nio.file.Paths
9
10   private val IMAGES = "src/test/resources/images/"
11
12   class PictureTest {
13       @Test
14       fun loadPictureFromFileTest() {
15           val file = Paths.get(IMAGES + "green_h50_w100.png").toFile()
16           val loaded = loadPictureFromFile(file)
17           Assert.assertEquals(loaded.height(), 50)
18           Assert.assertEquals(loaded.width(), 100)
19           val green = Color(0, 255, 0)
20           for (row in 0..49) {
21               for (column in 0..99) {
22                   Assert.assertEquals(loaded.pixelByRowColumn(row,
                        column), green)
23               }
24           }
25       }
26   }
```

Lines 14 and 15 define the image file as a variable and then pass it as the argument to `loadPictureFromFile`, keeping the returned `Picture` in the `val` called `loaded`. The rest of the test consists of various assertions about the object called `loaded`. Line 16 is a check that it has the correct number of rows. The next line checks the width. There follows a block of code that iterates through the pixels, row by row and column by column, and checks that they are all green. After you have copied this code into `PictureTest`, run it and check that the test passes.

PROGRAMMING CHALLENGE 14.7

There is a test file called yellow_h80_w30.png. Write a variant of the test that checks that this file is loaded correctly. The expected Color is Color(255, 255, 0).

With these tests in place, we can be reasonably confident that everything is working fine, so let's actually display a photograph. There is a Kotlin file called PhotoDisplayer.kt in our project that is currently almost empty. Replace what is in the file now with the following code:

```
package lpk.imaging

import java.nio.file.Paths

fun main() {
    PhotoDisplayer().show()
}

class PhotoDisplayer : PictureDisplayer() {
    private val IMAGES = "src/main/resources/images/"

    override fun createPicture() : Picture {
        val file = Paths.get(IMAGES + "bay.png").toFile()
        return loadPictureFromFile(file)
    }

    //Do not edit anything below here.
    fun show() {
        doLaunch()
    }
}
```

A Kotlin symbol should appear alongside the main function, allowing you to run this class. When you do so, a photo of a bay should appear, as in Figure 14-9.

Figure 14-9. *The result of running* PhotoDisplayer

14.4 Flipping an Image

We now have code in place that

- Reads an image file

- Turns it into a Picture object

- Displays the Picture

Let's make alterations to the Picture before displaying it. First of all, let's flip the image around its vertical axis. A pixel in the first column will move to the last column, the second column will be swapped with the second last column, and so on. We will add a function, called flipInVerticalAxis, to Picture that returns a flipped version of the Picture on which it is invoked.

PROGRAMMING CHALLENGE 14.8

Copy the following code into the Picture class. It should be a function of Picture, like width and height, not a function like loadPictureFromFile that is just in the same file as Picture.

```
fun flipInVerticalAxis(): Picture {
    val pixels = Array(height()) { row ->
        Array(width()) { column ->
            Color(0, 0, 0)
        }
    }
    return Picture(pixels)
}
```

This is just a stub of the function that we want.

What are the dimensions of the Picture that this function returns?

What color are the pixels?

The project test resources include the images blue_red.png and red_blue.png, shown in Figures 14-10 and 14-11. Each of these is a flipped version of the other, so we can use them as the basis of a test for flipInVerticalAxis. This test will be along the lines of

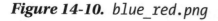

Figure 14-10. blue_red.png

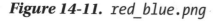

Figure 14-11. red_blue.png

- Load blue_red.png as a Picture, called blueRed.

- Load red_blue.png as a Picture, called redBlue.

- Check that blueRed.flipInVerticalAxis has the same pixels as redBlue.

For the last step, we need a way of comparing two Pictures, pixel by pixel.

PROGRAMMING CHALLENGE 14.9

Add this function to `PictureTest`:

```
1    fun checkPicture(picture: Picture, expected: Picture) {
2        Assert.assertEquals(picture.height(), expected.height())
3        Assert.assertEquals(picture.width(), expected.width())
4        for (row in 0..picture.height() - 1) {
5            for (column in 0..picture.width() - 1) {
6                val actualPixel = picture.pixelByRowColumn(row, column)
7                val expectedPixel = expected.pixelByRowColumn(row, column)
8                Assert.assertEquals(actualPixel, expectedPixel)
9            }
10       }
11   }
```

What does line 2 check?

What does line 3 check?

Can you describe in one sentence what the code block beginning at line 4 does?

Using this, we can write a test for our `Picture` flipping function:

```
@Test
fun flipInVerticalAxisTest() {
    val fileBR = Paths.get(IMAGES + "blue_red.png").toFile()
    val blueRed = loadPictureFromFile(fileBR)

    val fileRB = Paths.get(IMAGES + "red_blue.png").toFile()
    val redBlue = loadPictureFromFile(fileRB)

    val flipped = blueRed.flipInVerticalAxis()
    checkPicture(flipped, redBlue)
}
```

Copy this into `PictureTest` and run it. Of course, it should fail at this point.

With the support of a unit test, we can finish implementing the function. The code that we already have in place is creating a `Picture` of the correct dimensions. However, it is setting every pixel to be black. What we need to do is to work out a formula that gives, for any row and column, the Color of the pixel in the new Picture. Now because we are flipping in the vertical axis, a pixel is in the same row before and after the flip. So let's just think about the pixels in a single row. Consider a row of five pixels:

The flipped version of this is

$$\boxed{4}\;\boxed{3}\;\boxed{2}\;\boxed{1}\;\boxed{0}$$

The pattern is that pixel i in the result is pixel 4 - i in the original. Of course, the 4 here comes from the width minus 1. So in flipInVerticalAxis, rather than creating a black pixel at location (row, column), we should be returning

```
pixelByRowColumn(row, width() - 1 - column)
```

PROGRAMMING CHALLENGE 14.10

See if you can use this line instead of the Color(0, 0, 0) call in the current version of flipInVerticalAxis. Check that the unit test now passes.

To actually flip a photograph, we return to the PhotoDisplayer class and add a call to flip the Picture it reads from a file:

```
override fun createPicture() : Picture {
    val file = Paths.get(IMAGES + "bay.png").toFile()
    return loadPictureFromFile(file).flipInVerticalAxis()
}
```

When you run the main function of PhotoDisplayer, the image should appear flipped about the vertical axis as in Figure 14-12.

Figure 14-12. *The image flipped about its vertical axis*

Of course, we now want to flip images horizontally about their midline. Copy the function flipInVerticalAxis and rename the copied function to flipInHorizontalAxis.

PROGRAMMING CHALLENGE 14.11

The test resources directory of the project contains files red_green.png and green_red.png that represent flipped versions of each other. Write a unit test of flipInHorizontalAxis that makes use of these files.

PROGRAMMING CHALLENGE 14.12

Now implement the function properly, and check that your test passes.

PROGRAMMING CHALLENGE 14.13

Modify PhotoDisplayer to show the bay photo upside down. Then show the image flipped both horizontally and vertically.

14.5 Summary and Solutions to Challenges

In this chapter, we have developed a basic class for creating images and performing simple manipulations of them. In the coming chapters, we will build on the work done here. We also introduced some shorthand notation for creating double arrays and used it a lot in the creation of pictures of flags. As the book progresses, we will use this notation and related concepts a great deal, as they form a really important part of Kotlin and of other modern programming languages.

SOLUTION 14.1

The first image has red and blue at medium intensity, and no green. The second image has red, green, and blue all at low intensities. The third image has red and green, both at high intensity, and no blue.

SOLUTION 14.2

The Ukraine flag:

```kotlin
fun createPictureOfFlag(): Picture {
    val height = 300
    val width = 450
    val pixels = Array(height) {
            row ->
        if (row < height / 2) {
            Array(width, { column -> Color(51, 102, 255) })
        } else {
            Array(width, { column -> Color(254, 203, 0) })
        }
    }
    return Picture(pixels)
}
```

```
                           SOLUTION 14.3
```

The flag of Germany:

```
fun createPictureOfFlag(): Picture {
    val height = 300
    val width = 500
    val pixels = Array(height) {
            row ->
        if (row < 100) {
            Array(width, { column -> Color(0, 0, 0) })
        } else if (row < 200){
            Array(width, { column -> Color(255, 0, 0) })
        } else {
            Array(width, { column -> Color(255, 212, 0) })
        }
    }
    return Picture(pixels)
}
```

```
                           SOLUTION 14.4
```

The Italian flag:

```
fun createPictureOfFlag(): Picture {
    val height = 200
    val width = 300
    val pixels = Array(height) {
            row ->
        Array(width) {
                column ->
            if (column < 100) {
                Color(0, 145, 69)
            } else if (column < 200) {
                Color(255, 255, 255)
            } else {
                Color(207, 43, 56)
```

```
        }
      }
    }
    return Picture(pixels)
}
```

SOLUTION 14.5

Here's the complete code for Flag.kt after all of the refactoring:

```kotlin
package lpk.imaging

import java.awt.Color

fun main() {
    Flag().show()
}

class Flag : PictureDisplayer() {

val white = Color(255, 255, 255)
    val red = Color(255, 0, 0)

    fun createPictureOfFlag(): Picture {
        val height = 400
        val width = 400
        val pixels = Array(height) {
                row ->
            Array(width) {
                    column ->
                colorForLocation(row, column)
            }
        }
        return Picture(pixels)
    }

    fun colorForLocation(c: Int, r: Int): Color {
        if (r < 80) return red//top
        if (r > 320) return red//bottom
        if (c < 80) return red//left
```

```
        if (c > 320) return red//right
        return white//anything else
    }

    //Don't change anything below here.
    override fun createPicture(): Picture {
        return createPictureOfFlag()
    }

    fun show() {
        doLaunch()
    }
}
```

SOLUTION 14.6

Only the colorForLocation function needs to be changed:

```
fun colorForLocation(r: Int, c: Int): Color {
    if (c < 80) return red//left
    if (c >= 320) return red//right
    if (r < 80) return red//top
    if (r >= 320) return red//bottom,
    if (c < 160 && r < 160) return red
    if (c > 240 && r < 160) return red
    if (c < 160 && r > 240) return red
    if (c > 240 && r > 240) return red
    return white
}
```

SOLUTION 14.7

```
@Test
fun loadYellowPicture() {
    val file = Paths.get(IMAGES + "yellow_h80_w30.png").toFile()
    val loaded = loadPictureFromFile(file)
    Assert.assertEquals(loaded.height(), 80)
```

```
Assert.assertEquals(loaded.width(), 30)
val yellow = Color(255, 255, 0)
for (row in 0..79) {
    for (column in 0..29) {
        Assert.assertEquals(loaded.pixelByRowColumn(row, column), yellow)
    }
}
}
```

SOLUTION 14.8

The returned Picture has the same height and width as the original. Each pixel is black.

SOLUTION 14.9

Line 2 checks that the Pictures have the same height.

Line 3 checks that they have the same width.

The rest of the code checks that for each location in the Picture being tested, the pixel at that location is the same as the pixel in the corresponding location in the expected Picture.

SOLUTION 14.10

```
fun flipInVerticalAxis(): Picture {
    val pixels = Array(height()) {
            row ->
        Array(width()) {
                column ->
            Color(0, 0, 0)
        }
    }
    return Picture(pixels)
}
```

```
                    SOLUTION 14.11
```

```
@Test
fun flipInHorizontalAxisTest() {
    val fileGR = Paths.get(IMAGES + "green_red.png").toFile()
    val greenRed = loadPictureFromFile(fileGR)

    val fileRG = Paths.get(IMAGES + "red_green.png").toFile()
    val redGreen = loadPictureFromFile(fileRG)

    val flipped = greenRed.flipInHorizontalAxis()
    checkPicture(flipped, redGreen)
}
```

```
                    SOLUTION 14.12
```

```
fun flipInHorizontalAxis(): Picture {
    val pixels = Array(height()) { row ->
        Array(width()) { column ->
            pixelByRowColumn(height() - 1 - row, column)
        }
    }
    return Picture(pixels)
}
```

```
                    SOLUTION 14.13
```

This displays the image flipped both vertically and horizontally:

```
override fun createPicture() : Picture {
    val file = Paths.get(IMAGES + "bay.png").toFile()
    return loadPictureFromFile(file).
                flipInVerticalAxis().
            flipInHorizontalAxis()
}
```

CHAPTER 15

Pixel Transformations

In the previous chapter, we introduced a model for on-screen images that allowed us to load them from files and to change them by moving their pixels around. In this chapter, we will modify images by changing the colors of individual pixels.

To get started, create a new project in IntelliJ from this repository: `https://github.com/Apress/learn-to-program-w-kotlin-ch15.git`. The downloaded code is much the same as at the end of the previous chapter, but some extra image files are included, and the `Flag` class has been removed.

15.1 Blood Sunset

What happens if we change the colors in a photo by converting each pixel to a "red-only" version of that pixel? We can do this by creating a new `Color` from an existing one using the formula

```
newColor = Color(oldColor.red, 0, 0)
```

Let's implement this formula within a function called `makeRed` that creates a red-only version of a `Picture`. Add the following code to the `Picture` class:

```
1   fun makeRed(): Picture {
2       val pixelsRed = Array(height()) { row ->
3           Array(width()) { column ->
4               val pixel = pixelByRowColumn(row, column)
5               Color(pixel.red, 0, 0)
6           }
7       }
8       return Picture(pixelsRed)
9   }
```

© Tim Lavers 2021
T. Lavers, *Learn to Program with Kotlin*, https://doi.org/10.1007/978-1-4842-6815-5_15

PROGRAMMING CHALLENGE 15.1

Modify the `createPicture` function of `PhotoDisplayer` so that `makeRed` is called prior to an image being displayed. Now run the `main` function of `PhotoDisplayer`.

The modified picture will be a disturbingly red sunset image, shown in Figure 15-1.

Figure 15-1. *After transformation using makeRed*

Now suppose that instead of turning our image red, we want to turn it blue. We can add a function that does this:

```
1   fun makeBlue(): Picture {
2       val pixelsBlue = Array(height()) { row ->
3           Array(width()) { column ->
4               val pixel = pixelByRowColumn(row, column)
5               Color(0, 0, pixel.blue)
6           }
7       }
8       return Picture(pixelsBlue)
9   }
```

PROGRAMMING CHALLENGE 15.2

Copy this function into `Picture` and then invoke it, rather than `makeRed`, in `PhotoDisplayer`.

Write a `makeGreen` function and use it to change the image.

If we compare the `makeRed` and `makeBlue` functions (and `makeGreen` too), we notice that they are exactly the same, apart from line 7, which implements the pixel transformation logic. This transformation logic can be thought of as a function that takes one `Color` and turns it into another one:

$$(Color) \rightarrow (Color)$$

In fact, we can rearrange `makeRed` so that it has the form:

- Create a `Color` transformation function.

- Apply it to every pixel.

The rearranged version of `makeRed` is

```
fun makeRed(): Picture {
    val makePixelRed = { it: Color -> Color(it.red, 0, 0) }
    val pixelsRed = Array(height()) { row ->
        Array(width()) { column ->
            val pixel = pixelByRowColumn(row, column)
            makePixelRed(pixel)
        }
    }
    return Picture(pixelsRed)
}
```

Now let's take this a step further and extract the array-looping code as a function into which a transformation function can be passed:

```
fun transform(pixelTransformation: (Color) -> (Color)): Picture {
    val transformed = Array(height()) { row ->
        Array(width()) { column ->
            val pixel = pixelByRowColumn(row, column)
```

```
            pixelTransformation(pixel)
        }
    }
    return Picture(transformed)
}
```

The makeRed function can then be rewritten as

```
fun makeRed() : Picture {
    val makePixelRed = {it : Color -> Color(it.red, 0, 0)}
    return transform(makePixelRed)
}
```

PROGRAMMING CHALLENGE 15.3

Refactor makeBlue (and makeGreen) along the same lines as makeRed was rewritten earlier.

PROGRAMMING CHALLENGE 15.4

We can get some interesting results by swapping the red, green, and blue components of the pixels in a Picture. Define a function makeMess as follows:

```
fun makeMess() : Picture {
    val mess = { it : Color -> Color(it.green, it.blue, it.red)}
    return transform(mess)
}
```

Then show the bay photo with this transformation applied.

PROGRAMMING CHALLENGE 15.5

Consider the following code for changing pixels:

```
val function = {it : Color ->
    val average = (it.red + it.green + it.blue)/3
    Color(average, average, average)
}
```

How will this change a Picture?

Write a function that calls this and apply it before displaying a Picture.

15.2 A Unit Test

The transform function that we developed in the previous section is a powerful way of modifying images one pixel at a time. Before we go further, we should test it. The following unit test loads an image in which every pixel is green (line 5). It then creates a function from Color to Color, called toRed, that simply changes any input Color to red (line 8). The transform function is applied to the green image, with toRed as the argument (line 12). The result of the transformation should be an image of the same size as the original, but with every pixel red, and this is what is checked (lines 15 to 20).

```
1   @Test
2   fun transformTest() {
3       //Start with an image in which all pixels are green.
4       val file = Paths.get(IMAGES + "green_h50_w100.png").toFile()
5       val loaded = loadPictureFromFile(file)
6       //Create a transformation
7       //that turns each pixel red.
8       val red = Color(255, 0, 0)
9       val toRed = { it: Color -> red }
10      //Call the transform function
11      //using the red transformation.
12      val changed = loaded.transform(toRed)
13
```

```
14        //For each row in the result...
15        for (row in 0..49) {
16            //for each pixel in the row...
17            for (column in 0..99) {
18                Assert.assertEquals(changed.pixelByRowColumn(row, column),
                      red)
19            }
20        }
21    }
```

Copy this test function into PictureTest and check that it passes.

15.3 Conditional Transformations

The transform function can be used to create various artistic effects. For example, let's turn an image into pure black and white, choosing either shade based on the brightness of the input pixels. Start by modifying the PhotoDisplayer class to show the picture agent99.png in the resources directory:

```
override fun createPicture(): Picture {
    val file = Paths.get(IMAGES + "agent99.png").toFile()
    return loadPictureFromFile(file)
}
```

If you run the main function of PhotoDisplayer, you should see a photo of a cat.

Let's transform the cat image by changing each pixel to either black or white. All of the "bright" pixels will be made white, and all of the "dark" ones black. What do we mean by "bright" and "dark"? If we add the red, green, and blue components of a Color, and divide by three, we get the equivalent grayscale pixel, as we saw in Challenge 15.1. Let's just say that if this average is greater than 128, the pixel is bright and should be whitened, else it should be made black. In code:

```
val makeBW = { it: Color ->
    val brightness = (it.red + it.green + it.blue) / 3
    if (brightness > 128) {
        Color(255, 255, 255)
```

```
    } else {
        Color(0, 0, 0)
    }
}
```

This code snippet defines a val called makeBW that has type (Color) -> (Color), that is, it is a function that returns a Color from an input Color. Such a function can be passed into the transform function of Picture before the cat photo is displayed:

```
override fun createPicture(): Picture {
    val file = Paths.get(IMAGES + "agent99.png").toFile()
    val makeBW = { it: Color ->
        val brightness = (it.red + it.green + it.blue) / 3
        if (brightness > 128) {
            Color(255, 255, 255)
        } else {
            Color(0, 0, 0)
        }
    }
    return loadPictureFromFile(file).transform(makeBW)
}
```

If you run this version of PhotoDisplayer, you should see an "inkblot" version of the cat photo, as in Figure 15-2. The process of reducing the number of colors in an image by classifying the pixels according to levels of intensity and using a single color for each level is called *thresholding*.

(a) Agent 99.

(b) After the transformation.

Figure 15-2. *The "inkblot" transformation*

PROGRAMMING CHALLENGE 15.6

The images directory contains a file, `waratah.jpg`, that is a photo of a waratah bloom. Change the code in `createPicture` to load this file. Then change the transform function so that for a `Color`, `it`, the returned value is

- `it` itself if `it.red` is greater than 180.

- The grayscale version of `it` otherwise.

For the grayscale version of a pixel, you can use

```
val average = (it.red + it.green + it.blue) / 3
Color(average, average, average)
```

The original and modified images are shown in Figure 15-3a and 15-3b.

(a) The original image.

(b) After the transformation.

Figure 15-3. *Selective graying of the pixels in an image*

PROGRAMMING CHALLENGE 15.7

The file `skatingminister.png` in the images directory is a copy of *The Reverend Robert Walker Skating on Duddingston Loch* by Henry Raeburn, shown in Figure 15-4a. Let's see if we can change his dark clothes to something a bit more exciting, as in Figure 15-4b.

There are two steps in the transformation process: identifying the pixels in his clothing and then changing these to a purple hue. The pixels in the minister's clothes (including hat, skates, and stockings) are all much darker than any other pixels in the image. By experimentation, I have found that all of these pixels, and no others, have the following property:

```
it.red + it.green + it.blue < 140
```

To change one of these pixels to be purple, we can do something like this:

```
val halfGreen = it.green / 2
Color(it.red + halfGreen, 0, it.blue + halfGreen)
```

This formula produces a color that contains only red and blue, so it is a shade of purple. The complicated bit is the extraction of the green component and adding half of it to each of the red and blue components in the output. The reason that we do this is to maintain the total brightness of the transformed pixels. Putting this all together, we get the following transformation function:

```
val makeBlackPurple = { it: Color ->
    if (it.red + it.green + it.blue < 140) {
        val halfGreen = it.green / 2
        Color(it.red + halfGreen, 0, it.blue + halfGreen)
    } else {
        it
    }
}
```

Can you change `Picture.createPicture` to load the `skatingminister.png` file and then to apply the transformation to the loaded image?

(a) Original version.

(b) Now in purple.

Figure 15-4. *Recoloring of the dark pixels*

Our next transformation is a good review in computer arithmetic. Recall that for an integer x, x / y is the number of times that y goes fully into x. For example, 235 / 32 is 7. If we multiply this by 32, we get 224, which is close to, but not exactly the same as, the original value of 235. In summary:

$$(235/32) * 32 = 224$$

In fact:

$$(224/32) * 32 = 224$$

$$(225/32) * 32 = 224$$

$$(226/32) * 32 = 224$$

and so on, up to the next multiple of 32. We can use this to transform colors as follows:

```
override fun createPicture(): Picture {
    val file = Paths.get(IMAGES + "ladyagnew.png").toFile()
    val approximater = { it: Color ->
        Color((it.red / 32) * 32,
              (it.green / 32) * 32,
              (it.blue / 32) * 32
        )
    }
    return loadPictureFromFile(file).transform(approximater)
}
```

PROGRAMMING CHALLENGE 15.8

Calculate the result of applying the `approximater` to these colors:

- `Color(224, 67, 160)`
- `Color(239, 89, 172)`
- `Color(255, 97, 204)`

What is the effect of applying this transformation to every pixel in an image?

PROGRAMMING CHALLENGE 15.9

The file `ladyagnew.png` in the images directory is the portrait *Lady Agnew of Lochnaw* by John Singer Sargent, shown in Figure 15-5a. Change `PhotoDisplayer.createPicture` to load this file and then to apply the transformation. The result should be as in Figure 15-5b.

(a) Original version.
(b) After color reduction.

Figure 15-5. *The effects of color reduction*

There are 8 multiples of 32 between 0 and 255: 0, 32, 64, 96, 128, 160, 192, and 224, and the colors produced by this transformation can have any of them for their red, green, and blue components. This gives a total of

$$8 \times 8 \times 8 = 512$$

colors that could be produced by applying the mapping to an image. With fewer colors, an image can be stored in a smaller file than the original, which can have any of

$$256 \times 256 \times 256 = 16{,}777{,}216$$

different colors.

15.4 Position-Based Transformations

The transformations that we have seen so far have the signature

```
(Color) -> (Color)
```

That is, they take an input `Color` and change it to an output `Color`. Consider the two images of Cradle Mountain shown in Figure 15-6. The original image has been transformed using a function that darkens the border pixels. The formula for such a transformation needs not just the original `Color` but also the location of the pixel, that is, its `row` and `column` positions. A possible signature is

```
((Color), (Int), (Int)) -> (Color)
```

(a) Original version.   (b) With border.

Figure 15-6. *A transformation of the pixels according to their position*

The `Color` parameter in this signature is the pixel at the given `row` and `column`. This can actually be obtained from the image itself, so is redundant information. That is, we can achieve a border effect such as in Figure 15-6b using a function with signature

```
((Int), (Int)) -> (Color)
```

Let's see how.

Copy the following code into the `Picture` class:

```
fun transformByPosition(
    pixelTransformation: ((Int), (Int)) ->
    (Color)
): Picture {
    val transformed = Array(height()) { row ->
        Array(width()) { column ->
            pixelTransformation(row, column)
        }
    }
    return Picture(transformed)
}
```

This function builds a double array of Colors, representing the transformed pixels. The values in the array are set using the function pixelTransformation, which is passed in as a parameter. It will help our understanding of this new code to put it to work straight away. Rather than attempting anything really tricky, let's just see if we can change the top of an image to be a black bar. Copy this code into Picture:

```
1    fun blackBar(): Picture {
2        val blackAtTop = { row: Int, column: Int
3            ->
4            val originalPixel = pixelByRowColumn(row, column)
5            if (row < 50) {
6                Color(0, 0, 0)
7            } else {
8                originalPixel
9            }
10       }
11       return transformByPosition(blackAtTop)
12   }
```

Then change the createPicture function in PhotoDisplayer to be

```
override fun createPicture(): Picture {
    val file = Paths.get(IMAGES + "cradlemt.png").toFile()
    return loadPictureFromFile(file).blackBar()
}
```

Running PhotoDisplayer should show the image of Cradle Mountain with a black bar across the top. The blackBar function works as follows. On line 2, we declare a val which is our transformation function. It has two Int parameters, which are the row and column. On line 4, we get the pixel of the image being transformed at the current row and column. Line 5 decides whether or not this pixel is in one of the first 50 rows of the image. If it is, Color(0, 0, 0) is used, line 6. Otherwise, the original value is applied.

PROGRAMMING CHALLENGE 15.10

Change the blackBar function so that just the left-hand edge of the image becomes all black.

PROGRAMMING CHALLENGE 15.11

A single black bar on the left-hand side looks terrible. See if you can change your code to put bars at both the left- and right-hand edges.

We'd like to produce the image shown in Figure 15-6b, which has borders that are slightly darkened versions of the background, not just black. There is actually a library function that will do this recoloring for us. The function is called darker, and we can apply it as follows:

```
1    fun darkBorder(): Picture {
2        val borderWidth = 50
3        val darkSides = { row: Int, column: Int
4            ->
5            val originalPixel = pixelByRowColumn(row, column)
6            val isInBorder = column < borderWidth || width() - column <
7                    borderWidth
8            if (isInBorder) {
9                originalPixel.darker()
10           } else {
11               originalPixel
12           }
13       }
14       return transformByPosition(darkSides)
15   }
```

Line 6 calculates whether a pixel is within either the left or right border zone. If it is, then on line 8, the darker function is applied. The function darker returns a Color from an input Color.

PROGRAMMING CHALLENGE 15.12

Change the PhotoDisplayer.createPicture function to call darkBorder before displaying the Cradle Mountain photo.

If you run PhotoDisplayer, you will notice that the dark bars at the edges are not as dark as in Figure 15-6b. To fix this, we can change line 8 of darkBorder to call darker twice:

```
originalPixel.darker().darker()
```

To add the border at the top, we need to change the definition of isInBorder to include those in the first borderWidth rows:

```
val isInBorder = row < borderWidth || column < borderWidth || width() -
column < borderWidth
```

PROGRAMMING CHALLENGE 15.13

Can you modify the preceding line of code so that the pixels near the lower edge are included in the border?

With the darkBorder function as in the solution to Challenge 15.13, the displayed image should at last be as we want.

15.5 Summary and Solutions to Challenges

In this chapter, we have written functions that transform one Color into another. By passing these as parameters to functions that iterate over all of the pixels in an image, we have modified images in a variety of interesting ways. The style of programming in which functions themselves are used as parameters to other functions is called *Functional Programming*. There have been functional programming languages since the earliest days of computing. However, it is in the last 10 years or so that functional programming has become very popular. Many modern languages, such as Kotlin, combine functional and object-oriented features.

SOLUTION 15.1

Here is code that calls makeRed prior to showing the image:

```
override fun createPicture(): Picture {
    val file = Paths.get(IMAGES + "bay.png").toFile()
    return loadPictureFromFile(file).makeRed()
}
```

SOLUTION 15.2

Here is a function for turning a picture green:

```
fun makeGreen(): Picture {
    val pixelsRed = Array(height()) { row ->
        Array(width()) { column ->
            val pixel = pixelByRowColumn(row, column)
            Color(0, pixel.green, 0)
        }
    }
    return Picture(pixelsRed)
}
```

SOLUTION 15.3

Here is the makeBlue function:

```
fun makeBlue() : Picture {
    val makePixelBlue = {it : Color -> Color(0, 0, it.blue)}
    return transform(makePixelBlue)
}
```

SOLUTION 15.4

To apply the makeMess function, make this change to createPicture in PhotoDisplayer:

```
override fun createPicture(): Picture {
    val file = Paths.get(IMAGES + "bay.png").toFile()
    return loadPictureFromFile(file).makeMess()
}
```

You should get an image that looks like Figure 15-7.

Figure 15-7. *The bay with* makeMess *applied*

SOLUTION 15.5

The transformation makes the Picture grayscale. We can use it by wrapping it in a function:

```
fun makeGray() : Picture {
    val function = {it : Color ->
        val average = (it.red + it.green + it.blue)/3
        Color(average, average, average)
    }
    return transform(function)
}
```

and then applying it in PhotoDisplayer:

```
override fun createPicture(): Picture {
    val file = Paths.get(IMAGES + "bay.png").toFile()
    return loadPictureFromFile(file).makeGray()
}
```

It's interesting to note that "industrial-strength" grayscale algorithms use different proportions of red, green, and blue, because our eyes are naturally more sensitive to some colors than others.

SOLUTION 15.6

The code is

```
override fun createPicture(): Picture {
    val file = Paths.get(IMAGES + "waratah.jpg").toFile()
    val keepRed = { it: Color ->
        if (it.red > 180) {
            it
        } else {
            val average = (it.red + it.green + it.blue) / 3
            Color(average, average, average)
        }
    }
    return loadPictureFromFile(file).transform(keepRed)
}
```

SOLUTION 15.7

The full function is

```
override fun createPicture(): Picture {
    val file = Paths.get(IMAGES + "skatingminister.png").toFile()
    val makeBlackPurple = { it: Color ->
        if (it.red + it.green + it.blue < 140) {
            val halfGreen = it.green / 2
            Color(it.red + halfGreen, 0, it.blue + halfGreen)
```

```
        } else {
            it
        }
    }
    return loadPictureFromFile(file).transform(makeBlackPurple)
}
```

SOLUTION 15.8

The transformations are as follows:

- Color(224, 67, 160) → Color(224, 64, 160)

- Color(239, 89, 172) → Color(224, 64, 160)

- Color(255, 97, 204) → Color(224, 96, 196)

This transformation reduces the number of colors used in an image.

SOLUTION 15.9

The code is

```
override fun createPicture(): Picture {
    val file = Paths.get(IMAGES + "ladyagnew.png").toFile()
    val approximater = { it: Color ->
        Color((it.red / 32) * 32,
              (it.green / 32) * 32,
              (it.blue / 32) * 32
        )
    }
    return loadPictureFromFile(file).transform(approximater)
}
```

SOLUTION 15.10

To put the bar on the left:

```
fun blackBar(): Picture {
    val blackAtSide = { row: Int, column: Int
        ->
        val originalPixel = pixelByRowColumn(row, column)
        if (column < 50) {
            Color(0, 0, 0)
        } else {
            originalPixel
        }
    }
    return transformByPosition(blackAtSide)
}
```

SOLUTION 15.11

To put bars on both sides:

```
fun blackBar(): Picture {
    val borderWidth = 50;
    val blackAtSide = { row: Int, column: Int
        ->
        val originalPixel = pixelByRowColumn(row, column)
        val color = if (column < borderWidth ||
                        width() - column < borderWidth
        ) {
            Color(0, 0, 0)
        } else {
            originalPixel
        }
        color
    }
    return transformByPosition(blackAtSide)
}
```

SOLUTION 15.12

The code is

```
override fun createPicture(): Picture {
    val file = Paths.get(IMAGES + "cradlemt.png").toFile()
    return loadPictureFromFile(file).darkBorder()
}
```

SOLUTION 15.13

To get very dark borders:

```
fun darkBorder(): Picture {
    val borderWidth = 50
    val darkSides = { row: Int, column: Int
        ->
        val originalPixel = pixelByRowColumn(row, column)
        val isInBorder =
                row < borderWidth ||
                row > height() - borderWidth ||
                column < borderWidth ||
                width() - column < borderWidth
        if (isInBorder) {
            originalPixel.darker().darker()
        } else {
            originalPixel
        }
    }
    return transformByPosition(darkSides)
}
```

CHAPTER 16

Cropping and Resizing Images

In the previous two chapters, we have transformed pictures by rearranging their pixels or by applying color transformations. Now we will look at operations that change the size of an image, either by extracting a sub-image or by merging pixels to produce a compressed version of the original. We will also look at how to save our transformed images to file. The code for this chapter can be obtained from `https://github.com/Apress/learn-to-program-w-kotlin-ch16.git`. This code contains our familiar `Picture` class, but with the transformations introduced in the last couple of chapters removed.

16.1 Cropping

The operation of taking a part of an image and producing a new image from it is called *cropping*. Figure 16-1 shows an example. To crop a `Picture`, we need to specify the row and column at which the extracted `Picture` begins, plus the number of rows and columns in it. Each of these parameters is an `Int`. A good name for the function is `cropTo`, and the `Picture` class in the downloaded code for this chapter already contains a stub implementation:

(a) Original image.

(b) Cropped to the pelican.

Figure 16-1. *A photo and a cropped version of it*

© Tim Lavers 2021
T. Lavers, *Learn to Program with Kotlin*, https://doi.org/10.1007/978-1-4842-6815-5_16

```
1    fun cropTo(rowAt: Int, columnAt: Int, h: Int, w: Int): Picture {
2        val cropArray = Array(1) {
3            row ->
4            Array(1) {
5                column ->
6                Color(0, 0, 0)
7            }
8        }
9        return Picture(cropArray)
10   }
```

Let's have a quick look at this to review our understanding of Kotlin syntax:

- Line 1 defines the function name (cropTo), the list of parameters (four Ints), and the return type (Picture).

- On line 2, we define a val called cropArray, which is an array that has 1 row.

- On line 4, we define the first (and only) row of cropArray as being an Array that has just one element.

- On line 6, we define the single element to be a black Color object.

- On line 9, we build a Picture from the double array and return it.

- Lines 3 and 5 define parameters for the initialization functions. The arrow syntax row -> defines a function that takes an arbitrary row index as input and returns the array built on line 4. Similarly, column -> defines a function that takes an arbitrary column index and returns the black pixel created on line 6. When we define functions like this, with arrows pointing to code blocks, we are using what is called *lambda notation*.

So this stub implementation produces a Picture that consists of a single black pixel. Before replacing this stub with a correct implementation, we will write a test. Our tests use a simple Picture that can be cropped to easily described sub-Pictures. Figure 16-2a shows the test image. It has 100 rows and columns. If we crop this image at position (0, 0) with 50 rows and 50 columns in the cropped image, then the result should be a red square with side length 50. If we crop it at position (50, 10) with h = 10 and w = 20, then the result should be a blue rectangle of height 10 and width 20.

Finally, if we crop it at position (25, 25) and set both h and w to be 50, then the result should be a 50-by-50 version of the original image, as shown in Figure 16-2b.

(b) Cropped at position (25, 25) with h and w both 50.

(a) Input image.

Figure 16-2. *Test images*

The first of these scenarios corresponds to the following test function, which is already in PictureTest:

```
1   @Test
2   fun cropToRedSquare() {
3       val tiles100 = load("red_blue_tiles_50.png")
4       val cropped = tiles100.cropTo(0, 0, 50, 50)
5       val expectedColor = Color(255, 0, 0)
6       Assert.assertEquals(cropped.height(), 50)
7       Assert.assertEquals(cropped.width(), 50)
8       for (row in 0..49) {
9           for (column in 0..49) {
10              Assert.assertEquals(cropped.pixelByRowColumn(row, column),
                    expectedColor)
11          }
12      }
13  }
```

Line 1 of this code uses the load function in PictureTest to load the image into a val called tiles100. On line 4, the cropTo function is called with both row and column being 0 and h and w being 50. The return value from this function call is assigned to a val called cropped. The remainder of the test consists of assertions about cropped: line 6 checks that it is the right height, line 7 checks the width, and the double loops beginning on line 8 check that each pixel is red.

PROGRAMMING CHALLENGE 16.1

Let's write a test corresponding to the blue rectangle scenario.

- Copy the function cropToRedSquare and rename the copied function cropToBlueRectangle.

- Change the call to cropTo so that the starting point has row 50 and column 10 and so that there are 10 rows and 20 columns in the cropped image.

- Change the expectedColor to be blue rather than red.

- Check that the height of the cropped image is 10.

- Check that the width of the cropped image is 20.

- Change the outer loop to run from 0 to 9.

- Make a similar change to the inner loop.

When you run this new test, it should fail.

The third scenario, applying the cropTo at a central location, has already been written as a test function in PictureTest:

```
@Test
fun cropCenter() {
    val tiles100 = load("red_blue_tiles_50.png")
    val cropped = tiles100.cropTo(25, 25, 50, 50)
    val expected = load("red_blue_tiles_25.png")
    checkPicture(expected, cropped)
}
```

This test loads our familiar tile pattern image and then crops it at the point (25, 25) to a square of side length 50. Then the test loads a pre-prepared image that is what the cropped image should look like. The final line of the test is to compare the expected image with the actual image, using a function called checkPicture in PictureTest.

PROGRAMMING CHALLENGE 16.2

Have a look at checkPicture.

What does the first line do?

What does the second line do?

The last section of the function consists of nested loops. What does this code do?

To help us understand image cropping, it's very useful to have a particular example in mind. We will use the following multicolor square as our working example. This has seven pixels per side and is being cropped at position row=2,column=3. (Remember that rows and column indexes are zero based and that the top left hand of the square is (0,0).) The sub-image has two rows and three columns: height=2,width=3.

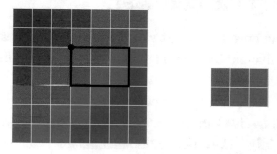

The cropped image is shown to the right of the square. Let's look at some of the pixels in this image and see what pixels they correspond to in the original.

Pixel	Location in result	Location in original
Yellow at top left	row=0, column=0	row=2, column=3
Green in top row	row=0, column=1	row=2, column=4
Green in second row	row=1, column=0	row=3, column=3

The pattern, as code, is as follows. If we crop at position (rowAt, columnAt), then the pixel at a given row and column in the result is in the original.

```
pixelByRowColumn(rowAt + row, columnAt + column)
```

PROGRAMMING CHALLENGE 16.3

Let's fix the stub implementation of cropTo.

On the first line, we currently create an array with 1 row. How many rows should there be in the cropped picture? Change the 1 to this value.

The third line creates an array with 1 column. Correct this.

Replace the current sixth line with the formula given earlier.

With these changes, the three tests should pass. If not, use the solution to this challenge to correct your code.

16.2 Improving the Unit Tests

In writing the second unit test for cropTo, we copied an existing test and then modified the code slightly. Now that our implementation of cropTo is working, we should go back and fix this code duplication.

The last seven lines of both cropToRedSquare and cropToBlueRectangle are essentially identical. They check the height and width of the image and then check that each pixel is expectedColor. Here's a function that makes exactly these checks:

```
fun checkSingleColorPicture(picture: Picture, expectedColor: Color,
expectedHeight: Int, expectedWidth: Int) {
    Assert.assertEquals(picture.height(), expectedHeight)
    Assert.assertEquals(picture.width(), expectedWidth)
    for (row in 0..expectedHeight - 1) {
        for (column in 0..expectedWidth - 1) {
            Assert.assertEquals(picture.pixelByRowColumn(row, column),
            expectedColor)
        }
    }
}
```

Copy this code into `PictureTest` and then change `cropToRedSquare` to use it:

```
@Test
fun cropToRedSquare() {
    val tiles100 = load("red_blue_tiles_50.png")
    val cropped = tiles100.cropTo(0, 0, 50, 50)
    val expectedColor = Color(255, 0, 0)
    checkSingleColorPicture(cropped, expectedColor, 50, 50)
}
```

PROGRAMMING CHALLENGE 16.4

Make similar changes to `cropToBlueRectangle`.

With these changes, our code is a lot less verbose and easier to understand and maintain. You may ask why we didn't extract the `checkSingleColorPicture` function before copying `cropToRedSquare` and so avoid the duplication from the beginning. The reason is that in programming it isn't always immediately clear what the correct abstractions are, but once we have found them, it is easy to refactor the code.

16.3 Shrinking an Image

Suppose that we have an image with 200 rows of pixels, and each row has 300 pixels in it, and that we want to shrink this by a factor of 2. The result will contain 100 rows of 150 pixels. Blocks of pixels in the original image get merged into single pixels in the smaller image. In this section, we will describe and implement algorithms for shrinking `Pictures`.

As a working example, consider the following `Picture` of a friendly black dog against a green background. This picture has 9 rows and 12 columns of pixels.

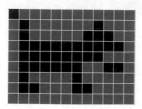

The first step in shrinking the image by a factor of 2 is to break it into 2-by-2 blocks:

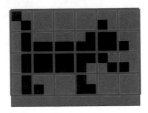

The pixels in the bottom row will be discarded, as they do not fit into complete blocks. The shrunken form of the image has a pixel for each block, and the color of that pixel is the average of the colors of the pixels in the block:

Consider now a particular block of pixels:

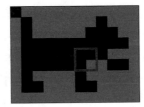

This block is just a double array of Colors, that is, a Picture, and it can be obtained by applying the cropTo function that we developed in Section 16.1.

To apply cropTo, we need to know the location of the top left-hand corner of the block. It is three blocks across from the left-hand side, so the column number is 3 × 2 = 6, because each block is 2-by-2. The block is two blocks down from the top, so the row number is 2 × 2 = 4. The other parameters required by cropTo are the width and height of the sub-Picture, and these are both 2. Thus, the red block can be obtained as the return of

```
cropTo(2 * 2, 3 * 2, 2, 2)
```

PROGRAMMING CHALLENGE 16.5

Remember that the height function tells us the number of rows of pixels in a Picture. If we break a Picture into square blocks with side length sideLength, how many rows of blocks are there?

How many columns of blocks are in each block row?

Consider the block in row blockRow and blockColumn of the blocks. How can we get this as a Picture using the cropTo function?

The solutions to the previous challenge give us the essentials of a function for breaking a Picture into blocks:

```
fun chopIntoSquares(sideLength: Int): Array<Array<Picture>> {
    val resultRows = height() / sideLength
    val resultColumns = width() / sideLength
    val result = Array(resultRows) { blockRow ->
        Array(resultColumns) { blockColumn ->
            cropTo(
                blockRow * sideLength, blockColumn * sideLength,
                sideLength, sideLength
            )
        }
    }
    return result
}
```

Copy this function into Picture.

PROGRAMMING CHALLENGE 16.6

The file red_blue_green.png in the test resources directory is shown in Figure 16-3. The red and blue squares are 50-by-50 pixels, and the green border at the right and bottom sides is 8 pixels wide.

Suppose that we break this into 10-by-10 blocks.

How many rows of blocks will there be?

How many columns of blocks?

Are any of the green pixels included in any of the blocks?

Describe the colors of the blocks.

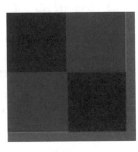

Figure 16-3. *Test image for chopIntoSquares*

The ideas from this challenge form the basis of the following test:

```
@Test
fun chopIntoSquaresTest() {
    val original = load("red_blue_green.png")
    val blocks = original.chopIntoSquares(10)
    Assert.assertEquals(10, blocks.size)//10 rows
    Assert.assertEquals(10, blocks[0].size)//10 columns
    val red = Color(255, 0, 0)
    val blue = Color(0, 0, 255)
    for (row in 0..4) {
        for (column in 0..4) {
            checkSingleColorPicture(blocks[row][column], red, 10, 10)
        }
        for (column in 5..9) {
            checkSingleColorPicture(blocks[row][column], blue, 10, 10)
        }
    }
    for (row in 5..9) {
        for (column in 0..4) {
            checkSingleColorPicture(blocks[row][column], blue, 10, 10)
        }
```

```
    for (column in 5..9) {
        checkSingleColorPicture(blocks[row][column], red, 10, 10)
    }
  }
}
```

Copy this function into `PictureTest` and check that it passes.

The function for calculating the average `Color` of the pixels in a `Picture` is relatively simple. Copy the following stub for it into `Picture`:

```
fun averageColor(): Color {
    return Color(0, 0, 0)
}
```

To test this function, we will make use of the image files red10.png, green10.png, and blue10.png in the test resources directory. These represent `Pictures` that consist of red, green, and blue pixels, respectively.

PROGRAMMING CHALLENGE 16.7

Here is a test for `averageColor` that uses the file red10.png:

```
@Test
fun averageColorTest() {
    val red10 = load("red10.png")
    Assert.assertEquals(Color(255, 0, 0), red10.averageColor())
}
```

Copy this function into `PictureTest` and check that it fails.

Then add sections of code to the test that make use of green10.png and blue10.png.

We should also do a test on a `Picture` that has more than one `Color`. Consider the image red_blue_tiles_50.png which was displayed in Figure 16-2. What do you think the average `Color` of pixels in this image is?

Add a section to the test that uses this image.

To implement averageColor, we will define variables for the total red, green, and blue values. Then we'll iterate through the pixels, adding the red, green, and blue values of each to the totals. Finally, we will construct a new Color that has red equal to the red total divided by the total number of pixels, and similar for green and blue.

PROGRAMMING CHALLENGE 16.8

In the algorithm described earlier, suppose that totalRed is the variable for the sum of the red values. Should this be defined as a val or as a var?

We can iterate through the pixels as follows:

```
1    for (row in 0..height() - 1) {
2        for (column in 0..width() - 1) {
3            val pixel = pixelByRowColumn(row, column)
4
5        }
6    }
```

Can you write an expression to put on line 4 that adds the red component of pixel to totalRed?

How many pixels are in the Picture?

What is the red component of the result?

PROGRAMMING CHALLENGE 16.9

From the previous challenge, we can write the following incomplete implementation of averageColor:

```
fun averageColor(): Color {
    var totalRed = 0
    for (row in 0..height() - 1) {
        for (column in 0..width() - 1) {
            val pixel = pixelByRowColumn(row, column)
            totalRed = totalRed + pixel.red
        }
```

```
    }
    val count = height() * width()
    return Color(totalRed / count, 0, 0)
}
```

Can you complete this? Check that the test now passes.

At last, we are ready to implement a scaling function.

PROGRAMMING CHALLENGE 16.10

Add the following function to `Picture`:

```
fun scaleDown(factor: Int) : Picture {
    return this
}
```

Can you explain the signature of this function and what it is doing?

With the stub in place, the following test should compile:

```
@Test
fun scaleDownTest() {
    val image1 = load("red_blue_green.png")
    val scaled1 = image1.scaleDown(10)
    val expected1 = load("red_blue_tiles_5.png")
    checkPicture(scaled1, expected1)

    val image2 = load("green_black_large.png")
    val scaled2 = image2.scaleDown(3)
    val expected2 = load("green_black_small.png")
    checkPicture(scaled2, expected2)
}
```

The first section scales down the `Picture` shown in Figure 16-3 and compares the result with a 10-by-10 version of the images shown in Figure 16-2. The second part of the test does a similar comparison, but using `Picture`s that are less symmetrical and contain different colors.

With a couple of tests in place, we can safely implement scaleDown. Replace the stub code with this:

```
fun scaleDown(factor: Int) : Picture {
    //First break it into a double array
    //of factor-by-factor square sub-pictures.
    val blocks = chopIntoSquares(factor)
    //Initialise a pixel array using the blocks.
    val newPixels = Array<Array<Color>>(blocks.size) {
        blocksRow ->
        Array<Color>(blocks[blocksRow].size) {
            blocksColumn ->
            //Each pixel is the average color of the
            //corresponding block.
            blocks[blocksRow][blocksColumn].averageColor()
        }
    }
    return Picture(newPixels)
}
```

Check that with this implementation, the unit tests pass. To see the function in action, change createPicture in PhotoDisplayer to

```
override fun createPicture(): Picture {
    val file = Paths.get(IMAGES + "ladyagnew.png").toFile()
    return loadPictureFromFile(file).scaleDown(5)
}
```

Try running the program with different values for the scale factor.

16.4 Storing Images

We have already seen, in Chapter 14, how to read an image from a file. Now we will add a function to save a Picture as a file. The function is a bit technical, and the hard work is done by a call to a built-in library function:

```kotlin
fun saveTo(file: File) {
    val image = BufferedImage(width(), height(), BufferedImage.TYPE_INT_RGB)
    val width = width()
    val height = height()
    for (row in 0..height - 1) {
        for (column in 0..width - 1) {
            image.setRGB(column, row, pixelByRowColumn(row, column).rgb)
        }
    }
    ImageIO.write(image, "png", file)
}
```

To test this function, we will load a test image as a Picture, then call saveTo to write it to a file, and then load this file as a Picture and check its pixels:

```kotlin
@Test
fun saveToTest() {
    val picture = load("green_black_small.png")
    val temp = Paths.get("temp.png").toFile()
    picture.saveTo(temp)
    val reloaded = loadPictureFromFile(temp)
    Assert.assertEquals(20, reloaded.height())
    Assert.assertEquals(40, reloaded.width())
    val green = Color(0, 255, 0)
    val black = Color(0, 0, 0)
    for (row in 0..9) {
        for (column in 0..39) {
            val pixel = reloaded.pixelByRowColumn(row, column)
            Assert.assertEquals(green, pixel)
        }
    }
    for (row in 10..19) {
        for (column in 0..39) {
            val pixel = reloaded.pixelByRowColumn(row, column)
            Assert.assertEquals(black, pixel)
        }
    }
}
```

This test contains a lot of code for checking the pixels of reloaded. Another option would be to simply use checkPicture to compare picture with reloaded. But if load were broken, such a test might pass, even if saveTo had problems. For this reason, it's probably better to make saveToTest complete in itself, as it is here.

16.5 Summary and Solutions to Challenges

In this chapter, we have written functions for cropping and shrinking Pictures. We were able to use the cropping function to implement shrinking, which greatly simplified what would otherwise have been a very complex algorithm. Additionally, we added a function for writing Pictures to file. We will use this in the next chapter to save transformed images.

SOLUTION 16.1

Here's the test:

```
@Test
fun cropToBlueRectangle() {
    val tiles100 = load("red_blue_tiles_50.png")
    val cropped = tiles100.cropTo(50, 10, 10, 20)
    val expectedColor = Color(0, 0, 255)
    Assert.assertEquals(cropped.height(), 10)
    Assert.assertEquals(cropped.width(), 20)
    for (row in 0..9) {
        for (column in 0..19) {
            Assert.assertEquals(cropped.pixelByRowColumn(row, column),
            expectedColor)
        }
    }
}
```

SOLUTION 16.2

The first line compares the heights of the actual and expected Pictures.

The second line compares their widths.

Following this is a loop over the indexes of the rows of the pictures, and within this a loop over the indexes of the columns. Within the inner loop, the actual and expected pixels for the (row, column) pair are extracted and then compared.

SOLUTION 16.3

```
fun cropTo(rowAt: Int, columnAt: Int, h: Int, w: Int): Picture {
    val cropArray = Array<Array<Color>>(h) {
        row ->
        Array<Color>(w) {
            column ->
            pixelByRowColumn(rowAt + row, columnAt + column)
        }
    }
    return Picture(cropArray)
}
```

SOLUTION 16.4

```
@Test
fun cropToBlueRectangle() {
    val tiles100 = load("red_blue_tiles_50.png")
    val cropped = tiles100.cropTo(50, 10, 10, 20)
    val expectedColor = Color(0, 0, 255)
    checkSingleColorPicture(cropped, expectedColor, 10, 20)
}
```

SOLUTION 16.5

There are

```
height() / sideLength
```

rows and

```
width() / sideLength
```

columns. The `Picture` for the block at row `blockRow` and column `blockColumn` can be obtained as

```
cropTo(blockRow * sideLength, blockColumn * sideLength, sideLength,
sideLength)
```

SOLUTION 16.6

There will be ten rows and ten columns of blocks. None of the green pixels will be included in any of the blocks. Each block will contain pixels of just one color. The first five blocks in the first five rows are all red. The last five blocks in the last five rows are also all red. All of the other blocks are blue.

SOLUTION 16.7

Here is the complete test function:

```
@Test
fun averageColorTest() {
    val red10 = load("red10.png")
    Assert.assertEquals(Color(255, 0, 0), red10.averageColor())

    val green10 = load("green10.png")
    Assert.assertEquals(Color(0, 255, 0), green10.averageColor())

    val blue10 = load("blue10.png")
    Assert.assertEquals(Color(0, 0, 255), blue10.averageColor())
```

```
val redblue = load("red_blue_tiles_50.png")
Assert.assertEquals(Color(127, 0, 127), redblue.averageColor())
}
```

Note that the average of red and blue is Color(127, 0, 127), *not* Color(128, 0, 128), because in integer arithmetic

$$255 / 2 = 127.$$

SOLUTION 16.8

The variable totalRed needs to be a var, as its value will change.

On line 4, we can write

```
totalRed = totalRed + pixel.red
```

The number of pixels in Picture is

```
val count = height() * width()
```

For the red component of the result, we can use totalRed/count.

SOLUTION 16.9

```
fun averageColor(): Color {
    var totalRed = 0
    var totalGreen = 0
    var totalBlue = 0
    for (row in 0..height() - 1) {
        for (column in 0..width() - 1) {
            val pixel = pixelByRowColumn(row, column)
            totalRed = totalRed + pixel.red
            totalGreen = totalGreen + pixel.green
            totalBlue = totalBlue + pixel.blue
        }
    }
```

```
    val count = height() * width()
    return Color(totalRed / count, totalGreen / count, totalBlue / count)
}
```

SOLUTION 16.10

The function is called scaleDown. It has a single parameter, which is an Int that we call factor. The function returns a Picture. The current implementation simply returns the Picture object on which it is called.

CHAPTER 17

Project Dino

We will finish this part of the book by writing a CGI (computer-generated imagery) program using the code developed over the previous three chapters. Our program will create a picture of a dinosaur standing in Dove Lake, Tasmania, as shown in Figure 17-1. As well as implementing a really interesting algorithm, this project will demonstrate how software engineers often have to find the balance between a technically perfect implementation and one that is fit for purpose and a lot less work. We will need to solve a lot of problems to get a good image, and some of our solutions will be nontechnical. This is typical in applied programming.

Figure 17-1. *The finished image*

The fundamental algorithm that we will use is called "green screen." It is used a lot in film and television. The trick is to take a photo of the dinosaur against a background that consists of a single color, which is not present in the dinosaur, and then to merge the

© Tim Lavers 2021
T. Lavers, *Learn to Program with Kotlin*, https://doi.org/10.1007/978-1-4842-6815-5_17

landscape photo into the dinosaur photo by switching any pixels of the screen color with ones from the landscape.

The source code for the chapter includes landscape and dinosaur photographs, but you can easily use your own. The main steps in our CGI project are as follows:

- Produce the screen background against which the dinosaur can be photographed. This uses techniques from Chapter 14.

- Take the photo of the dinosaur and then use the thresholding algorithms from Chapter 15 to correct for various errors.

- Write a function that does the selective superposition.

- Shrink the image and display it.

To get started, download the code from `https://github.com/Apress/learn-to-program-w-kotlin-ch17.git`.

17.1 Producing the Screen

The dinosaur that we will use is painted a mixture of colors that includes green. This means that using a shade of green as a screen color will not work—parts of the dinosaur would get replaced with the background. Instead, we will use magenta. It's best if the screen is a light source, so that there is no shadow when we photograph the dinosaur in front of it. A computer screen will do fine. If we can lay the screen flat, then we can place the dinosaur on the screen, which makes it easy to get the entire model in the photo.

To turn the computer screen magenta, we can modify the `Flag` program from Chapter 14 to show a giant rectangle of that color. The following code, which is in the file `Flag.kt` in the project source, shows how this is done. Note that the flag dimensions must match the screen. If the rectangle is too big, the program will probably crash.

```
package lpk.imaging

import java.awt.Color

fun main() {
    Flag().doLaunch()
}
```

```
class Flag : PictureDisplayer() {

    val magenta = Color(255, 0, 255)

    fun createPictureOfFlag(): Picture {
        val height = 2000//Use your screen
        val width = 3000//resolution here!
        val pixels = Array(height) {
            Array(width) {
                magenta
            }
        }
        return Picture(pixels)
    }

    //Don't change anything below here.
    override fun createPicture(): Picture {
        return createPictureOfFlag()
    }
}
```

17.2 Photographing the Dinosaur

Once we've got the screen magenta, we can line the dinosaur up against it and take a photo. The results might be something like Figure 17-2, in which the background changes color as we move away from the center of the screen. The reason for this is probably that the pixels at the edges are more "side on" to our camera than those at the center, and so we are seeing more of the blue subpixels than the red. Whatever the exact problem is, we can fix it with thresholding: we will write a program that changes any pixel that is almost magenta to be exactly magenta. (This is another reason why there needs to be a strong contrast between the background color and the colors in the dinosaur model.)

Figure 17-2. *The raw dinosaur photo*

Save your dinosaur photo and paste it into the src/images directory of the project, as shown in Figure 17-3.

Figure 17-3. *The photo of the dinosaur against the magenta screen is to be saved in the* images *directory*

Now we can write a program that loads this file as Picture, applies a thresholding function, and then saves the modified Picture. Create a new file called Thresholder.kt in the lpk.imaging directory and paste the following code into it. Note that the code assumes that the dinosaur image is called "a_dinosaur.png". You need to use the name of your photo.

```
package lpk.imaging

import java.awt.Color
import java.nio.file.Paths
```

```
fun main() {
    val IMAGES = "src/main/resources/images/"
    val dinoFile = Paths.get(IMAGES + "a_dinosaur.png").toFile()
    val dino = loadPictureFromFile(dinoFile)
    val magenta = Color(255, 0, 255)
    val makeMagenta : ((Color) -> (Color)) = {
        color ->
        if (color.red > 150 && color.green < 120  && color.blue > 150) {
            magenta
        } else {
            color
        }
    }
    val transformed = dino.transform(makeMagenta)
    val dinoFileFixed = Paths.get(IMAGES, "a_dinosaur_fixed.png").toFile()
    transformed.saveTo(dinoFileFixed)
}
```

When you run this code, a new file should appear in the `images` directory. Open this in IntelliJ and check that the background is uniformly magenta. You may need to adjust the cutoffs to achieve this. My first attempt produced the image shown in Figure 17-4. My second attempt missed some pixels in the middle of the screen that were actually whiter than pure magenta. I'm not sure why these were present. In any case, the code listed earlier fixed all problems.

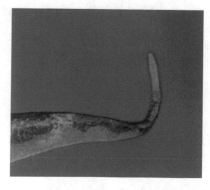

Figure 17-4. *A partially successful attempt at fixing the parallax problems*

17.3 First Attempt at Superposition

The algorithm to do the pixel swapping is pretty complicated, so let's start with
something easier: producing a picture that simply puts the dinosaur photo into the top-
left corner of the background, with no conditional pixel swapping. For this first attempt,
we will be using `cliffs.png` in the images directory. This is a 3840-by-2160 photograph
taken on the Ulan river in Australia. Of course, you're welcome to use your own
photograph. To do so, paste it into the `images` directory. Anyhow, to get started, replace
the code in `PhotoDisplayer.createPicture()` with this:

```kotlin
override fun createPicture(): Picture {
    val backgroundFile = Paths.get(IMAGES + "cliffs.png").toFile()
    val background = loadPictureFromFile(backgroundFile)
    val dinoFile = Paths.get(IMAGES +
            "a_dinosaur_fixed.png").toFile()
    val dino = loadPictureFromFile(dinoFile)
    val dinoWidth = dino.width()
    val dinoHeight = dino.height()
    val newPixels = Array(background.height()) {
            row ->
        Array(background.width()) {
                column ->
            if (row >= dinoHeight) {
                background.pixelByRowColumn(row, column)
            } else if (column >= dinoWidth) {
                background.pixelByRowColumn(row, column)
            } else {
                dino.pixelByRowColumn(row, column)
            }
        }
    }
    return Picture(newPixels).scaleDown(5)
}
```

The looping code in the second half of this function is where the pixel swapping
occurs.

The first `if` statement says that for a `row` greater than or equal to the height of the foreground image, a background pixel is used.

The second `if` statement says that for `column` greater than or equal to the width of the foreground image, we also take a background pixel.

For any other location, which in fact only leaves the top left-hand corner, a foreground pixel is taken. Note that on the last line we are scaling down the image before showing it. If you run this code, you should see something like Figure 17-5.

Figure 17-5. *First step in image superposition*

Let's now try to position the dinosaur a bit better. We will add `vals` called `rowOffset` and `columnOffset`, which represent the position of the top left-hand corner of the dinosaur foreground picture within the background picture. Suppose that we want to move the dinosaur image 500 pixels down and 400 pixels to the right, so

```
val rowOffset = 500
val columnOffset = 400
```

Now consider the pixel for a particular `row` and `column` location. If `row` is less than 500, or it is greater than or equal to 500 + `dinoHeight`, then the background pixel is to be used. If `column` is less than 400, or it is greater than or equal to 400 + `dinoWidth`, then we also use the background pixel. For any other location, we use the foreground pixel.

Putting this all together, we can replace our implementation by

```
override fun createPicture(): Picture {
    val backgroundFile = Paths.get(
        IMAGES + "cliffs.png").toFile()
    val background = loadPictureFromFile(backgroundFile)
    val dinoFile = Paths.get(
        IMAGES + "a_dinosaur_fixed.png").toFile()
    val dino = loadPictureFromFile(dinoFile)
    val dinoWidth = dino.width()
    val dinoHeight = dino.height()
    val rowOffset = 500
    val columnOffset = 400
    val newPixels = Array(background.height()) { row ->
        Array(background.width()) { column ->
            if (row < rowOffset || row >= rowOffset + dinoHeight) {
                background.pixelByRowColumn(row, column)
            } else if (column < columnOffset || column >=
                columnOffset + dinoWidth
            ) {
                background.pixelByRowColumn(row, column)
            } else {
                dino.pixelByRowColumn(
                    row - rowOffset, column - columnOffset
                )
            }
        }
    }
    return Picture(newPixels).scaleDown(5)
}
```

If you run this, you should see the foreground image pushed down and to the right, as in Figure 17-6.

Figure 17-6. *The foreground has been shifted*

17.4 Letting the Background Through

Now that we know how to move the foreground image around, let's try letting the
background through wherever there are magenta pixels in the foreground. Our current
implementation has this loop code:

```
1   val newPixels = Array(background.height()) { row ->
2       Array(background.width()) { column ->
3           if (row < rowOffset || row >= rowOffset + dinoHeight) {
4               background.pixelByRowColumn(row, column)
5           } else if (column < columnOffset || column >=
6               columnOffset + dinoWidth
7           ) {
8               background.pixelByRowColumn(row, column)
9           } else {
10              dino.pixelByRowColumn(
11                  row - rowOffset, column - columnOffset
12              )
13          }
14      }
15  }
```

We need to replace line 10 by

```
1   val foregroundPixel = dino.pixelByRowColumn(
2       row - rowOffset,column - columnOffset)
3   if (foregroundPixel == Color(255, 0, 255)) {
4       background.pixelByRowColumn(row, column)
5   } else {
6       foregroundPixel
7   }
```

Once this is done, the merged image appears as in Figure 17-7.

Figure 17-7. *A first attempt at foreground switching*

This looks ok, so let's move the picture a bit so that the dinosaur is at least on the ground. This is achieved by adjusting the offsets. Values of

```
val rowOffset = 950
val columnOffset = 1300
```

produce a fair result, as shown in Figure 17-8. The dinosaur does look a little lost in this image, partly because its head, which is quite dark, is superimposed against a dark section of the background image. We could try to do something clever such as programmatically brightening the dinosaur's head, but an easier solution is to flip the dinosaur in the vertical axis, as shown in Figure 17-9:

Figure 17-8. *Moving the dinosaur to its final location*

```
val dino = loadPictureFromFile(dinoFile).flipInVerticalAxis()
```

Figure 17-9. *The dinosaur can be flipped before display*

With all of these changes and some refactoring to consolidate the multiple calls to get a pixel from the background picture, createPicture() is

```
override fun createPicture(): Picture {
    val backgroundFile = Paths.get(IMAGES + "cliffs.png").toFile()
    val background = loadPictureFromFile(backgroundFile)
```

```
val dinoFile = Paths.get(IMAGES +
        "a_dinosaur_fixed.png").toFile()
val dino = loadPictureFromFile(dinoFile).flipInVerticalAxis()
val dinoWidth = dino.width()
val dinoHeight = dino.height()
val rowOffset = 950
val columnOffset = 1300
val newPixels = Array(background.height()) {
        row ->
    Array(background.width()) {
            column ->
        val backgroundPixel = background.pixelByRowColumn(row,
            column)
        if (row < rowOffset || row >= rowOffset + dinoHeight) {
            backgroundPixel
        } else if (column < columnOffset || column >=
            columnOffset + dinoWidth) {
            backgroundPixel
        } else {
            val foregroundPixel = dino.pixelByRowColumn(row -
                    rowOffset, column - columnOffset)
            if (foregroundPixel == Color(255, 0, 255)) {
                backgroundPixel
            } else {
                foregroundPixel
            }
        }
    }
}
return Picture(newPixels).scaleDown(5)
}
```

17.5 Hiding the Feet

If we look closely at the feet of the dinosaur, we notice that the toes have an unnatural magenta tinge. Green-screen techniques are least effective in the detailed parts of images, because some of the pixels end up being a mixture of the screen color and the target object. There are various programmatic improvements we could try to fix this. For example, we could detect the edge pixels and reduce the amount of magenta in them. However, sometimes, it's better to look for a nontechnical solution to a problem. What we will do is replace the background image with one containing a lake and have the dinosaur standing in the lake, so that the toes are hidden. We can use the Cradle Mountain image from Chapter 15 as the new background.

The changes we need to make are

- Set the value of backgroundFile to

```
val backgroundFile = Paths.get(IMAGES + "cradlemtbig.jpg").
toFile()
```

(note that this has a "jpg" extension).

- Remove the call to flipInVerticalAxis.

- Set the offsets to

```
val rowOffset = 1100
val columnOffset = 1200
```

The results of these changes are shown in Figure 17-10.

Figure 17-10. *Choosing a better background*

To give the effect of submerged feet, we can use background pixels in the lower portion of the foreground image. Removing the last 200 rows gives pretty good results. This is done by changing the if statement about rows to

```
if (row < rowOffset || row >= rowOffset + dinoHeight - 200) {
```

As a final detail, we can darken the border of the combined image by a call to darkBorder after the image scaling. The complete listing for createPicture is

```
override fun createPicture(): Picture {
    val backgroundFile = Paths.get(IMAGES +
            "cradlemtbig.jpg").toFile()
    val background = loadPictureFromFile(backgroundFile)
    val dinoFile = Paths.get(IMAGES +
            "a_dinosaur_fixed.png").toFile()
    val dino = loadPictureFromFile(dinoFile)
    val dinoWidth = dino.width()
    val dinoHeight = dino.height()
    val rowOffset = 1100
    val columnOffset = 1200
```

```
    val newPixels = Array(background.height()) {
            row ->
        Array(background.width()) {
                column ->
            val backgroundPixel = background.pixelByRowColumn(row,
                column)
            if (row < rowOffset || row >= rowOffset + dinoHeight -
                200) {
                backgroundPixel
            } else if (column < columnOffset || column >=
                columnOffset + dinoWidth) {
                backgroundPixel
            } else {
                val foregroundPixel = dino.pixelByRowColumn(row -
                        rowOffset, column - columnOffset)
                if (foregroundPixel == Color(255, 0, 255)) {
                    backgroundPixel
                } else {
                    foregroundPixel
                }
            }
        }
    }
    return Picture(newPixels).scaleDown(5).darkBorder()
}
```

This gives the image shown at the start of the chapter.

One thing worth noting here is that the dinosaur has been placed in a dark patch of water, where it would not have a shadow. The absence of shadows in green-screen images is one of the reasons they can be unconvincing. Rather than making a shadow programmatically, we have avoided the problem altogether.

17.6 Summary

We have produced a pretty good green-screen effect just using the code we developed over the previous few chapters. This is a great result for beginner programmers! In several situations, we worked around a problem rather than attempting a complex technical fix. This is the kind of pragmatic decision that professional software engineers make all the time.

PART IV

Vision

In Part IV, we use all the programming skills that we learned in earlier parts to create software that reads speed signs.

CHAPTER 18

Overview

Computer vision is the use of software to extract information from images. This is an important topic, with applications in fields such as medicine (finding tumors), astronomy (finding planets), and security (finding criminals). In this last part of the book, we will solve the problem of reading speed signs, which is necessary for self-driving cars.

The speed signs that our software will read consist of black numerals inside a red circle, all on a white background. By the end of the book, we will have written software that can find the speed sign in a photo and read it.

Our software will do this in two main steps. First, the part of the image that contains the sign will be located and will be broken into sub-images. The output of this process will be a list of `Pictures`, each representing a numeral of the speed. The second step will be to determine what numbers these images represent.

The implementation of the software is spread across the next four chapters, as follows. In this chapter, we will enhance the `Picture` class from Part III to allow the kind of slicing that is required in locating important features of images. In the next chapter, these new functions will be applied to speed sign photos to extract the digit sub-images. In Chapter 20, we will develop the code that can take a black and white image and determine what digit it represents. Finally, in the last chapter of the book, we will put all of these pieces together to produce what is really a very sophisticated program.

18.1 A Bit More Kotlin

Before we get started on our computer vision code, there are a couple of concepts to learn. We will do so using a tool called the Kotlin REPL (read, evaluate, print loop), which is a part of IntelliJ. The REPL is started using the menus Tools ➤ Kotlin ➤ Kotlin REPL. The tool itself is a sort of command-line interface to Kotlin and is shown in Figure 18-1.

© Tim Lavers 2021
T. Lavers, *Learn to Program with Kotlin*, https://doi.org/10.1007/978-1-4842-6815-5_18

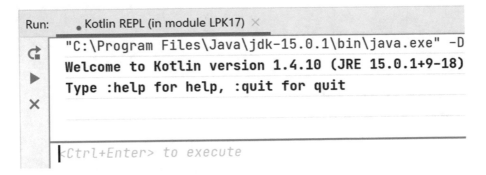

Figure 18-1. *The Kotlin REPL*

In Chapter 20, we will need to talk about proportions, which are fractional numbers, such as ".65". These can be modeled in Kotlin using a class called Float. If we want to divide two Ints using ordinary arithmetic (rather than integer arithmetic), we convert them to Floats first. For example, if we enter the expression

```
1.toFloat() / 3.toFloat()
```

in the Kotlin REPL, the answer 0.33333334 is printed out. There's not much really to say about Floats. They are very easy to use. We usually only get problems when we forget to convert Ints to Floats before making a division, for example:

```
(1/3).toFloat()
```

gives the result 0.0 because 1/3 is the Int 0, which is then converted to the Float 0.0.

The second new programming concept that we need is that of *filtering*, which is the application of some decision process to the elements of a List, to keep the important ones and discard the rest. To see this in action, let's filter the integers between 1 and 10, keeping just the even ones. To do this, type

```
(1..10).filter { i -> i % 2 == 0 }
```

into the REPL and press Ctrl+Enter. You should get the printout:

```
[2, 4, 6, 8, 10]
```

The expression

```
i -> i % 2 == 0
```

is a function from type Int to type Boolean. This function returns true if the remainder of dividing i by 2 is equal to 0, that is, if i is even. Recall, from the previous chapter, that this is called a lambda function. In fact, lambda functions like this are so useful that Kotlin allows a shorthand in which the i -> i part of the expression is replaced by it, which is a nice shorthand for "any element of the collection that we are iterating over." Using this, we can write

```
(1..10).filter { it % 2 == 0 }
```

The filter function applies this to all of the elements of the original list and builds a new list consisting of those for which the function was true. We can use filtering to answer questions such as "What is lowest multiple of 41 that is greater than 1000?":

```
(1001..1100).filter{it % 41 == 0}.first()
```

We will use filtering in Chapter 19, where we slice images into lists of sub-images and need to discard those that are too small to be of interest.

18.2 Project Structure

The code for this chapter can be downloaded from https://github.com/Apress/learn-to-program-w-kotlin-ch18.git. This contains the Picture class from previous chapters, with some unnecessary functions removed, PictureTest, and a directory of test images.

18.3 Image Slicing

The first lot of image slicing we need to do is to break a Picture into a List of Pictures that contain red pixels. To do this, we need to identify rows and columns that contain red pixels. Add this function to Picture:

```
fun columnContainsRedPixel(column: Int): Boolean {
    for (row in 0..height() - 1) {
        if (pixelByRowColumn(row, column) == Color.RED) {
            return true
        }
    }
    return false
}
```

Notice the term Color.RED in the if statement. In the interests of introducing as little syntax as possible, we have been creating Color objects as we needed them, but in fact there are constants for the most commonly used Colors, which we will be using from now on. The test function uses presupplied images:

```
@Test
fun columnContainsRedPixelTest() {
    val allBlue = load("blue10.png")
    for (column in 0..9) {
        Assert.assertFalse(allBlue.columnContainsRedPixel(column))
    }
    val allRed = load("red10.png")
    for (column in 0..9) {
        Assert.assertTrue(allRed.columnContainsRedPixel(column))
    }

    //100 rows, 200 columns, all black apart from
    //a 50-by-50 square with top left corner at
    //row 50 and column 100.
    val someRed = load("red_in_black.png")
    for (column in 0..99) {
        Assert.assertFalse(someRed.columnContainsRedPixel(column))
    }
    for (column in 100..149) {
        Assert.assertTrue(someRed.columnContainsRedPixel(column))
    }
    for (column in 150..199) {
        Assert.assertFalse(someRed.columnContainsRedPixel(column))
    }
}
```

Copy these functions into Picture and PictureTest, respectively, and check that the test passes.

PROJECT STEP 18.1

Add a function for checking if a row contains any red pixels.

Add a test for this, and check that the test passes.

To slice a `Picture` vertically into pieces that each contain red pixels, we can work as follows. Starting on the left side, we look for the first column that contains a red pixel. When we have found this, we start looking for a column that does not contain a red pixel. The columns in between form the first slice. We turn this slice into a `Picture` and add it to the result, which is a `List<Picture>`. Then we start again, looking for a column containing red pixels, and so on.

This is best understood with an example. Consider the following `Picture`, which has 4 rows and 13 columns of pixels.

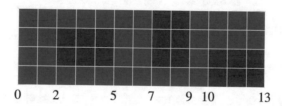

Define vars called `leftLimit` and `rightLimit`. These represent the start and end columns of a section of `Picture` in which every column contains a red pixel. Initially, these vars both contain the value -1. We start at column 0 and take action as follows:

Column	Contains red?	leftLimit	rightLimit	Action
0	false	-1	-1	
1	false	-1	-1	
2	true	2	2	
3	true	2	3	
4	true	2	4	
5	false	-1	-1	Add Picture to result
6	false	-1	-1	
⋮	⋮	⋮	⋮	

PROJECT STEP 18.2

See if you can complete the preceding table.

Pictures are added to the result when a column with no red pixels follows a column that does contain red. This occurs at columns 5 and 7. A Picture is also added at column 12, as that is the last column. The Pictures that are added consist of all of the pixels in the columns containing red, not just the red pixels. These are shown in Figure 18-2.

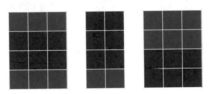

Figure 18-2. *After slicing*

Here is an implementation of this algorithm:

```
fun sliceVerticallyIntoPicturesContainingRed(): List<Picture> {
    val result = mutableListOf<Picture>()
    var leftLimit = -1
    var rightLimit = -1
    for (i in 0..width() - 1) {
        if (columnContainsRedPixel(i)) {
            if (leftLimit == -1) {
                leftLimit = i
            }
            rightLimit = i
        } else {
            //This is a gap.
            if (leftLimit >= 0) {
                //The current sub-picture is complete.
                val columnsInCurrentPiece = rightLimit - leftLimit + 1
                val piece = cropTo(0, leftLimit, height(),
                columnsInCurrentPiece)
```

```
            result.add(piece)
            //Reset the markers.
            leftLimit = -1
            rightLimit = -1
        }
    }
}
//There may be a piece left over
//that extends to the edge of the picture.
//Add it, if it exists.
if (leftLimit >= 0) {
    val columnsInCurrentPiece = rightLimit - leftLimit + 1
    val piece = cropTo(0, leftLimit, height(), columnsInCurrentPiece)
    result.add(piece)
}
return result
}
```

This is very complicated, but a couple of things can help us understand it. First, we can try to step through the code using the values from the preceding example. Second, we can compare this code to the init block of Line from Chapter 10. It's really the same algorithm, as this comparison shows:

	Line.init	Picture **slicing**
What is being split	A String	A Picture, in one dimension
Boundaries	Spaces	Columns with no red pixels
Output	List<String>	List<Picture>

The general form of the algorithm is the same in both cases, consisting of a main loop followed by a call to add any leftover pieces.

Of course, a unit test always helps us to get on top of code. The test for the slicing function makes use of the test image shown in Figure 18-3. The test splits this vertically, checks that there are three pieces, and then compares each piece with an expected test image.

Figure 18-3. *The test image*

```
@Test
fun sliceVerticallyIntoPicturesContainingRedTest() {
    val picture = load("slice_test_v.png")
    val slices = picture.sliceVerticallyIntoPicturesContainingRed()
    Assert.assertEquals(3, slices.size)
    checkPicture(load("v0.png"), slices[0])
    checkPicture(load("v1.png"), slices[1])
    checkPicture(load("v2.png"), slices[2])
}
```

Copy the function and test into `Picture` and `PictureTest`, respectively, and check that the test passes.

PROJECT STEP 18.3

Copy the vertical slicing function and modify it to slice horizontally. Don't worry about a bit of repetition; we will refactor everything later.

Note   Be careful with the lines using `cropTo`, as these will change a little.

Create a unit test for it that uses the test image `slice_test_h.png` and the three small images `h0.png`, `h1.png`, and `h2.png`.

18.4 Summary and Step Details

In this chapter, we have used the Kotlin REPL to experiment with some new syntax. We have also added some functions to Picture that will slice up images in just the way required for detection of speed signs, as we will see soon.

18.1.1 Details of Project Step 18.1

Here is the function:

```
fun rowContainsRedPixel(row: Int): Boolean {
    for (column in 0..width() - 1) {
        if (pixelByRowColumn(row, column) == Color.RED) {
            return true
        }
    }
    return false
}
```

And here is the test:

```
@Test
fun rowContainsRedPixelTest() {
    val allBlue = load("blue10.png")
    for (row in 0..9) {
        Assert.assertFalse(allBlue.rowContainsRedPixel(row))
    }
    val allRed = load("red10.png")
    for (row in 0..9) {
        Assert.assertTrue(allRed.rowContainsRedPixel(row))
    }

    val someRed = load("red_in_black.png")
    for (row in 0..49) {
        Assert.assertFalse(someRed.rowContainsRedPixel(row))
    }
```

```
    for (row in 50..99) {
        Assert.assertTrue(someRed.rowContainsRedPixel(row))
    }
}
```

18.2.2 Details of Project Step 18.2

The table continues:

Column	Contains red?	leftLimit	rightLimit	Action
7	true	7	7	
8	true	7	8	
9	false	-1	-1	Add Picture to result
10	true	10	10	
11	true	10	11	
12	true	10	12	Add Picture to result

18.3.3 Details of Project Step 18.3

Here's the function for slicing horizontally:

```
fun sliceHorizontallyIntoPicturesContainingRed(): List<Picture> {
    val result = mutableListOf<Picture>()
    var upperLimit = -1
    var lowerLimit = -1
    for (i in 0..height() - 1) {
        if (rowContainsRedPixel(i)) {
            if (upperLimit == -1) {
                upperLimit = i
            }
            lowerLimit = i
        } else {
```

```
            //This is a gap.
            if (upperLimit >= 0) {
                //The current sub-picture is complete.
                val rowsInCurrentPiece = lowerLimit - upperLimit + 1
                val piece = cropTo(upperLimit, 0, rowsInCurrentPiece, width())
                result.add(piece)
                //Reset the markers.
                upperLimit = -1
                lowerLimit = -1
            }
        }
    }
    //There may be a piece left over
    //that extends to the edge of the picture.
    //Add it, if it exists.
    if (upperLimit >= 0) {
        val rowsInCurrentPiece = lowerLimit - upperLimit + 1
        val piece = cropTo(upperLimit, 0, rowsInCurrentPiece, width())
        result.add(piece)
    }
    return result
}
```

And here's the test:

```
@Test
fun sliceHorizontallyIntoPicturesContainingRedTest() {
    val picture = load("slice_test_h.png")
    val slices = picture.sliceHorizontallyIntoPicturesContainingRed()
    Assert.assertEquals(3, slices.size)
    checkPicture(load("h0.png"), slices[0])
    checkPicture(load("h1.png"), slices[1])
    checkPicture(load("h2.png"), slices[2])
}
```

CHAPTER 19

Finding Digits

In this chapter, we will write a class that, given a `Picture` containing a speed sign, will extract a `List` of `Pictures` representing the individual digits in the sign. To get started, open https://github.com/Apress/learn-to-program-w-kotlin-ch19.git.

19.1 DigitFinder

In addition to `Picture`, the project contains a class called `DigitFinder`:

```
1   package lpk.imaging
2
3   import java.awt.Color
4
5   class DigitFinder(val input : Picture) {
6       fun digits() : List<Picture> {
7           val result = mutableListOf<Picture>()
8           result.add(input)
9           return result
10      }
11  }
```

The purpose of `DigitFinder` is to take an input image that contains a speed sign and produce a `List` of `Pictures`, one for each of the digits in the sign. The preceding implementation just adds the `input` image to the `result` list. It does no analysis at all.

There is also a class called `DigitFinderTest`. This is not really a test; rather, it is a convenient way of running code so that we can find the threshold values and slicing techniques that work best. We will work with just one image for now.

© Tim Lavers 2021
T. Lavers, *Learn to Program with Kotlin*, https://doi.org/10.1007/978-1-4842-6815-5_19

Here is the complete listing of DigitFinderTest, apart from the package and import statements:

```
1    val SIGNS = "src/test/resources/images/signs/"
2
3    fun loadSign(name: String): DigitFinder {
4        val file = Paths.get(SIGNS + name).toFile()
5        return DigitFinder(loadPictureFromFile(file))
6    }
7    fun saveInTempDir(picture: Picture, name: String) {
8        val tempDir = File("temp")
9        tempDir.mkdirs()
10       val file = File(tempDir, name)
11       picture.saveTo(file)
12   }
13   class DigitFinderTest {
14       @Test
15       fun analyse() {
16           val s80 = loadSign("80.png")
17           val digitPictures = s80.digits()
18           saveInTempDir(digitPictures[0], "p0.png")
19       }
20   }
```

Figure 19-1. *The speed sign*

On line 16, we create a `DigitFinder` for the sign shown in Figure 19-1. Next, we call the `digits` function to get the list of `Pictures` that `DigitFinder` has discovered. By the end of the chapter, there should be two of these, but for now there is just one. On line 18, we save this image in a temporary location so that we can have a look at it and check our thresholds.

When we run the `analyse` function in `DigitFinderTest`, a directory called `temp` is created, and a file called `p0.png` is written there, as shown in Figure 19-2. We can open this in IntelliJ, and of course it just shows our original input image for now.

Figure 19-2. *The project layout, with the extracted images (there is only one right now) written to the* `temp` *directory*

19.2 Thresholding the Sign Images

The Picture class has functions that can slice an instance into components containing red. One of the most distinctive features of a speed sign is the red circle surrounding the numbers. Our plan is to slice the speed sign image to retrieve a slice containing the red circle. Of course, speed signs do not contain pure colors, but we can overcome this problem by thresholding. This can be achieved by creating a function:

```
(Color) -> (Color)
```

and then passing this in as the argument to the transform function of Picture. The thresholding function should map pixels to whichever of red, white, or black they are closest.

So, for a Color that is vaguely white, it should return Color.WHITE; for a Color that is close to Color.RED, it should return that; and otherwise it should return Color.BLACK. To this end, change DigitFinder to be

```
class DigitFinder(val input : Picture) {
    val blackWhitRedThresholder: ((Color) -> (Color)) = {
        if (it.red > 196 && it.green > 196 && it.blue > 196) {
            Color.WHITE
        } else if (it.red > 196) {
            Color.RED
        } else {
            Color.BLACK
        }
    }

    fun digits() : List<Picture> {
        val result = mutableListOf<Picture>()
        val blackWhitRedVersion = input.transform(blackWhitRedThresholder)
        result.add(blackWhitRedVersion)
        return result
    }
}
```

In this new version of the class, there is a `val` called `blackWhiteThresholder` that performs the thresholding. This is then applied to produce a new version of the input image, and it is this thresholded version that is added to the result.

After making these changes, run the test. You should see that the thresholding has not worked very well. As shown in Figure 19-3, almost everything is black, including parts of the sign that should be white. To understand what is going on, it's useful to open the original image in a drawing program and have a look at what the actual colors in it are. It turns out that the "white" background of the sign has a red value of about 185, which is below the 196 in our thresholder. Even more surprisingly, the pixels in the "red" circle have red values of about 155 and blue values of about 80. They are a long way from being a pure red.

Figure 19-3. *First attempt at thresholding*

For a second attempt, let's try changing `blackWhitRedThresholder` to

```
val blackWhitRedThresholder: ((Color) -> (Color)) = {
    if (it.red > 128 && it.green > 128 && it.blue > 128) {
        Color.WHITE
    } else if (it.red > 128) {
        Color.RED
    } else {
        Color.BLACK
    }
}
```

This gives a better result, but brown parts of the picture, such as the grass, are being changed to be red, as in Figure 19-4. This will make it hard to find the sign.

Figure 19-4. *Second attempt*

For our third attempt, let's change emphasis and think about what information in the image is most important for our purpose. The digits in the sign are really what we are most interested in. These are pretty dark in the photo. So let's only change pixels to black if they really are very dark. Next in importance are the red pixels in the circle. As we learned from our second attempt, pixels that have high red values but also have high green or blue values should not be changed to red. Anything else can be changed to white without loss of the information that really counts. So let's try changing the thresholder to

```
val blackWhitRedThresholder: ((Color) -> (Color)) = {
    if (it.red < 96 && it.green < 96 && it.blue < 96) {
        Color.BLACK
    } else if (it.red > 128 && it.green < 96 && it.blue < 96) {
        Color.RED
    } else {
        Color.WHITE
    }
}
```

The result, shown in Figure 19-5, at last gives us something that we can work with.

Figure 19-5. *Third attempt*

19.3 Slicing the Thresholded Image

With a nicely thresholded Picture, we can now find the horizontal slice that contains the
speed sign. We can do this by changing the digits function to

```
fun digits(): List<Picture> {
    val result = mutableListOf<Picture>()
    val blackWhitRedVersion = input.transform(blackWhitRedThresholder)

    val slicesH = blackWhitRedVersion.
            sliceHorizontallyIntoPicturesContainingRed()
    val sliceH0 = slicesH.first()

    result.add(sliceH0)
    return result
}
```

Note that we are taking just the first Picture from the list produced by the horizontal
slicing function. We will tidy this up later on. With the new code, we get just a narrow
section of the thresholded image, as shown in Figure 19-6.

There is still a lot of image here that is not the sign. We can get rid of the excess by slicing this image vertically. To do so, change `digits` to

```
fun digits(): List<Picture> {
    val result = mutableListOf<Picture>()
    val blackWhitRedVersion = input.transform(blackWhitRedThresholder)

    val slicesH = blackWhitRedVersion.
            sliceHorizontallyIntoPicturesContainingRed()
    val sliceH0 = slicesH.first()

    val slicesV = sliceH0.
            sliceVerticallyIntoPicturesContainingRed()
    val sliceV0 = slicesV.first()

    result.add(sliceV0)
    return result
}
```

Figure 19-6. *Thresholded and then sliced horizontally*

The result is a nicely trimmed speed sign, in just three colors, as shown in Figure 19-7.

Figure 19-7. *After the vertical slicing*

19.4 A More General Slicing Function

To get to the actual digits in the thresholded and twice-sliced speed sign of Figure 19-7, we need to get rid of the red circle and the white space around the digits. We can do this by more slicing! If we change our slicing functions to match any required color, then we will be able to slice horizontally and then vertically to obtain pure black and white images that are trimmed to the digits.

Let's start by deleting the function rowContainsRedPixel and replacing it with a new function that takes the Color that is to be found as a parameter:

```
fun rowContainsPixelMatching(row: Int, toMatch: Color): Boolean {
    for (column in 0..width() - 1) {
        if (pixelByRowColumn(row, column) == toMatch) {
            return true
        }
    }
    return false
}
```

When we do this, we will have a couple of problems. First, within Picture, the call to rowContainsMatchingPixel in the body of sliceHorizontallyIntoPicturesContainingRed will need to change to

```
if (rowContainsPixelMatching(i, Color.RED)) {
```

Second, the unit test for the deleted function needs to be replaced with this:

```
@Test
fun rowContainsPixelMatchingTest() {
    val allBlue = load("blue10.png")
    for (row in 0..9) {
        Assert.assertTrue(allBlue.rowContainsPixelMatching(row,
        Color.BLUE))
        Assert.assertFalse(allBlue.rowContainsPixelMatching(row,
        Color.RED))
    }
    val allRed = load("red10.png")
    for (row in 0..9) {
        Assert.assertTrue(allRed.rowContainsPixelMatching(row, Color.RED))
        Assert.assertFalse(allRed.rowContainsPixelMatching(row, Color.BLUE))
    }
```

```
val someRed = load("red_in_black.png")
for (row in 0..49) {
    Assert.assertFalse(someRed.rowContainsPixelMatching(row, Color.RED))
}
for (row in 50..99) {
    Assert.assertTrue(someRed.rowContainsPixelMatching(row, Color.RED))
}
}
```

PROJECT STEP 19.1

Make similar changes to `columnContainsRedPixel` and its test.

Let's now turn to the slicing functions themselves. We can rename the horizontal slicing function to `sliceHorizontallyIntoPicturesContaining` and introduce a Color parameter, so that the function begins:

```
fun sliceHorizontallyIntoPicturesContaining(toMatch: Color): List<Picture> {
    val result = mutableListOf<Picture>()
    var upperLimit = -1
    var lowerLimit = -1
    for (i in 0..height() - 1) {
        if (rowContainsPixelMatching(i, toMatch)) {
            ...
```

Note that the call to `rowContainsPixelMatching()` in the `if` statement now uses the argument `toMatch` rather than `Color.RED`.

We need to change the call to the function in `DigitFinder` to pass in `Color.RED` as a parameter. We should also change the test to

```
@Test
fun sliceHorizontallyIntoPicturesContainingTest() {
    val picture = load("slice_test_h.png")
    val slices = picture.sliceHorizontallyIntoPicturesContaining(Color.RED)
    Assert.assertEquals(3, slices.size)
    checkPicture(load("h0.png"), slices[0])
```

```
    checkPicture(load("h1.png"), slices[1])
    checkPicture(load("h2.png"), slices[2])

    val slicesBlack = picture.sliceHorizontallyIntoPicturesContaining(
    Color.BLACK)
    Assert.assertEquals(1, slicesBlack.size)
    checkPicture(load("slice_test_h.png"), slicesBlack[0])
}
```

Note that we've added code to check that the function works when it has as its parameter a color other than red.

PROJECT STEP 19.2

Make similar changes to `sliceVerticallyIntoPicturesContainingRed` and its test.

19.5 Filtering the Slices

Using our more generalized slicing functions, we can attempt to extract the digits from a speed sign. Our strategy will be to slice horizontally to get a section containing black pixels. This should remove the parts of the image above and below the numbers. What is left will then be sliced vertically to get the individual digits. Let's first make a change to do the horizontal slicing:

```
fun digits(): List<Picture> {
    val result = mutableListOf<Picture>()
    val blackWhitRedVersion = input.transform(blackWhitRedThresholder)

    val slicesH = blackWhitRedVersion
            .sliceHorizontallyIntoPicturesContaining(Color.RED)
    val signSlice = slicesH.first()

    val slicesV = signSlice.sliceVerticallyIntoPicturesContaining(Color.RED)
    val sign = slicesV.first()

    val slices2H = sign.sliceHorizontallyIntoPicturesContaining(Color.BLACK)
    val digitsSlice = slices2H.first()
```

```
    result.add(digitsSlice)
    return result
}
```

Running this shows a bizarre output, a `Picture` so narrow that it is virtually impossible to see without zooming. Under magnification, the problem becomes apparent. There is a black dot in the image, and the rows containing it are being counted as a slice, as shown in Figure 19-8.

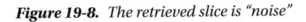

Figure 19-8. *The retrieved slice is "noise"*

We need to ignore such "noise." The `List` filtering that we saw in Chapter 18 provides a lovely way of doing this. We need a function:

```
(Picture) -> (Boolean)
```

that can be used to select the `Pictures` large enough to be important. This will do the job:

```
val sizeAtLeast20: ((Picture) -> (Boolean)) = {
    it.width() > 20 && it.height() > 20
}
```

PROJECT STEP 19.3

Add the `sizeAtLeast20` val to `DigitFinder`. Then use it to filter the slices:

```
val slices2H = sign.
        sliceHorizontallyIntoPicturesContaining(Color.BLACK).
        filter(sizeAtLeast20)
val digitsSlice = slices2H.first()
```

With these changes, the output is nicely trimmed, as Figure 19-9 shows. A close look at this output shows an isolated black pixel on the left-hand side. This will need to be filtered out when we slice this image vertically. However, the digits themselves are quite narrow (the output that is shown has been magnified), so filtering to size 20 will not work. Let's add a finer filter than that used for horizontal slicing and apply it to the vertical slices. Here is a version of DigitFinder with these changes:

Figure 19-9. *After filtering out the extremely thin slices*

```
class DigitFinder(val input: Picture) {
    val blackWhitRedThresholder: ((Color) -> (Color)) = {
        if (it.red < 96 && it.green < 96 && it.blue < 96) {
            Color.BLACK
        } else if (it.red > 128 && it.green < 96 && it.blue < 96) {
            Color.RED
        } else {
            Color.WHITE
        }
    }

    val sizeAtLeast20: ((Picture) -> (Boolean)) = {
        it.width() > 20 && it.height() > 20
    }

    val sizeAtLeast10: ((Picture) -> (Boolean)) = {
        it.width() > 10 && it.height() > 10
    }

    fun digits(): List<Picture> {
        val blackWhitRedVersion = input.transform(blackWhitRedThresholder)

        val slicesH = blackWhitRedVersion.
                sliceHorizontallyIntoPicturesContaining(Color.RED)
        val signSlice = slicesH.first()
```

CHAPTER 19   FINDING DIGITS

```
        val slicesV = signSlice.
                sliceVerticallyIntoPicturesContaining(Color.RED)
        val sign = slicesV.first()

        val slices2H = sign.
                sliceHorizontallyIntoPicturesContaining(Color.BLACK).
                filter(sizeAtLeast20)
        val digitsSlice = slices2H.first()

        return digitsSlice.
                sliceVerticallyIntoPicturesContaining(Color.BLACK).
                filter(sizeAtLeast10)
    }
}
```

We now expect two `Pictures` in the output, so let's change the test function to save them both:

```
@Test
fun analyse() {
    val s80 = loadSign("80.png")
    val digitPictures = s80.digits()
    saveInTempDir(digitPictures[0], "p0.png")
    saveInTempDir(digitPictures[1], "p1.png")
}
```

Running this code gives two files in the temp directory. These are just black and white and are neatly trimmed to the digits, as shown in Figure 19-10.

(a) The first extracted digit.

(b) The second extracted digit.

Figure 19-10. *Two images representing individual digits have been extracted from the image containing the speed sign*

344

19.6 Summary and Step Details

We now have a program that will take a photo containing a speed sign and break it into a List of Pictures of individual digits. In the next chapter, we will write code that can determine the digits that these images represent.

19.1.1 Details of Project Step 19.1

The refactored function is

```kotlin
fun columnContainsPixelMatching(column: Int, toMatch: Color): Boolean {
    for (row in 0..height() - 1) {
        if (pixelByRowColumn(row, column) == toMatch) {
            return true
        }
    }
    return false
}
```

The test can be changed to

```kotlin
@Test
fun columnContainsPixelMatchingTest() {
    val allBlue = load("blue10.png")
    for (column in 0..9) {
        Assert.assertFalse(allBlue.columnContainsPixelMatching(column,
        Color.RED))
        Assert.assertTrue(allBlue.columnContainsPixelMatching(column,
        Color.BLUE))
    }
    val allRed = load("red10.png")
    for (column in 0..9) {
        Assert.assertTrue(allRed.columnContainsPixelMatching(column,
        Color.RED))
        Assert.assertFalse(allRed.columnContainsPixelMatching(column,
        Color.BLUE))
    }
```

```
//100 rows, 200 columns, all black apart from
//a 50-by-50 square with top left corner at
//row 50 and column 100.
val someRed = load("red_in_black.png")
for (column in 0..99) {
    Assert.assertFalse(someRed.columnContainsPixelMatching(column,
    Color.RED))
}
for (column in 100..149) {
    Assert.assertTrue(someRed.columnContainsPixelMatching(column,
    Color.RED))
}
for (column in 150..199) {
    Assert.assertFalse(someRed.columnContainsPixelMatching(column,
    Color.RED))
}
}
```

19.2.2 Details of Project Step 19.2

The refactored test is

```
@Test
fun sliceVerticallyIntoPicturesContainingTest() {
    val picture = load("slice_test_v.png")
    val slices = picture.sliceVerticallyIntoPicturesContaining(Color.RED)
    Assert.assertEquals(3, slices.size)
    checkPicture(load("v0.png"), slices[0])
    checkPicture(load("v1.png"), slices[1])

    val slicesBlack =
        picture.sliceVerticallyIntoPicturesContaining(Color.BLACK)
    Assert.assertEquals(1, slicesBlack.size)
    checkPicture(load("slice_test_v.png"), slicesBlack[0])
}
```

19.3.3 Details of Project Step 19.3

The new version of DigitFinder is

```kotlin
package pfb.imaging

import java.awt.Color

class DigitFinder(val input: Picture) {
    val blackWhitRedThresholder: ((Color) -> (Color)) = {
        if (it.red < 96 && it.green < 96 && it.blue < 96) {
            Color.BLACK
        } else if (it.red > 128 && it.green < 96 && it.blue < 96) {
            Color.RED
        } else {
            Color.WHITE
        }
    }

    val sizeAtLeast20: ((Picture) -> (Boolean)) = {
        it.width() > 20 && it.height() > 20
    }

    fun digits(): List<Picture> {
        val blackWhitRedVersion = input.transform(blackWhitRedThresholder)

        val slicesH = blackWhitRedVersion.
            sliceHorizontallyIntoPicturesContaining(Color.RED)
        val signSlice = slicesH.first()

        val slicesV = signSlice.
            sliceVerticallyIntoPicturesContaining(Color.RED)
        val sign = slicesV.first()

        val slices2H = sign.
            sliceHorizontallyIntoPicturesContaining(Color.BLACK).
            filter(sizeAtLeast20)

        return slices2H
    }
}
```

CHAPTER 20

Parsing the Images

We finished the last chapter with a program, `DigitFinder`, that was able to load a photo of a speed sign and extract from it a list of black and white images of the individual digits. In this chapter, we will write code for determining the numbers that these extracted images represent.

Applying `DigitFinder` to different speed signs gives output images such as those shown as follows:

$$0 \quad 1 \quad 2 \quad 3 \quad 4$$
$$5 \quad 6 \quad 7 \quad {}_8 \quad 9$$

To determine what digit an image represents, our software will build a description of the image and then make a decision based on the description. For example, if the image is "very narrow," it will be classified as representing "1." If it is "white centered," then it will be classified as "0." Because the images we are classifying vary in size and angle of presentation and are missing the occasional black pixel, our software will only be able to use fairly broad descriptions, such as "narrow" or "white centered," in deciding what digit an image represents.

We will mostly use information about the density of black pixels in different parts of an image to describe it. A class called `Regions` will identify which part of an image a pixel lies in. A class called `PictureSummary` will run through the pixels in an image and, with the help of a `Regions` object for that image, will gather statistics about where the black pixels are. This information will be summarized as properties such as `hasCenterBlank`, `hasCenterDark`, and so on. Finally, a function called `read`, in a file

© Tim Lavers 2021
T. Lavers, *Learn to Program with Kotlin*, https://doi.org/10.1007/978-1-4842-6815-5_20

called `DigitReader.kt`, will contain the decision-making logic that uses the information from a `PictureSummary` to decide which digit an image represents.

Our goal in this chapter is to develop the classes `Regions`, `PictureSummary`, and `DigitReader.kt`, and their tests, to the point where we can programmatically distinguish "0," "1," "2," "5," and "7." The code that does this can then be easily extended to deal with the remaining digits. Rather than explain all the details, we will just present the finished classes as the starting point of the next chapter.

20.1 Terminology

All of our number images are rectangular. As outlined earlier, we will summarize an image by describing the regional density of its black pixels within this rectangle. The images come in different sizes, so we can only talk in relative terms.

The *left*, *right*, *top*, and *bottom* refer to the quarters of the image in those locations. We are interested in the proportions of all the black pixels in the image that are in each of these regions. Consider, for example, Figure 20-1. Ignoring the red border, the proportion of the black pixels that are in the left quarter is 0.5, and the proportion in the top quarter is 0.25.

Figure 20-1. *Half of the pixels that are black are in the left quarter*

The *center* of the image is the part that is surrounded by these quarters. The *top bar* is the top seventh of the image, and the *bottom bar* is the bottom seventh. For the center and for the bars, we are interested in the proportion of all of the pixels *in these regions* that are black. The following table gives examples of some of the terms that we will use.

Term	Meaning	Example
hasCenterBlank	At most 10% of center pixels are black	"0"
hasDarkCenter	At least 65% of center pixels are black	"4"
hasTopBar	The top seventh is at least 75% black	"5"
hasBottomBar	The bottom seventh is at least 75% black	"2"

20.2 Project Structure

The code for this chapter can be downloaded from https://github.com/Apress/learn-to-program-w-kotlin-ch20.git. The Picture and DigitFinder classes are as we left them at the end of the previous chapter. There are also basic versions of PictureSummary, Regions, and DigitReader and tests for these.

Two new directories of test data have been added. The summary directory contains images that we will use in the unit tests for PictureSummary. The digits directory contains the images shown at the start of this chapter, which will be used for testing DigitReader. Another change is that the signs test data directory now contains signs that cover all numerals. DigitFinderTest has been enhanced to process all of the files in this directory, rather than just 80.png, and this is how the images in the digits directory were created.

20.3 Identifying the Digit "1"

The freshly downloaded code already contains a version of DigitReader that can identify "1." To see how it does this, it's easiest to work backward from the test:

```
1   val DIGITS = "src/test/resources/images/digits"
2
3   class DigitReaderTest {
4       @Test
5       fun readTest() {
6           Assert.assertEquals(1, read(loadSummary("1.png")))
7       }
8
```

```
9       fun loadSummary(name: String): PictureSummary {
10          val file = Paths.get(DIGITS + "/" + name).toFile()
11          return PictureSummary(loadPictureFromFile(file))
12      }
13  }
```

The first line of this code is a constant that identifies the relevant test data directory. On line 9, we have a function that takes the name of an image file, loads it as a Picture, and then creates a PictureSummary. This function is used in the test function, on line 6. This line of code applies read to the summary and checks that it returns 1.

If we go now to the read function itself, which is in a file called DigitReader.kt, we see that is simply looking at the image height to width ratio, which is obtained from PictureSummary:

```
fun read(summary : PictureSummary) : Int {
    if (summary.heightToWidth > 3.0) return 1
    return -1
}
```

Let's now look at PictureSummary:

```
1    package lpk.imaging
2
3    import java.awt.Color
4
5    class PictureSummary(picture: Picture) {
6        val heightToWidth: Float
7        val hasBottomBar : Boolean
8        val proportionBlackRight : Float
9
10       init {
11           heightToWidth = picture.height().toFloat() / picture.width().
             toFloat()
12           val regions = Regions(picture.height(), picture.width())
13           var rightQuarterBlack = 0
14           var bottomBarBlack = 0
15           var black = 0
```

```
16              for (row in 0..picture.height() - 1) {
17                  for (column in 0..picture.width() - 1) {
18                      val isBlack = picture.pixelByRowColumn(row, column) ==
                        Color.BLACK
19                      if (isBlack) {
20                          black++
21                          if (regions.isInBottomBar(row)) bottomBarBlack++
22                          if (regions.isInRightQuarter(column))
                            rightQuarterBlack++
23                      }
24                  }
25              }
26              proportionBlackRight = rightQuarterBlack.toFloat() /
                black.toFloat()
27              val bottomBarRatio = bottomBarBlack.toFloat() /
                regions.bottomBarArea().toFloat()
28              hasBottomBar = bottomBarRatio > .75
29          }
30      }
```

Line 5 shows that a PictureSummary is created with a Picture. There are three vals in PictureSummary. We have already seen that heightToWidth is used to identify "1." The vals hasBottomBar and proportionBlackRight summarize information about where the black pixels are. The init block, which begins on line 10, calculates these vals.

At first, the init block looks very complicated. Let's go through the details of it. On line 11, the heightToWidth is set as the height to width ratio of the image. On line 12, we create an instance of Regions that will be used to classify where in the image a pixel is. Lines 13 to 15 set up three vars that are used to count black pixels. Lines 16 and 17 define a double loop through the pixels of the image. We have seen this row-column double looping before.

Within the loop, on line 18, we check whether the current pixel is black. If the pixel is black, then we want to record statistics about it. This is done by incrementing the relevant counters, on lines 20 to 22. To increase the counters, we use the notation ++, by which c++ is shorthand for c = c + 1. On lines 21 and 22, we are using the Regions object to decide whether or not to increment the region-specific counters we set up earlier.

After the pixel iteration double loop is finished, the counter values are used to set proportionBlackRight and hasBottomBar. Note that we convert the integer counts to floats before doing the divisions. Also note that for proportionBlackHigh, we are dividing the number of black pixels in the region by the total number of black pixels in the image, whereas for hasBottomBar we are dividing the number of black pixels in the lower seventh by the total number of pixels in that region.

The unit test for PictureSummary loads files from the summary directory that have been specially prepared to have easily calculated proportions of black pixels in the regions of interest. For example, here's proportionBlackRightTest:

```
@Test
fun proportionBlackRightTest() {
    Assert.assertEquals(0.0F, summary("bwbw_v.png").proportionBlackRight)
    Assert.assertEquals(0.5F, summary("wbwb_v.png").proportionBlackRight)
    Assert.assertEquals(0.25F, summary("bwbw_h.png").proportionBlackRight)
    Assert.assertEquals(0.25F, summary("wbwb_h.png").proportionBlackRight)
}
```

The first assertion uses the image shown in Figure 20-1 on page 350.

The Regions class is another one that looks more complicated than it really is:

```
1    package lpk.imaging
2
3    class Regions(val rows: Int, val columns: Int) {
4        val seventhHeight: Int
5        val sixSeventhsHeight: Int
6        val quarterWidth: Int
7        val threeQuarterWidth: Int
8        val quarterHeight: Int
9        val threeQuarterHeight: Int
10
11       init {
12           seventhHeight = rows / 7
13           sixSeventhsHeight = rows - seventhHeight
14           quarterWidth = columns / 4
15           threeQuarterWidth = columns - quarterWidth
16           quarterHeight = rows / 4
```

```
17              threeQuarterHeight = rows - quarterHeight
18          }
19
20      fun isInRightQuarter(column: Int): Boolean {
21          return column >= threeQuarterWidth
22      }
23
24      fun isInBottomBar(row: Int): Boolean {
25          if (row >= sixSeventhsHeight) return true
26          return false
27      }
28
29      fun bottomBarArea(): Int {
30          return columns * seventhHeight
31      }
32  }
```

The constructor on line 3 has rows and columns declared as vals. This means that they are available throughout the code in the class, as are the vals declared on lines 4 to 9. These other vals are calculated from the constructor parameters. The calculations are done in the init block. The functions in the class are pretty self-explanatory and have unit tests that further clarify their meaning.

To check that these classes are all correct so far, we can run the unit tests. The fact that readTest passes means that our code is in fact reading the digit "1" from an image.

20.4 Identifying the Digit "2"

It's possible to recognize "2" using the current version of PictureSummary, as "2" is the only digit containing a bottom bar. Let's first add a line for this in readTest:

```
@Test
fun readTest() {
    Assert.assertEquals(1, read(loadSummary("1.png")))
    Assert.assertEquals(2, read(loadSummary("2.png")))
}
```

The change to the read function itself is also a one-liner:

```
fun read(summary: PictureSummary): Int {
    if (summary.heightToWidth > 3.0) return 1
    if (summary.hasBottomBar) return 2
    return -1
}
```

With this version of read, the modified test passes.

20.5 Identifying "5" and "7"

To recognize "5" and "7," we need to implement the hasTopBar concept in
PictureSummary.

PROJECT STEP 20.1

Add a function isInTopBar to Regions.

Also, add a test for this in RegionsTest.

PROJECT STEP 20.2

Add a val hasTopBar to PictureSummary and calculate it in the init block. You can do this
by copying and modifying each line of code relating to hasBottomBar.

For an image, the top bar and bottom bar have the same area. So, in the calculation of the
topBarRatio, just use regions.bottomBarArea.

For the test, copy and modify hasBottomBarTest. The images directory already contains
the files topbar.png and notopbar.png for use in this test.

PROJECT STEP 20.3

Add lines to readTest that check that "5" and "7" can be recognized. Check that the test fails.

With these pieces in place, it's quite easy to write the code for identifying "5" and "7." A picture that has a top bar can only represent either of these. To choose between them, we look at the proportion of pixels on the right-hand side. For "7," this is very low, whereas for "5" it is about a quarter. Expressing this in code, we can change read to

```kotlin
fun read(summary: PictureSummary): Int {
    if (summary.heightToWidth > 3.0) return 1
    if (summary.hasBottomBar) return 2
    if (summary.hasTopBar) {
        if (summary.proportionBlackRight < .2) {
            return 7
        }
        return 5
    }
    return -1
}
```

With these changes, the tests should pass, and two more digits are done!

20.6 Identifying "0"

Zero is characterized by having an empty center, so if we can enhance the class PictureSummary to indicate this, then we will be able to deal with "0."

PROJECT STEP 20.4

Add these three new functions: isInLeftQuarter, isInTopQuarter, and isInBottomQuarter to Regions.

These should all be quite similar to isInRightQuarter.

Also, add the corresponding tests.

Using these new functions, we can add an isInCenter function to Regions:

```
fun isInCenter(row: Int, column: Int): Boolean {
    if (isInTopQuarter(row)) return false
    if (isInBottomQuarter(row)) return false
    if (isInLeftQuarter(column)) return false
    if (isInRightQuarter(column)) return false
    return true
}
```

PROJECT STEP 20.5

Add a test for this function, using a Regions created with 40 rows and 60 columns.

To know the density of black pixels in a region, we need to know the total number of pixels in that region.

PROJECT STEP 20.6

With our definition of the center region, what proportion of a rectangle is in this region?

I always draw a picture for this kind of problem.

Add a function for this, called centerPixelCount.

Also, add a test, assuming the usual test region with 40 rows and 60 columns.

Let's add a property called hasCenterBlank to PictureSummary. To initialize this, we add a counter called centerBlack in the init block. If a black pixel is in the center, the counter is incremented:

```
if (regions.isInCenter(row, column)) centerBlack++
```

After iterating through all of the pixels, at the end of init, we can set the val hasCenterBlank, as follows:

```
val centerRatio = centerBlack.toFloat() /
    regions.centerPixelCount().toFloat()
hasCenterBlank = centerRatio < .1
```

Now let's use this new property in the digit recognition code. First, we add a test.

PROJECT STEP 20.7

Add this line to `readTest`:

```
Assert.assertEquals(0, read(loadSummary("0.png")))
```

To get this test passing, we can add this line to the read function:

```
if (summary.hasCenterBlank) return 0
```

20.7 Summary and Step Details

Our code can recognize the numerals "0," "1," "2," "5," and "7" from images. We will use an extended form of this code, which can recognize all digits, in the next chapter.

20.1.1 Details of Project Step 20.1

The new function is

```
fun isInTopBar(row: Int): Boolean {
    if (row < seventhHeight) return true
    return false
}
```

The test is

```
@Test
fun isInTopBarTest() {
    val regions = Regions(70, 60)
    for (i in 0..9) {
        Assert.assertTrue(regions.isInTopBar(i))
    }
    for (i in 10..69) {
        Assert.assertFalse(regions.isInTopBar(i))
    }
}
```

20.2.2 Details of Project Step 20.2

To calculate hasTopBar in the init block, we add a counter:

```
var topBarBlack = 0
```

This is incremented for black pixels that are in the top bar:

```
if (regions.isInTopBar(row)) topBarBlack++
```

The count is used to determine the proportion of black pixels in the top bar region, which is used to set hasTopBar:

```
val topBarRatio = topBarBlack.toFloat() /
        regions.bottomBarArea().toFloat()
hasTopBar = topBarRatio > .75
```

Here's a test:

```
@Test
fun hasTopBarTest() {
    Assert.assertTrue(summary("bwbw_h.png").hasTopBar)
    Assert.assertTrue(summary("topbar.png").hasTopBar)
    Assert.assertFalse(summary("wbwb_h.png").hasTopBar)
    Assert.assertFalse(summary("notopbar.png").hasTopBar)
}
```

20.3.3 Details of Project Step 20.3

The enhanced test is

```
@Test
fun readTest() {
    Assert.assertEquals(1, read(loadSummary("1.png")))
    Assert.assertEquals(2, read(loadSummary("2.png")))
    Assert.assertEquals(5, read(loadSummary("5.png")))
    Assert.assertEquals(7, read(loadSummary("7.png")))
}
```

20.4.4 Details of Project Step 20.4

The new functions are

```
fun isInTopQuarter(row: Int): Boolean {
    return row < quarterHeight
}

fun isInBottomQuarter(row: Int): Boolean {
    return row >= threeQuarterHeight
}

fun isInLeftQuarter(column: Int): Boolean {
    return column < quarterWidth
}
```

The corresponding tests are

```
@Test
fun isInTopQuarterTest() {
    val regions = Regions(40, 60)
    for (i in 0..9) {
        Assert.assertTrue(regions.isInTopQuarter(i))
    }
    for (i in 10..39) {
        Assert.assertFalse(regions.isInTopQuarter(i))
    }
}

@Test
fun isInBottomQuarterTest() {
    val regions = Regions(40, 60)
    for (i in 0..29) {
        Assert.assertFalse(regions.isInBottomQuarter(i))
    }
    for (i in 30..39) {
        Assert.assertTrue(regions.isInBottomQuarter(i))
    }
}
```

```
@Test
fun isInLeftQuarterTest() {
    val regions = Regions(40, 60)
    for (i in 0..14) {
        Assert.assertTrue(regions.isInLeftQuarter(i))
    }
    for (i in 15..59) {
        Assert.assertFalse(regions.isInLeftQuarter(i))
    }
}
```

20.5.5 Details of Project Step 20.5

The test is

```
@Test
fun isInCenterTest() {
    val regions = Regions(40, 60)
    for (i in 0..39) {
        for (j in 0..59) {
            if (i >= 10 && i < 30 && j >= 15 && j < 45) {
                Assert.assertTrue(regions.isInCenter(i, j))
            } else {
                Assert.assertFalse(regions.isInCenter(i, j))
            }
        }
    }
}
```

20.6.6 Details of Project Step 20.6

When we remove the side quarters, half of the image remains. Of the remainder, the top and bottom quarters are then removed. At the end of this process, there is

$$\frac{1}{2} \times \frac{1}{2} = \frac{1}{4}$$

of the original rectangle remaining.

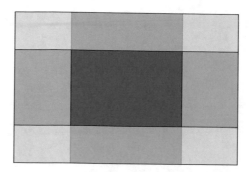

So

```
fun centerPixelCount() : Int {
    return columns * rows / 4
}
```

The test is

```
@Test
fun centerPixelCountTest() {
    val regions = Regions(40, 60)
    Assert.assertEquals(600, regions.centerPixelCount())
}
```

CHAPTER 21

Reading Speed Signs

In this chapter, we will put together the code from the previous chapters to finish our sign-reading software. The starting point is an enhanced version of the code from Chapter 20. This can be downloaded from `https://github.com/Apress/learn-to-program-w-kotlin-ch21.git`. The new code base is more complete than at the end of the last chapter:

- `Regions` and `PictureSummary` contain code for determining pixel densities in other parts of an image, such as the top quarter.

- The read function in `DigitReader.kt` now correctly identifies all digits.

- There are tests for the new functions.

- The slicing functions in `Picture` have been refactored so as to remove code duplication.

21.1 SpeedReader

In addition to the changes listed earlier, there is a new class called `SpeedReader` and a test for it. The test contains a check for each of the sign images in the test data directory. Here's the code, without the `package` and `import` statements:

```
val SPEED_SIGNS ="src/test/resources/images/signs/"

classSpeedReaderTest {
    @Test
    fun readTest() {
        Assert.assertEquals(5, reader("5.png").speed())
        Assert.assertEquals(10, reader("10.png").speed())
        Assert.assertEquals(20, reader("20.png").speed())
```

© Tim Lavers 2021
T. Lavers, *Learn to Program with Kotlin*, https://doi.org/10.1007/978-1-4842-6815-5_21

```
        Assert.assertEquals(40, reader("40.png").speed())
        Assert.assertEquals(60, reader("60.png").speed())
        Assert.assertEquals(70, reader("70.png").speed())
        Assert.assertEquals(80, reader("80.png").speed())
        Assert.assertEquals(90, reader("90.png").speed())
        Assert.assertEquals(130, reader("130.png").speed())
    }

    fun reader(name: String): SpeedReader {
        val file = Paths.get(SPEED_SIGNS +"/"+ name).toFile()
        returnSpeedReader(file)
    }
}
```

The function called reader in this code takes the name of a speed sign file, creates a File object from it, and then uses it as the parameter in creating a SpeedReader. The assertions in the test function check that the numbers returned by SpeedReader are correct.

The SpeedReader class is only partially implemented:

```
classSpeedReader(signImageFile : File) {
    val digits = mutableListOf<Int>()

    init {

    }

    fun speed() :Int {
        return-1
    }
}
```

The val called digits is a List of Ints. The elements of this list will be the individual numerals read from the speed sign image file that is passed into the constructor. This is to be done in the init block, which has not been written. The other outstanding job is to write the speed function, which will turn the list of digits into an Int.

21.2 Base 10 Numbers

Let's deal with the implementation of speed as our first task. The digits variable
contains a List of Ints. How do we turn these into a number? If the digits in the list are
a, b, and c, then the number that they represent is just the base 10 expansion:

$$a \times 100 + b \times 10 + c \times 1$$

There may just be one or two numbers in the list, so our conversion code is going
to be reasonably complex. In order that we can test the code, let's put it into a helper
function that takes any List of Ints and converts it to a number.

PROJECT STEP 21.1

Add the following function to the file SpeedReader.kt. The function is to be put just before
the line beginning class SpeedReader....

```kotlin
fun convertDigits(digits: List<Int>) : Int {
    return-1
}
```

Then change the implementation of speed to

```kotlin
fun speed(): Int {
    return convertDigits(digits)
}
```

PROJECT STEP 21.2

Add this test function to SpeedReaderTest:

```kotlin
@Test
fun convertDigitsTest() {
    val list1 = mutableListOf(1)
    Assert.assertEquals(1, convertDigits(list1))

    val list45 = mutableListOf(4,5)
    Assert.assertEquals(45, convertDigits(list45))
```

```
    val list150 = mutableListOf(1, 5, 0)
    Assert.assertEquals(150, convertDigits(list150))
}
```

When you paste the code, IntelliJ should show a suggestion to import the `convertDigits` function, as in Figure 21-1. As suggested, press `Alt` and the `Enter` keys simultaneously. You should then see the line

```
import lpk.imaging.convertDigits
```

added among the other `import` statements.

Check that this test fails.

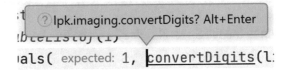

Figure 21-1. *IntelliJ offers to import the new function*

One way of implementing `convertDigits` is as follows:

- Have a running total, called `total`.

- Have a `var` called `multiplier`, which will always be a power of 10.

- Run through the list backward, and at each step

  – Multiply the current digit by `multiplier`.

  – Add the result to `total`.

  – Make `multiplier` ten times bigger, ready for the next digit.

PROJECT STEP 21.3

See if you can implement the preceding algorithm.

The refactoring that we have done here—to implement key logic as a "helper" function that can be easily tested—is very common in software engineering.

21.3 Putting It All Together

It only remains for us to fill in the `init` block. This is much easier than the digit conversion. The code will need to convert the image file to digits and add these to the `digits` field. Here is how this can be done:

- Create a `Picture` from the `File`.

- Create a `DigitFinder` from the `Picture`.

- Get a list of digit images from the `DigitFinder`.

- For each digit image:

  - Create a `PictureSummary`.

  - Pass the `PictureSummary` to the read function, to get an `Int`.

  - Add the `Int` to digits.

PROJECT STEP 21.4

Implement the preceding algorithm in the `init` block of `SpeedReader`. Check that the tests for `SpeedReader` all pass.

This concludes the project—the tests prove that our software is successfully reading speed signs. This is a fantastic achievement. Well done!

You may be wondering how "industrial-strength" image recognition software is written. Much of the code is fundamentally the same as what we have implemented. One of the main differences is that our read function, with its delicately chosen cutoffs and particular order of digit selection, is replaced by robust statistical models that are built from the analysis of thousands of images in a process called "machine learning."

21.4 Summary

In reading this book and, above all, in doing the challenges and project steps, you will have learned the fundamental skills required for serious programming:

- Modeling the real world with object-oriented software

- Unit testing

- Functional programming

- Code refactoring

Additionally, you will have gained experience with professional tools such as Git and IntelliJ. Finally, you have learned the basic syntax of the beautiful language Kotlin. Good luck with your future programming!

21.5 Project Steps

21.5.1 Details of Project Step 21.1

The new version of SpeedReader.kt is

```
packagelpk.imaging

importjava.io.File

fun convert(digits: List<Int>): Int {
    return-1
}

classSpeedReader(signImageFile: File) {
    val digits = mutableListOf<Int>()

    init {

    }

    fun speed(): Int {
        returnconvert(digits)
    }
}
```

21.5.2 Details of Project Step 21.3

Here is the implementation:

```kotlin
fun convertDigits(digits: List<Int>): Int {
    var total = 0
    var multiplier = 1
    val n = digits.size
    for(i in 0..n - 1) {
        val digit = digits[n - i - 1]
        total = total + digit * multiplier
        multiplier = multiplier * 10
    }
    return total
}
```

21.5.3 Details of Project Step 21.4

Here is how all of the components work together to read the sign:

```kotlin
init {
    val sign = loadPictureFromFile(signImageFile)
    val digitImages = DigitFinder(sign).digits()
    digitImages.forEach {
        digitImage ->
        val pictureSummary = PictureSummary(digitImage)
        val digit = read(pictureSummary)
        digits.add(digit)
    }
}
```

Index

Symbols

&&, 40
!!, 212
?:, 97, 131
*, 49
>, 41
<, 41
/, 54
%, 54
+, 49
++, 353
-, 49
!=, 81
==, 36
$, 52

A

Addition, 49
Anagrams, 157–183
And operator, 40
Annotation, 114
Argument,
      14, 15, 52
Array, 14, 21
arrayOf, 15

B

Boolean, 82, 140

C

Char, 75, 78, 80
Class, 111, 112
    constructor, 115
    data, 164
    field, 119
    init, 120
    instance variable, 119
col loop, 25
Comma-Separated Variable (CSV)
       format, 150
Constructor, 115, 119, 131, 136, 164, 198,
       209, 218, 233

D

Data type, 77, 102, 111, 140
Division, 54

E

Edge case, 167
Elvis operator, 97, 131
Equals, 22, 50, 66

F

Field, 119, 120, 130
File system, 101–103, 106
    reading, 102, 103
    writing, 104, 106

© Tim Lavers 2021
T. Lavers, *Learn to Program with Kotlin*, https://doi.org/10.1007/978-1-4842-6815-5

Printed in the United States
by Baker & Taylor Publisher Services